DEATH AND DYING

DEATH AND DYING
INDIVIDUALS
AND INSTITUTIONS

Barbara A. Backer, M.S., M.A., R.N.
Clinical Specialist, Psychiatric/Mental Health Nursing
Lecturer, Department of Nursing
Lehman College
New York, New York

Natalie Hannon, Ph.D.
Formerly Assistant Dean
Graduate School of Arts and Sciences
New York University
New York, New York

Noreen A. Russell, M.S.W., A.C.S.W.
Social Service Department
New York University Medical Center
New York, New York

A WILEY MEDICAL PUBLICATION
John Wiley & Sons
New York • Chichester • Brisbane • Toronto • Singapore

Cover design by Wanda Lubelska
Production Editor: Cheryl Howell

ISBN 0-471-08715

Printed in the United States of America

10   9   8   7

Preface

The past decade has been marked by many publications in the field of thanatology. As members of a "death-denying" society, professionals and lay people welcomed these new publications since each represented different sociological, psychological, and medical concepts. This proliferation of materials, though refreshing and rewarding, has now presented educators and practitioners with a different dilemma. Very few of these writings provide an overall framework integrating the various theories and concepts developed by the different disciplines. In view of this, most instructors are faced with the necessity of assigning a wide variety of books. Students often are discouraged by the difficulty they encounter in creating a "small library" to meet course requirements and by the lack of an overall framework for organizing this disparate material. From our experiences in working with dying patients and their families, and from having team-taught courses on death, dying, and bereavement, we have developed a text that provides an integration of the thanatological literature.

In this book we identify patterns and responses to dying and death in American society, discuss problems related to the termination of life, and examine the structure and processes of interaction among the terminally ill, their families, and helping professionals. Motivated by our belief that caregivers must be exposed to a humanistic approach to counterbalance the industrialization of health care in the United States, we emphasize the caring aspects rather than the curing aspects of health care for dying people. We also discuss a variety of modes of intervention based on the individual's unique response to his or her own death, rather than a universal recipe approach. This, too, represents our philosophy that facing death encompasses a complex set of human behaviors.

Content material is organized into eleven chapters. Chapters 1 and 2 discuss attitudes and perceptions concerning death and dying and review the dying process. Chapter 3 discusses how hospitals or institutions with cure-oriented goals affect dying patients with care-oriented needs. How health caregivers are educated for, and socialized in, the care of dying patients is reviewed in Chapter 4. Interaction and communication between caregivers and dying patients are also analyzed. Chapter 5 discusses children's perceptions, concepts, and reactions to death and how families respond to the death of children. Chapter 6 is concerned with ethical issues of death, such as euthanasia, the right to refuse treatment, and definitions of death. Theories of the causes of suicide and interventions for suicidal patients are reviewed in Chapter 7. Chapter 8 deals with the functions of funerals and the funeral rites of major religions. The processes of grief and bereavement are discussed in Chapter 9, along with suggestions for interventions in these processes. Chapter 10 views death from a cross-cultural perspective. Chapter 11 presents ideas and concepts about death education.

We think that this book, with its interdisciplinary approach and emphasis on individualized, humanistic care of dying people, is a significant and important text for students in the fields of nursing, social work, sociology, psychology, and medicine. Health care practitioners should also find this a valuable text.

It would be impossible to thank all of the people who have supported and encouraged us in developing this book. We would like to acknowledge and thank Serena Nanda, Ph.D., for providing her anthropological perspectives on death and dying in Chapter 10. Special thanks also go to Andrea Stingelin, Editor, and Janet Walsh, Editorial Assistant, for their ongoing assistance and answers to countless questions! We would also like to express our gratitude and appreciation to our students and patients, who have been continuing sources of motivation and enrichment and who provided us with the impetus for writing this text.

Barbara A. Backer
Natalie Hannon
Noreen A. Russell

Contents

DEATH AND DYING

1

Death in American Society

Try talking about dying and death at a party. Watch people's reactions: many people will move away; some people will tell jokes about the subject; and others may just say, "I don't want to talk about such a morbid topic." But there will also be a group of people who will be fascinated by the topic, and a lively conversation may ensue. Most of us do not want to deal with the fact that sooner or later, all of us, including those at the party, will die. Yet there is in our society an increased realization that dealing with the subject of death will allow us to live our lives more fully now.

Thanatologists, those people who are specialists in studying the various aspects of death and dying, have called us a "death-denying" society. Death is considered to have taken the place of sex as pornography (Gorer, 1965) in our society. Yet to make the general assumption that we all deny death is too simple. At the same time that most of us do not wish to talk about death and dying at a party, *On Death and Dying* by Elisabeth Kübler-Ross was a best-seller among trade paperbacks. We may not wear seatbelts, but we carry organ donor cards in our wallets just in case something happens to us. And although the death of a loved one is probably not experienced until adulthood, children view death on television practically every night. It is probably more accurate to say that instead of denial, we are ambivalent in our feelings toward death and dying. How have we come to these attitudes and feelings of ambivalence? What helps to explain the attitudes of society toward death and dying?

ATTITUDES TOWARD DEATH AND DYING

Philippe Aries in *Western Attitudes Towards Death* (1974) presents four attitudes toward death found in the history of Western civilization: resignation to death; acceptance of one's own death; fear of and fascination with death; and regarding death as shameful and prohibited. The first attitude, resignation to death, or "tamed death," occurred before and during the Middle Ages. "Tamed death" was the familiar resignation to the collective destiny of the species and can be summarized by the phrase, 'we shall all die'" (p. 55). Death and life were considered to exist simultaneously. Aries labeled this attitude "tamed death" since death was both "familiar and near, evoking no great fear or awe" (p. 13). During the Middle Ages, with the growing importance of religion and Catholicism and the effects of the Black Death, "tamed death" was slightly modified in that people not only resigned themselves to the deaths of others but also accepted their own death and their own dying.

One could not be isolated from death. In the fourteenth century the Black Death was said to have killed over 25 percent of the population of Europe. In 1603, one-fifth of the population of London was killed by the plague (Thomlinson, 1965, p. 84). People were surrounded by death during "tamed death," as shown by the diary entries of the British Admiralty secretary in 1665 (Samuel Pepys, as quoted in Thomlinson, 1965):

June 15th, 1665. The Towne grows very sickly, and people to be afeard of it; there dying this last week of the plague 112, from 43 the week before.

August 10th, 1665. By and by to the office, where we sat all the morning; in great trouble to see the Bill this week rise so high, to above 4,000 in all, and of them above 3,000 of the plague. . . . The town growing so unhealthy, that a man cannot depend upon living two days to an end.

September 20th, 1665. But, Lord! what a sad time it is to see no boats upon the River; and grass grows all up and down White Hall court, and nobody but poor wretches in the streets! And, which is worst of all, the Duke showed us the number of the plague this week, brought in the last night from the Lord Mayor; that it is encreased from about 600 more than the last, which is quite contrary to all our hopes and expectations, from the coldness of the late season. For the whole general number is 8,297, and of them the plague 7,165. (p. 84)

With the ascendance of Catholicism and then Protestantism, death became viewed as a form of justice, and in order to have a good life after death, it was imperative for the dying person to have behaved well. People had to prepare to meet their maker in a proper manner. "In death, man encountered one of the great laws of the species, and he had no thought of escaping it or glorifying it" (Aries, 1974, p. 29). As Jacques Choron (1963) points out:

> The hereafter has become through the efforts of the Church, a source of terror and not consolation. Instead of reward, most people could only expect retribution. In order to secure a blissful existence in the other world . . . it was necessary to lead such a life in this world as was beyond the endurance of most people, except for a few over-zealous ascetics. (p. 91)

True salvation could only be found if all mortal passions were renounced; humanity was only to concentrate on God (Stannard, 1977, p. 21).

Beginning in the eighteenth century, people again became concerned with the death of others, which Aries calls "thy death." Death was no longer considered to be banal. Rather than being viewed as part of life, death was seen as a break with life. Death was both frightening and fascinating, while also being romaticized. This may seem contradictory, but the contradiction can be explained by Aries' hypothesis that the romanticization of death was a psychological sublimation of the erotic view of death held in the seventeenth century. "Like the sexual act, death was henceforth increasingly thought of as a transgression which tears man from his daily life, from rational society, from monotonous work, in order to make him undergo a paroxysm, plunging him into an irrational, violent, beautiful world" (p. 57). If we accept Aries' hypothesis, then death can be both frightening and romantic.

Death of another became much more fearful than the death of oneself. Mourning became exaggerated. Memorials and monuments were built for the dead. The American colonies exemplified this: funerals were extravagant social gatherings wherein hundreds of pounds were spent to mark the death of an individual (Jackson, 1977, p. 8).

In the mid-nineteenth century, we entered the period of "forbidden death." Death was no longer a dramatic act but rather a technological phenomenon. Important here is the fact that death no longer occurred in the home, but in the hospital, which eliminated any ceremony between the family and the dying person. Death had become pornography (Gorer, 1976):

> The natural processes of corruption and decay have become disgusting, as disgusting as the natural processes of birth and copulation were a cen-

tury ago; preoccupation about such processes is (or was) morbid and unhealthy, to be discouraged and punished in the young. Our great-great-
parents were told that babies were found under gooseberry bushes or
cabbages; our children are likely to be told that those who have passed on
are changed into flowers, or be at rest in lovely gardens. The ugly facts
are relentlessly hidden; the art of the embalmers is an art of complete denial. (p. 74)

The factors accounting for "forbidden death" include changing mortality patterns, the American value structure, the institutionalization of
dying, the potential for mass death, and our family structure.

Changing Mortality Patterns

Calvin Goldschneider (1971, pp. 102–134) points out that in the
change from a preindustrial to an industrial society, we have gone
from uncontrolled to controlled mortality. Uncontrolled mortality involved three characteristics: mortality was high, it fluctuated over short
periods, and it varied widely at any point in time. Under controlled
mortality, the opposite conditions prevail: mortality is low, and it does
not fluctuate widely either over time or geographic area.

The United States estimated that between the thirteenth and seventeenth centuries, life expectancy ranged from 20 to 40 years (Goldschneider, 1971, p. 107). Table 1.1 shows the expectation of life at
birth in eighteenth-century Europe and America (Dublin, Lotka, &
Spiegelman, 1949, pp. 35–36). Not only was the life span short, but
mortality conditions were such that they could fluctuate to as high as
400 per 1,000 population during times of famine or epidemics. There
were smallpox, cholera, and typhus epidemics: in the eighteenth century, 25 percent of all Frenchmen were killed, crippled, or disfigured
by smallpox (p. 85).

Famine was also a contributor to high mortality. In Western Europe
alone, 450 more or less localized famines were recorded from the years
1000 to 1855 (p. 79). A famine could easily have a severe effect on one
area of a country while not affecting an adjacent area because of inadequate transportation. Under uncontrolled mortality, death was constantly present, and it was, therefore, necessary for society to incorporate it into the ongoing system.

Today, under conditions of controlled mortality, the average life expectancy is over 70 years of age, with a death rate of 10.9 per 1,000
population for males and 8.1 per 1,000 population for females (U.S.

Table 1.1. Expectation of Life at Birth in Eighteenth-Century Europe and America

Period Covered	Area	Expectation of Life at Birth
1746	French convents and monasteries	37.5
1735–1780	Northampton, England	30.0
1782, 1788–1790	Part of Philadelphia	25.0
A period before 1789	Massachusetts and New Hampshire	35.5
1772–1792	Montpellier, France	
	Males	23.4
	Females	27.4
A period before 1789	Different parts of France	28.8

Reprinted with permission from *Length of Life* by Louis Dublin et al. Copyright © 1949 by Ronald Press.

Department of Commerce, 1976, p. 194). Furthermore, these death rates have hardly fluctuated for the past 30 years. Another effect of controlled mortality was the change in terms of who died. One of the most privileged groups in preindustrial society, the British aristocracy, had an infant mortality rate of 200 per 1,000 live births (Goldschneider, 1971, p. 107). If you were able to live beyond infancy, as pointed out previously, you or your spouse was likely to die in the middle of adulthood. Death had to be confronted.

In 1974 in the United States, the infant mortality rate was 16.7 per 1,000 live births (U.S. Department of Commerce, 1976, p. 193). Furthermore, it is the elderly who are most likely to die. Since the elderly are not defined as important in our society, and since it is the elderly who are expected to die, it is not necessary to incorporate death into our lives before we are old. Charles Corr (1979) states that in societies that have controlled mortality:

It is possible to have lengthy courtship patterns emphasizing romantic love, marriages at a later age, longer marriages, and serial monogamy—divorces and remarriages; to have more time to devote to formal education and training programs; to have more energy available for research and therapy aimed at curing disease and further extending life; and to foster future-oriented attitudes of planning, saving and deferred gratification. (p. 13)

Clearly, our concentration is on prolonging life; our expectations are that we will have many years to live in order to accomplish and to achieve our goals. Death is no longer relevant.

AMERICAN VALUE STRUCTURE

Implicit in American values are the notions of innovation, efficiency, and progress (Williams, 1970). Basically, we feel that we should be able to conquer all natural problems, and that all natural phenomena can eventually become not only rationally understood but even manipulated. We approach death in the light of these values. Our major concern when someone dies is what the cause of death was. When a number of American Legionnaires died in Philadelphia a couple of years ago, people in the United States were upset since there seemed to be no cause for the deaths. We were all very relieved to find out that death was caused by a virus.

The illusion that we can conquer death has been strengthened by the fact that we have increased our life span by over 20 years since the year 1900. In 1900 the average life span was 47.3 years; today, it is 71.9 years. Table 1.2 shows the causes of death in 1900 (Lerner, 1970, p. 14) and 1972 (U.S. Public Health Service, 1973). Tuberculosis, gastritis, and diphtheria are no longer leading causes of death. Today, we die of diseases of old age: diseases of the heart, cancer, and stroke cause over 65 percent of our deaths.

If we could only find a cure for heart disease or cancer, people believe that death would go away. Yet as Table 1.3 shows, if we found a cure for heart disease, we would only gain 5.86 years in life expectancy, and we would still die (U.S. Department of Commerce, 1976, p. 197).

Our belief in our ability to conquer death is further shown by the use of life tables. At any given age, one can calculate how much longer one should live and what the probability of death is at any given age (U.S. Public Health Service, 1971). For example, from the life table (Table 1.4), one can see that at age 6, a white person is likely to live 68.3 more years. The chance of death at age 10 is 189 out of 98,027.

Parsons and Lidz (1967) see this response to death, not as a denial of death, but as a response of "instrumental activism" stemming from our values. It does not matter whether we can talk about dying or have euphemisms concerning death; what is important is that we value prolongation of life and that we develop a highly rationalized system for identifying the controllable components of death—the effects of pre-

Table 1.2. The Ten Leading Causes of Death in the United States, 1900 and 1972

Rank	Cause of Death	Deaths per 100,000 Population	Percent of All Deaths
1900			
1	Influenza and pneumonia	202.2	11.8
2	Tuberculosis	194.4	11.3
3	Gastritis, enteritis, etc.	142.7	8.3
4	Diseases of the heart	137.4	8.0
5	Vascular lesions affecting the central nervous system	106.9	6.2
6	Chronic nephritis	81.0	4.7
7	All accidents	72.3	4.2
8	Malignant neoplasms (cancer)	64.0	3.7
9	Certain diseases of early infancy	62.6	3.6
10	Diphtheria	40.3	2.3
	All other causes	615.3	35.9
1972			
1	Diseases of the heart	361.3	38.3
2	Malignant neoplasms (cancer)	166.6	17.7
3	Cerebrovascular diseases	100.9	10.7
4	Accidents	54.6	5.8
5	Influenza and pneumonia	29.4	3.1
6	Diabetes mellitus	18.8	2.0
7	Certain diseases of early infancy	16.4	1.7
8	Arteriosclerosis	15.8	1.7
9	Cirrhosis of the liver	15.7	1.7
10	Bronchitis, emphysema, and asthma	13.8	1.5
	All other causes	148.9	15.8

Data for 1900 reprinted with permission from "When, Why and Where People Die" by Monroe Lerner in O. Brim et al. (Eds.), *The Dying Patient* (Russell Sage Foundation). Copyright © 1970. Data for 1972 from the Public Health Service.

mature death, the physical suffering of dying, and deliberately imposed death. As summed up by Robert Veatch (1976, pp. 16–17), Parsons and Lidz see death as "an enemy to be conquered by our own activist faith in man's ability to solve its own problems and an unknown

Table 1.3. Gain in Expectation of Life at Birth That Would Result If Specified Causes of Death Were Eliminated, 1969–1971

Cause of Death	Gain in Expectation of Life in Years
Diseases of the heart	5.86
Vascular-renal diseases	5.90
Malignant neoplasms	2.47
Certain diseases of early infancy	.82
Motor vehicle accidents	.70
All other accidents	.63
Suicide and homicide	.49

Table 1.4. Abridged Life Tables, United States, 1971 (by Race)

		Of 100,000 Born Alive		
Age Interval	Proportion Dying	Number Living at Age Interval	Number Dying at Age Interval	Average Remaining Years
White				
0–1	0.0169	100,000	1,687	71.9
1–5	.0029	98,313	286	72.1
5–10	.0019	98,027	189	68.3
10–15	.0019	97,838	185	63.5
15–20	.0052	97,653	508	58.6
20–25	.0063	97,145	610	53.9
25–30	.0059	96,535	570	49.2
30–35	.0069	95,965	658	44.5
35–40	.0099	95.307	945	39.8
40–45	.0159	94,362	1,500	35.1
45–50	.0250	92,862	2,318	30.6
50–55	.0392	90,544	3,550	26.4
55–60	.0604	86,994	5,250	22.3
60–65	.0912	81,744	7,453	18.6
65–70	.1308	74,291	9,715	15.2
70–75	.1942	64,576	12,544	12.1
75–80	.2836	52,032	14,755	9.4
80–85	.3902	37,277	14,547	7.1
85 and over	1.0000	22,730	22,730	5.1

Table 1.4. (Continued)

Age Interval	Proportion Dying	Of 100,000 Born Alive		
		Number Living at Age Interval	Number Dying at Age Interval	Average Remaining Years
Other				
0–1	0.0293	100,000	2,930	65.2
1–5	.0045	97,070	436	66.2
5–10	.0026	96,634	251	62.5
10–15	.0027	96,383	256	57.6
15–20	.0079	96,127	756	52.8
20–25	.0137	95,371	1,306	48.2
25–30	.0158	94,065	1,488	43.8
30–35	.0205	92,577	1,897	39.4
35–40	.0284	90,680	2,579	35.2
40–45	.0377	88,101	3,317	31.2
45–50	.0513	84,784	4,349	27.3
50–55	.0728	80,435	5,855	23.6
55–60	.0947	74,580	7,059	20.3
60–65	.1436	67,521	9,695	17.1
65–70	.1916	57,826	11,081	14.6
70–75	.3021	46,745	14,121	12.4
75–80	.2929	32,264	9,554	11.7
80–85	.3140	23,070	7,243	10.5
85 and over	1.0000	15,827	15,827	9.2

of infinite proportions." What we seem to have difficulty with is that death ultimately denies rational analysis. We want answers; we are used to being supplied with answers, and we find it difficult to live with the uncertainties and ambiguities of death.

Another value important in our society is happiness. Our advertising media, with its emphasis on youth, have contributed to our thinking that we must be happy. We are the "Pepsi generation," and happiness is one of our goals. Dying and death interfere with this, and we do not want to accept the interference. As the historian Arnold Toynbee (1968, p. 131) says: "For Americans, death is unAmerican, and an affront to every citizen's inalienable right to life, liberty and the pursuit of happiness."

The Institutionalization of Dying

With our control over mortality and our belief that death can be cured, dying has become institutionalized. No longer do people die at home with their families; they die within hospitals. As Quint (1979) points out, the first half of the twentieth century saw the chronic and long-term diseases take over from the communicable diseases. Along with this came greater diagnostic and treatment techniques and the development of scientific medicine. "More and more, hospitals came to be places designed and organized for the purpose of controlling death" (pp. 142–143). Besides hospitals, after World War II came the development of nursing homes. Although it is a myth that Americans put all their old people in nursing homes (only 3 percent of the population over 65 are in nursing homes), the percentage of people over 80, the frail elderly, who are in nursing homes is 11 percent (U.S. Department of Commerce, 1976, p. 204). In a sense, the population of nursing homes may be defined as dying.

The rise in the percentage of people who die in institutions has been noted by Monroe Lerner (1970, pp. 20–23). In 1949, 49 percent of all deaths in the United States took place in institutions; in 1969, the percentage rose to 61. (The data cited by Monroe Lerner are the most recent available national data.) If we look at New York City, the trend continues: 73 percent of all deaths in New York City in 1967 occurred in institutions. Hence, the family no longer plays a major part in the dying ritual.

Since people die in hospitals, dying has become invisible. We do not have any idea of what dying looks like. Neither the dying patient nor the family is at the center of the ritual of dying—it is the health care professional. The difficulty, however, is that hospitals are not set up to deal with dying; rather, they are places to go to be cured. As such, there is very little room for the dying in the rituals of the hospital. As is discussed in Chapter 3, many dying patients must pretend that they are getting better in order to be defined as "good patients" and to get good care.

The Effect of Mass Death

Another reason for "forbidden death" has been the development of the nuclear age. As Lifton (1964) points out, the nuclear age affects our symbolic immortality. In order for us to contemplate our lives and our deaths, we must be sure that we will somehow live on. For example, we have children so that our names will continue; we write books so that the world will know we existed; we have friends so that memories of us will live on.

Seventeen years after the bombing of Hiroshima, Lifton interviewed Japanese people who had had possible exposure to significant amounts of radiation at the time of the bombing. Lifton's concern was to explore the psychological elements of what he referred to as the "permanent encounter with death" that the atomic bomb created in those exposed to it. Lifton formulated the premise that

> we are not absolutely convinced of our immortality, but rather have a need to maintain a sense of immortality in the face of inevitable biological death; and that this need represents not only the inability of the individual unconscious to recognize the possibility of its own demise but also a compelling universal urge to maintain an inner sense of continuous symbolic relationship, over time and space, to the various elements of life. (p. 203)

He suggests that this sense of immortality may be achieved through any of several modes:

1. *Biosocially:* We can express our immortality by means of biological reproduction, living on through our sons and daughters, and through their sons and daughters.
2. *Theologically:* We may feel that when we die, we transcend our earthly life for one of a higher existence.
3. *Creatively:* Our writings, art, inventions, and influences upon other people may give us a sense of immortality.
4. *Naturally:* A sense of immortality may be achieved through being survived by nature itself; that is, when we die, we perceive that nature will remain, and that we become part of nature.

However, the concept of nuclear death totally annihilates our sense of immortality. We cannot live on in others since no others would exist. Everything that gave substance to our existence would die with us.

Our Family Structure

The major reason that families are held together in our society is basically for emotional gratification. The emotional dependency within the nuclear family is rarely diffused by other relations. This situation makes separation appear very threatening. The notion of marrying for love developed after industrialization. Before that, marriage was an economic necessity. The roles of the husband and wife were defined in terms of economic production. The extended kinship network also played an important role. With today's emphasis on psychological companionship and the nuclear family, it is more difficult to conceive of a spouse or another loved one dying. One can understand the feelings of the wife on the radio commercial after her husband says he spent his lunch hour shopping for life insurance; the woman does not want to talk about it. To contemplate her husband's death is too painful.

THE EFFECTS OF FORBIDDEN DEATH

"Forbidden death" is seen in our language, our funeral practices, the way we handle the dying, and in the presentation of death and dying in the media.

No one ever dies in our society. We either "pass on," "rest in peace," or "sleep eternally." Even in hospitals, patients do not die—they expire. Feifel, writing in 1959 (pp. 115–116), points out that the *Christian Science Monitor* did not permit the word *death* to be mentioned in its newspaper until recently. Our funeral practices are such that we attempt to make the corpse look as alive as possible. Special fashions and cosmetics may be used. We are also concerned with the comfort of the body within the casket. (Chapter 8 surveys funeral practices and the funeral industry in greater depth.)

Hospitals attempt to make the dying invisible. Kübler-Ross (1969) discusses how there suddenly were no dying patients in the hospital in which she worked when she asked to interview a dying patient for a seminar she was giving. In many cases, patients are not told that they are dying, so that the interaction between the health professionals and the patient may focus on the patient's getting well. Dumont and Foss (1972) provide a quote from a textbook, *Modern Concepts in Hospital Administration*, that they consider highly suggestive of death denial in American hospitals:

> The hospital morgue is best located on the ground floor and placed in an area inaccessible to the general public. It is important that the unit have a suitable exit leading onto a private loading platform which is concealed from the hospital patient and the general public. (p. 37)

Another example of death denial occurred in the planning of the renovation of a major medical center in New York City: no space was allocated for the morgue. It was not until the renovation was under way that someone realized the omission. As a result, the morgue is located in a very inconvenient area of the hospital.

In terms of the media, death tends either to be romanticized or depicted as violent. One of the authors at one time did not know that people died with their eyes open, since all the movies she had seen showed dying people closing their eyes upon death. Most of us will not die with smiles on our faces, holding hands with our loved ones, nor in the violent fashion portrayed in police stories.

Dumont and Foss (1972, p. 43) point out that newspapers tend to isolate death into specific sections. Impersonal forms of death, such as death from plane crashes, may be front-page news, but the more personal, emotional aspects of death are segregated. A good example of this was the news handling of the subject during the Vietnamese War, where deaths were reported as head counts and numbers.

Lofland (1978, pp. 35–37) discusses three clusters of "problems and potentials" arising from our attitudes toward death and dying:

Role problems: The dying role is a new role for people dying from chronic, rather than acute, disease. How is a person supposed to act in this role? Since the dying are generally elderly and isolated in hospitals, we have not seen how people act in this role. We have no experience in dealing with death or dying in our families; and we are not socialized as children into the proper role behaviors for dealing with the dying and the bereaved. As adults, we then find it difficult to face either our own deaths or the deaths of others.

Organizational problems: The organization, the hospital, is designed for curing, not caring. As such, it is difficult for hospital personnel to care for the dying properly.

Belief problems: We are without beliefs concerning the meaning of death. We are no longer comforted by knowing a reason for death.

Along with these problems are potentials for solutions: new roles can be developed in which the dying can, if they so choose, talk about their feelings and their dying; new organizations can be designed, such as the hospice, where the care and comfort of the terminally ill are the primary goals; and new meanings to death can be constructed. To realize these potentials, we must leave the period of "forbidden death," which we are beginning to do.

DEATH IN SOCIETY TODAY

Throughout the 1970s, people began to talk about death and dying. We have become concerned about the various ethical and practical issues that arise from our dealing with death as a technological phenomenon. For example, questions concerning euthanasia have received a great deal of attention. Books are being published about various aspects of death and dying; and educators are becoming concerned with death education. Although not accepting death, we are beginning to discuss death. Why has this change taken place?

Kastenbaum and Aisenberg (1972, pp. 234–236) discuss five reasons why mental health specialists have become interested in death. These reasons can be applied to many of us:

1. "We face the prospect of mass death." Just as the idea of mass death may justify the denial of death, it has also led people to question the meaning of life, and to bring forth a new death awareness.
2. "We are less isolated from violent death." Television news has brought death into our lives. Whether we see the results of an airplane crash or a fire, death comes into our living rooms every evening at six o'clock. This was especially true throughout the sixties during the Vietnamese War.
3. "We now have more 'mental healthers' who have been through the mill." Kastenbaum and Aisenberg note that mental health professionals, psychologists and psychiatrists, have become part of the establishment. Many of them are elderly and now have to deal with death in their own lives. They are now writing about death and dying.
4. "Simple faith in material progress is on the ebb." There has become an awareness that technology may cause as many problems as it alleviates—for example, the use of nuclear energy. In the past 20 years the life span of an American has hardly changed at all; nor have we increased our maximum longevity. The technology of dying has not seemed to alleviate the suffering of the dying. As a result, many ethical questions have been raised concerning our use of technology in handling the dying.
5. "We suspect our very way of life has lethal components." We must start to become concerned with death since our way of life may be the largest reason for premature death.

There is perhaps one more important reason for our new interest in death: we are becoming an older society. In 1977, almost 11 percent of the population was 65 or older. In 2020, the aged are expected to make up almost 16 percent of our population (U.S. Bureau of the Census, 1977, p. 327). This means that dying is becoming relevant to more of us.

As our attitudes toward death and dying change, Peter Steinfels (1975, pp. 3–4) cautions us as to how we should proceed. Death must be viewed as a mystery, not a problem; that is, death should be something we contemplate, rather than a problem we must solve. We must be aware that death has an "underside," that inherent in death are fears and contradictions. Ultimately, though, "discussions of death must be discussions about life." The question must not be, How should we order our dying? but, How should we order our living?

SUMMARY

According to Aries, Western civilization has experienced four attitudes toward death: resignation to death; acceptance of one's own death; fear of and fascination with death; and regarding death as shameful and prohibited. Many thanatologists feel that we exhibit the last attitude. The reasons for our denial of death are changing mortality patterns, the American value structure, the institutionalization of dying, the potential for mass death, and our family structure. Our society, though, is beginning to change—we are starting to talk about death. One major reason for this is that our society is graying: a larger proportion of the population is becoming elderly. However, we must come to realize that "discussions of death must be discussions about life" (Steinfels, 1975, p. 4).

LEARNING EXERCISES

1. Read a newspaper and note the following:
   a. How often is death mentioned?
   b. What deaths are reported?
   c. How is death reported in the obituary column?
   d. How is death reported in the rest of the newspaper?
2. Tell your friends that you are taking a course in death and dying. What are their reactions?
3. Talk about your feelings about death and dying with the person sitting next to you. After five minutes analyze what has happened in your conversation. What conclusions can you draw from this?
4. Observe how old people are portrayed on TV. What do your observations tell you about society's attitudes toward old people? Do the same with dying people.

AUDIOVISUAL MATERIAL

What Man Shall Live and Not See Death. 57 min/color/1971 Films, Inc.
A film showing the attitudes of Americans toward death, with conversations with doctors and clergymen as well as with bereaved and the terminally ill.

To Be Aware of Death. 13 min/color/1974. University of Minnesota or Billy Budd Films.
American youths' feelings toward death. Presented through a collage of photography, interviews, poetry, and stills with accompanying folk music.

The Meaning of Death in American Society. 28 min/audiocassette/1970. Dr. Herman Feifel, Charles Press.
Dr. Herman Feifel lectures on contemporary American attitudes toward death.

REFERENCES

Aries, P. *Western attitudes towards death.* Baltimore, Md.: Johns Hopkins University Press, 1974.

Choron, J. *Death and Western thought.* New York: Collier Books, 1963.

Corr, C. Reconstructing the changing face of death. In H. Wass (Ed.), *Dying: Facing the facts.* New York: McGraw-Hill, 1979.

Dublin, L., Lotka, A., & Spiegelman, M. *Length of life.* New York: Ronald Press, 1949.

Dumont, R., & Foss, D. *The American view of death: Acceptance or denial.* Cambridge, Mass.: Schenkman, 1972.

Feifel, H. Attitudes toward death in some normal and mentally ill populations. In H. Feifel (Ed.), *The meaning of death.* New York: McGraw-Hill, 1959.

Goldschneider, C. *Population modernization and social structure.* Boston: Little, Brown, 1971.

Gorer, G. *Death, grief and mourning.* New York: Doubleday, 1965.

Gorer, G. The pornography of death. In E. Shneidman (Ed.), *Death: Current perspectives.* Palo Alto, Calif.: Mayfield, 1976.

Jackson, C. *Passing.* Westport, Conn.: Greenwood Press, 1977.

Kastenbaum, R., & Aisenberg, R. *The psychology of death.* New York: Springer, 1972.

Kübler-Ross, E. *On death and dying.* New York: Macmillan, 1969.

Lerner, M. When, why and where people die. In O. Brim, H. Freedman (Eds.), *The dying patient*. New York: Russell Sage Foundation, 1970.

Lifton, R. J. On death and death symbolism: The Hiroshima disaster. *Psychiatry*, August 1964, *27*, 191–210.

Lofland, L. *The craft of dying*. Beverly Hills, Calif.: Sage Publications, 1978.

Parsons, T., & Lidz, V. Death in American society. In E. Shneidman (Ed.), *Essays in self-destruction*. New York: Science House, 1967.

Quint, J. Dying in an institution. In H. Wass (Ed.), *Dying: facing the facts*. Washington, D.C.: Hemisphere, 1979.

Stannard, D. *The puritan way of death*. Oxford: Oxford University Press, 1977.

Steinfels, P. Introduction. In P. Steinfels & R. Veatch (Eds.), *Death inside out*. New York: Harper & Row, 1975.

Thomlinson, R. *Population dynamics*. New York: Random House, 1965.

Toynbee, A. Changing attitudes toward death in the modern western world. In A. Toynbee, A. K. Man, N. Smart, et al. (Eds.), *Man's concern with death*. New York: McGraw-Hill, 1968.

U.S. Bureau of the Census. *Statistical abstract of the United States 1977*. Washington, D.C.: U.S. Government Printing Office, 1977.

U.S. Department of Commerce. *Social indicators*. Washington, D.C.: U.S. Goverment Printing Office, 1976.

U.S. Public Health Service. *Monthly Vital Statistics Report, 1971, 19(2)*.

U.S. Public Health Service. *Monthly Vital Statistics Report, 1973, 21(13)*.

Veatch, R. *Death, dying and the biological revolution*. New Haven: Yale University Press, 1976.

Williams, R. *American society*. New York: Knopf, 1970.

2

Death
and the Process
of Dying

As we have noted in Chapter 1, mortality patterns have changed throughout the years. In our society, people are living longer, and they are not dying at home anymore, but in institutions—away from family, friends, and pets. These changing mortality patterns can affect the way in which we perceive death. Our general lifestyle leads us toward viewing death as an isolated event. We do not live with death on our minds; when we do think of death, we find it difficult to concentrate on it for any period of time. It has been the experience of the authors in teaching classes on death, dying, and bereavement that it is difficult both for students and teachers to focus on a discussion of death for more than one hour at a time; somehow, at this point, the content of the discussion becomes very technical—for example, "How does embalming really work!"—and/or very dramatic, in that students begin to relate stories of bizarre deaths they have heard about. The reality of our own death remains remote and difficult to imagine, let alone to discuss. We can talk about death in theory; we can state that indeed we all shall die; then we relegate our own death to an abstract future. Kübler-Ross (1972) describes denial as one of our first defense mechanisms when we are confronted with the immediacy of our own death. Perhaps denial is not a stage of dying as much as it is an integral part of our current lifestyle in dealing with death. Freud (1957) has stated:

Picasso, Pablo. *Guernica.* (1937, May–early June).

It is indeed impossible to imagine our own death; and whenever we attempt to do so we can perceive that we are in fact still present as spectators. Hence the psychoanalytic school could venture on the assertion that at bottom no one believes in his own death, or, to put the same thing in another way, that in his unconscious, every one of us is convinced of his own immortality. (p. 289)

What death is, we cannot define, but we do attribute certain meanings to death and to dying. This chapter focuses on these various meanings, the process of dying, and the fears surrounding death and dying.

PERCEPTIONS OF DEATH

Although we do not have a definitive idea of what death is, we have various perceptions of it. Jung (1969) saw life and death as part of a continuing process:

Life is an energy process, like every energy process, it is in principle irreversible and is therefore unequivocally directed towards a goal. That goal is a state of rest. In the long run everything that happens is, as it were, nothing more than the initial disturbance of a perpetual state of rest which forever attempts to reestablish itself. (pp. 405–406)

Weisman (1972) proposes that for almost everyone, the meaning of death is that of a universal negative, repudiating and nullifying the objectives so sought in life (p. 8). The negative aspects of death include separation, loneliness, illness, injury, failure, humiliation, and defeat.

Death may be seen as a leveler by some people (Kastenbaum, 1977b, p. 41). Despite power, money, or fame, each person will die just as anyone else will. This view of death helps some of us to accept our current life states, since we know that eventually all of us—rich or poor—will die. When someone wealthy and powerful dies, such as Howard Hughes, we can say: "You see, even with all his money, he died like everyone else." Death may also be seen as a validator (p. 44). We can see this exemplified in the elaborate funeral arrangements that are prepared to make one last statement to society about the quality of the person's life, and to show the esteem felt by the survivors for the dead person. People pay to insure themselves a "proper funeral." The elaborateness of the funeral is seen as confirming not only the individual's worth but that of the survivors as well. The survivors have participated in an appropriate rite of passage, approved by society, that validates their status in the community.

Death may be perceived as a relief for people who are in pain, either physically or emotionally. A woman severely burned from her waist to her feet, who was valiantly struggling to live, sighed one day and said, "You know, it would be so easy just to close my eyes and die."

DYING AS A PROCESS

Just as it is difficult to define death, it is difficult to explain what it means to say that someone is dying. In a sense, we are all dying; yet we do not define ourselves as such. Do we define an 89-year-old man who is recovering from pneumonia as dying? Probably not, although we will define a 24-year-old with terminal cancer as dying. Yet the two will very likely have the same remaining time alive. When, then, does dying begin?

Kastenbaum (1977b, pp. 156–160) points out that there are a number of pragmatic definitions of dying based on levels of thoughts, feelings, and interpersonal communication. One may say that dying begins when a physician ascertains the facts and decides that the person is dying. Or dying may begin for the person when the prognosis is told; but a patient who denies the prognosis may not be dying to him- or herself. A person may not be considered dying until he or she realizes the true situation. Or a person may not be defined as dying until it is felt that nothing more can be done to preserve life.

Once a physician arrives at the conclusion that the person is dying however, the patient will enter a "dying trajectory":

> The course of dying—or "dying trajectory"—of each patient has at least two outstanding properties: first, it takes place over time. It has duration. Second, a trajectory has shape. It can be graphed. It plunges straight down, it moves slowly, moving slightly up and down before diving downward radically; it moves slowly down at first, then hits a long plateau, then plunges abruptly to death. Dying trajectories themselves are perceived, rather than the actual course of dying. (Glaser & Strauss, 1968, pp. 5–6)

There are various types of trajectories: (1) certain death at a known time; (2) certain death at an unknown time; (3) certain death but a known time when the prognosis will be made; and (4) uncertain death and an unknown time when certainty can be known. Within the dying trajectory, certain junctures or stages are passed: (1) the patient is de-

fined as dying; (2) staff and family prepare for the patient's death; (3)
it is decided that nothing more can be done; (4) the final descent occurs, leading to (5) the final hours; (6) the death watch; and finally (7)
the death itself (Glaser & Strauss, 1968, p. 7). These junctures may be
more easily ascertained during trajectories 1 and 3. During trajectories
2 and 4 caregivers must be more watchful in determining the critical
junctures. If the trajectory goes as it should, as perceived by the health
care professional, then the caregivers can be prepared for the critical
juncture and feel they have done the most that was possible.

What, however, is the patient going through once he or she is defined as dying? The work that has been most influential in terms of
answering this question is the book *On Death and Dying* by Elisabeth
Kübler-Ross (1972). Kübler-Ross divides dying into five stages:

1. *Denial and isolation*: This is the first response Kübler-Ross found
once patients were informed that they were dying. The people could
not believe that the prognosis was true. Kübler-Ross notes that she regards this as a healthy way of dealing with the uncomfortable and
painful situation. Denial can function as a buffer after the unexpected
news, which allows patients to collect themselves and mobilize other
defenses. After learning of his diagnosis of inoperable cancer, one patient talked about "being relieved surgery was not necessary—now I
can take my vacation and return to work. Surgery would have interfered with my plans."

2. *Anger*: Denial gets replaced by feelings of rage, and patients ask
themselves the question: "Why me?" Anger may be taken out on the
people around them—for example, a 20-year-old patient who, dying,
smashed an IV bottle since the nurse did not answer her call quickly
enough.

3. *Bargaining*: Here there is an attempt to postpone the death. People bargain with God in order to gain more time. Usually family events
or new projects are mentioned. "God knows I have a good book in me.
I'm sure this chemotherapy will give me enough time to finish it."

4. *Depression*: When patients finally realize that they are dying, the
rage turns to feelings of depression and loss. It is the anticipatory grief
that one goes through in order to prepare for one's own death.

5. *Acceptance*: When the patient has worked through the preceding
stages, the time will come when the death is accepted. A patient wrote
a letter to a friend a few months before her death in which she described her reconciliation and the shifts in her philosophy of life:
"There is so much importance in the here and now. I know this may

sound strange to you but this has been an intensely happy period for me."

Throughout all these stages, the patient will maintain hope. For example, patients who realistically acknowledge that they are dying may still hope for a miracle.

Kübler-Ross's work has become the accepted model for the care of the dying. The major problem is that health care professionals view the stages as normative rather than descriptive. At conferences on death and dying, one may hear a physician talk about waiting for an angry patient to enter the depression stage. Caregivers tend to fit patients into the stages rather than using the stages as a descriptive tool.

Most thanatologists agree that the feeling states described by Kübler-Ross do exist; however, they are not necessarily stages, with one feeling following the other. For example, Shneidman (1973) concluded from his work with the dying that the stages of the dying process are not necessarily lived through in any order:

> What I do see is a complicated clustering of intellectual and affective states, some fleeting, lasting for a moment or a day or a week; set, not unexpectedly against the backdrop of that person's total personality, his "philosophy of life" (whether an essential optimism and gratitude to life or a pervasive pessimism and dour or suspicious orientation to life). (p. 6)

The other major critique of Kübler-Ross's work is that there has been no further scientific testing of her findings. There have been no objective studies of the stage theory. As Kastenbaum (1977b) says, "For the better part of a decade, then, the basic stage conceptualization has been taken on faith" (p. 210).

However, Kübler-Ross's theory may be used as a guideline for listening to patients (Benoliel, 1970, pp. 265–266). While patients are denying, they may not be ready to confront their dying. Patients may make statements and plans for the future that indicate they are not thinking about dying. We need to be careful of how we interpret the use of denial. The label "denial" implies that the patient is not coping. However, this may be the only defense mechanism available at this time. It is equally important to listen for cues that may indicate that the patient is becoming more ready to discuss the situation.

Anger can be difficult both for patients and health care professionals. The patient may project anger about dying onto the environment. Patients may become noncompliant with the treatment regime and find fault with all that the staff tries to do. It is beneficial to reflect with patients on these angry feelings to help them focus more on what it is they are actually feeling. Anger often hides feelings of frustration, powerlessness, and helplessness—emotions that patients may be experiencing in trying to deal with their dying.

It was the third hospital admission for a 24-year-old woman with an inoperable spinal cord tumor. During the course of her illness, she experienced increasing loss of control— first, her lower extremities; next, bladder and bowel control. On this admission she rapidly lost the use of her arms and could only move her neck and head. She was coping with her fears and frustrations by constantly finding fault with hospital rules and regulations. In many instances the nursing staff agreed with her complaints and went out of their way to bend rules, and complied with all her requests. This included her refusal to use a call bell because she would not work with the physical therapist to learn to manipulate an oral device to produce enough pressure to trigger the light. She told the staff that she refused "to become a machine" just to satisfy a hospital rule to "use a bell." Whenever she needed assistance, she would call out her nurse's name. To the staff's surprise, her response to all their compliance was only an escalation of her demands. They soon started feeling angry and frustrated, and she was labeled a "problem patient." A patient care conference was arranged to discuss ways of handling her care. In the course of the meeting, the nurses were able to express their anger and explore their motivation for wanting "to do everything" to help the patient. It soon became apparent that their identification with her and their own sense of helplessness (not being able to stop her disease process) had reinforced the patient's feelings of not being in control. They agreed that she needed to be encouraged to explore her feelings about "becoming a machine," which had little to do with hospital regulations. They also saw that the anxiety she was feeling was related to her inability to "make sense" out of what was happening to her body. In many ways she no longer had "rules" to follow, and structure would be more helpful to her than total compliance with her demands. They agreed to discuss with her the necessity for certain rules to maximize her care, and to shift the emphasis of their interventions back to her underlying feelings. This approach was much more successful, and during the course of her hospitalization, the patient was able to mobilize herself and look forward to returning home.

During bargaining, patients often attempt to make "deals" to postpone their death until a certain goal or purpose is accomplished. A dedicated nursing instructor who was dying negotiated with her doctor to try to keep her well enough so she could finish teaching the semester. Depression, like anger, is difficult both for patients and staff. Patients are beginning to confront the reality of the losses death involves—loss of goals, family and, ultimately, of oneself. Staff members often find themselves experiencing depression with their patients. Again, if patients can be helped to talk about their feelings, they may not feel so overwhelmed, helpless, and alone. If there are some definitive concerns, such as financial or family matters, problem solving may help to relieve them. At other times, sitting in silence with patients—perhaps offering a touch now and then to let them know someone is with them—can be most helpful. Patients may not always be able to disucss their feelings of depression, but the presence and availability of another person can provide much comfort.

Not all patients accept their own death. If they do, they may express themselves in various ways. Some may wish to withdraw quietly, limiting their interpersonal relationships to a few friends or relatives. Others may wish to continue living their lives as they always have for as long as that is possible. Patients may want to reminisce, to do a life review in order to affirm their value and worth as people. Listening can be vital here, as patients come to terms with their lives. A component of dying is the fear of losing control. One way of giving control back is to ask: "What do you want?"—not what the doctor wants, or a spouse or relative, but what the patient wants—from whom and when (Ufema, 1977, p. 96).

Another view of the dying process is presented by E. Mansell Pattison (1977b). He sees dying patients going through three clinical phases once they are aware that they are dying: the acute crisis phase, the chronic living–dying phase, and the terminal phase. In the acute crisis phase, the patient will use the defense mechanisms described by Kübler-Ross—denial, anger, and bargaining—because of feelings of anxiety and inadequacy. Once patients begin to deal with their anxieties, they enter a chronic living–dying phase where they must deal with their fears. (These are discussed later in this chapter.) Patients enter the terminal phase when they begin to withdraw into themselves (see Figure 2.1). At this time, the patient's type of hope changes: he or she goes from having expectational hope to desirable hope. Expectational hope is the expectation that a miracle will happen: a cure will be discovered or a remission will occur. Desirable hope is the feeling that it would be good if one could be cured, but a cure is no longer expected.

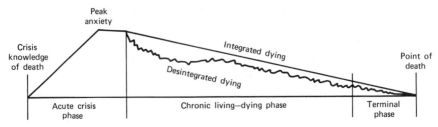

Figure 2.1 Clinical phases of dying. (E. Mansell Pattison, *The Experience of Dying*, © 1979. Reprinted by permission of Prentice-Hall Inc., Englewood Cliffs, New Jersey.)

Pattison (1977a, p. 306) does not view these phases as stages, but as convenient ways of dividing the living–dying process into three aspects to aid in understanding the dying process.

Kastenbaum and Weisman (1972), using the technique of the psychological autopsy, found that the terminally ill did not go through stages or phases. The psychological autopsy, first·developed by Shneidman and Farberow (1961), attempts to reconstruct the patient's dying. It provides insights into why the patient died, how the patient died, and the psychological state of the patient before death. Kastenbaum and Weisman found that everyone died in their own fashion. Once patients found out that they were dying, they tended to maintain a pattern of behavior that continued until death. Two major orientations were the acceptance of death, and the view of death as an interruption. The first orientation generally led to withdrawal, whereas people with the latter orientation kept actively engaged. From their studies, "the investigators learned to respect individual differences in the face of death and would not conclude that people either do die or should die in any one standardized way" (Kastenbaum, 1977b, p. 178). The dying process is influenced by our different perceptions of death throughout the life cycle.

Although we all will have idiosyncratic responses, age-related tasks will color and shape the "meaning" of death for the dying. Under the age of 3, illness and death are sources of separation anxiety. Children do not understand why their parents are not protecting them and feel angry and abandoned. The very young child is concerned with physical comfort and the knowledge that mother and/or other consistent caretakers are available. The preschooler (3 to 5) is in a period of struggle with sexually aggressive impulses directed against parents and siblings. Preschoolers often experience feelings of shame and fear of mutilation and invasion of the body. Illness is often viewed as punishment and impinging on their beginning sense of independence. School-age children (6 to 10) react similarly to preschoolers in that they feel responsible for the illness and attribute it to bad thoughts and actions. Their major concerns focus on an increased sense of competency and mastery. In working with these three age groups, it is essential to provide a constancy of caring to assuage the fears of abandonment. Children should be given every opportunity to work through their fantasies and to attempt to gain mastery over their situation. (Chapter 5 has a more detailed discussion.)

Adolescence is a time of intense emotional and intellectual preoccupation. The individual is in the process of separation from parents. Adolescents can be extremely sensitive about their physical appearance; their image is very important, both to themselves and to how they feel others view them. Garfield (1978) asserts that the adolescent does not have a sense of longevity and, therefore, develops a romantic notion of death. This lack of futurity is also confirmed by Kastenbaum's (1977a) study of adolescents. Adolescents are less concerned with the quantity of life and more concerned with quality, in that they seek affirmation of their worthiness and sense of self. Hospitalization and illness impinge on adolescents' growing sense of selfhood. They are very involved in the process of separation from parental authority and find themselves in a situation where all decisions concerning their bodies are left to their parents. Medical staff, if sensitive enough, may discuss procedures and the like, but parents sign consent forms. If the adolescent objects, this objection is often met with "You're not old enough yet." Treatment often involves loss of hair, weight, and energy. In helping the adolescent to cope with the crisis of illness, Garfield (1978) suggests that "the affirmation, confirmation and clarification of an adolescent as a unique and real being may be the most important task" (p. 156). An 18-year-old boy recently undergoing renal dialysis discussed his response to treatment very much with a "here and now" orientation. He was most concerned that he "really wasn't any different" and that "his fistula wasn't even noticeable." He was unclear about telling his peers because "he wasn't sure they'd understand" and he didn't "want to be treated like a sick person." He conceptualized his need for dialysis as a mode for increasing his independence: "Now my parents have promised to buy me a car."

For the young adult, life is just beginning; life tasks for this period include establishing a work identity and intimacy with a loved partner, including marriage and having children. Facing death at this stage of the life cycle is frustrating and disappointing. The young adult feels cheated and speaks about how "unfair" life can be. During this stage of life the individual will often cope with death by expressing rage at the world or by turning it inward and becoming depressed. If the individual is married and has children, he or she will experience anxiety about "who will care for the children" and "how my spouse will manage." A 22-year-old with Burkett's lymphoma became increasingly depressed and refused to see visitors. When asked to share her feelings, she became outraged and, in an outburst, screamed, "Talking isn't going to help. Unless you can give me back the use of my legs so I can put on my backpack and hike across the Rockies with my boyfriend, you're useless to me."

The middle years have a deeper interpersonal tone. This is a time of meaningful ongoing relationships, attainment of work goals, and expansion of the self. This is a time devoted to "establishing and guiding the next generation" (Erikson, 1963, p. 267). Kastenbaum (1977a) contends that the middle years can be particularly difficult because they often present a first major encounter with death. With increased longevity, parents generally do not die until this period in the life cycle, and the individual is faced with the double task of incorporating a major loss and facing personal mortality. Society's emphasis on beauty, youth, and strength contributes to the stress of this age. LeShan (1973) comments: "The greatest burden we carry into middle age is the burden of our masks. To some degree each of us is an island. We devote enormous amounts of time and energy to keeping up appearances and maintaining a good front while each of us weeps in the privacy of our own souls" (p. 188). Kastenbaum (1977a) refers to this phenomenon as "developmental death" (p. 39). People facing death during this phase of life must reconcile themselves to losing the opportunity to enjoy family and life successes, as well as new horizons of growth, and to feeling the failure of not "guiding the next generation." A 42-year-old woman with leukemia spoke about her eagerness to return home. She was looking forward to spending more time playing the piano. She had devoted most of her time to rearing her children and helping in her husband's business. She questioned whether this "had been the best thing," for perhaps her children needed an example of "taking time out for yourself. I want to devote more time to myself. I always used my family as an 'excuse.' I just couldn't allow myself the time I really deserve."

The older person faces multiple contradictions. The time to "sit back and take life easy" often is a period of multiple losses: spouse, peers, well-being, and work. Kastenbaum (1977a) calls this a time of "bereavement overload" (p. 42). This is a period when the individual thinks of death in practical terms. The elderly fear that they will become burdensome. Institutionalization is the response to increasing infirmity, fragmentation of family life, and inadequate health care supports within the community. The older person may "welcome" death as an escape from an otherwise unbearable situation. A recently widowed 89-year-old woman was admitted to the hospital because of increasing weakness and dizzy spells. Prior to her hospitalization, she had lived with her daughter, son-in-law, and five grandchildren. She very much wanted to return there, but said: "I know I can't go back. I feel like such a burden. None of this makes sense anymore. I've outlived my usefulness. Why doesn't God just take me?"

What is significant from this discussion is that death can have a variety of meanings for different people. We must listen to ourselves to discover what death means to us and to others—for the meaning of death for them may be different from what it is for us.

TALKING WITH PEOPLE ABOUT THEIR DYING

One difficulty in the dying process is that physicians are often reluctant to tell patients they are dying. Physicians themselves have different opinions of telling people about diagnosis of a terminal illness, or death; they may state "I always tell my clients" or "I never tell my clients." Oken's (1961) study, in which a questionnaire and interviews were used to study the policies of 219 physicians about "telling" cancer patients, showed that 90 percent indicated a preference for not telling. Fitts and Ravdin (1953) questioned 443 Philadelphia physicians about what they told their clients with cancer, and found that 70 percent of the physicians seldom or never told the clients their diagnoses whereas 30 percent always informed the clients of their disease. Physicians' own opinions, attitudes, beliefs, and convictions may influence their decisions rather than individual assessments of each unique client. Such convictions and beliefs may be heard in such statements as: "Most people don't want to know," or "People will lose hope if they are told," or "People will become too emotionally upset." These convictions may be based on the physician's own life experiences and/or on what he or she would like to be told, rather than on what the patient's actual needs are. According to Hinton (1966), there is little published evidence of suicide as a result of people being told in a thoughtful manner that they have a potentially fatal disease. However, serious illness may well contribute to suicide. The pain people feel; the disruption of their lives, of their physical image, of their social roles; the fear of dying— all are factors that could lead to suicide. The real roots, then, of physicians' policies about "telling" people are likely not to be actual clinical experience and/or research findings, but prejudices, inconsistencies, and perhaps underlying feelings of pessimism and futility if a particular disease is involved. Oken (1961) concluded that our strong feelings of concern for cancer patients and our difficulties in helping them stimulate denial mechanisms that, in turn, interfere with our abilities to respond to our patients' needs (p. 1120).

The traditional one-to-one relationship between a patient and a physician must be examined here to understand further what contributes to telling or not telling. The ethical foundations of Western medicine have been derived from the works of Hippocrates, with the physician emerging from this philosophic view as a benign but authoritarian figure. Pellegrino (1975) notes that "there is little or nothing in the Hippocratic works about dialogue with patients as consenting adults, and there are no prescriptions to engage them in the decisions that affect them or even to disclose what will be happening to them" (p. 399). Although a great many interactions between physicians and patients are still conducted in the more traditional mode of parent–child, there are some changes occurring here. Joseph Fletcher (1967) supports our rights as patients to know the medical facts about ourselves, and gives the following reasons for this: "first that as persons our human, moral quality is taken away from us if we are denied whatever knowledge is available; second, that the doctor is *entrusted* by us with what he learns, but the facts are ours, not his, and to deny them to us is to steal from us what is our own, not his; third, that the highest conception of the physician–patient relationship is a personalistic one, in the light of which we see that the fullest possibilities of medical treatment and cure in themselves depend upon mutual respect and confidence, as well as upon technical skill; and, fourth, that to deny a patient knowledge of the facts as to life and death is to assume responsibilities which cannot be carried out by anyone but the patient, with his own knowledge of his own affairs" (pp. 60–61).

Physicians are expected by patients and society to use judgment and discretion in the disclosure of information. If a patient has no desire to know the truth, this wish should be respected. Patients who are very ill, anxious, too young, very old, or of varying cultural backgrounds will have different needs for knowledge about their illness. However, as our society becomes more consumer oriented, and as health care is seen more in terms of prevention and self-care, people are becoming more protective of their rights to self-determination. Patients who are able to understand and cope with their illness will increasingly expect the physician and other caregivers to act as technical experts and advisers and to invite and include the patients' participation in treatment plans.

In a research study conducted by Kelly and Friesen (1950), two groups of 100 individuals each were polled regarding whether or not they would want to know if they had cancer; one group contained people with known cancer, and the other group consisted of people who were not known to have cancer. Questionnaire and interview returns indicated that the majority of people in both groups wanted to be told of the presence of cancer. Many people stated they wanted to know if they had cancer because even if it was bad news, it would make the situation definite. While this research indicates a need for patients to know about their illness, we should keep several factors in mind in our interpretation of such a study:

1. Patients who have been told they have cancer often cannot permit doubts about the people who have told them; they need to trust these people so very much.
2. For people who are cancer free, whether to tell or not to tell is only academic; it is not a personal issue with them.

Patients will vary in their needs to be aware, and in their abilities to cope with knowledge, of their illness. Caregivers' assessments of these needs and abilities for each individual patient are of utmost significance. Braver (1965) suggests that in considering whether or not a patient and family should be told the truth about dying, we need to ask ourselves, "Which patient? What truth?" (p. 178). It is important to assess very carefully the patient's and the family's understanding of the disease, their ways of dealing with stress and crises in the past as well as the present, their cultural orientation to death and grieving, and their support systems. It is also important to assess the patient's and family's understanding of certain words: *cerebrovascular accident* may not mean much to some people; *stroke* may convey much more (Brauer, 1965).

Some patients always want to know exactly what is happening to them; others do not want to know much about it. Denial, according to Kübler-Ross (1972), is experienced by most people as part of the dying process. Tolstoy, in *The Death of Ivan Ilych* (1896), aptly describes denial:

> Ivan Ilych saw that he was dying, and he was in continual despair. In the depth of his heart he knew he was dying, but not only was he not accustomed to the thought, he simply did not and could not grasp it. (p. 131)

If patients have a great need to deny a diagnosis and are told about it, they may forget it, distort it, disbelieve it, or repress it. It is therefore important for caregivers to communicate with other members of the health team as to what has been told to patients about their diagnoses. A team assessment of the patient's need to know about a diagnosis of fatal illness is helpful.

Caregivers themselves may use denial to cope with the reality that, although they have tried their best and have utilized all the knowledge that medicine, nursing, and technology have to offer, their patients do die. Goldstein (1972) reports on this use of denial in a study he conducted with chronic hemodialysis patients. Patients who were involved in this study were informed that they would receive some kind of remuneration for their participation. The remuneration was not yet established for the first patient-participant, and the researcher half-jokingly told the patient that the payment would be sufficient to cover dinner at a French restaurant. Neither patient nor researcher thought this was an unusual comment at the time. It was not until later that the researcher realized that suggesting dinner at a French restaurant to a patient who was on a strict diet, deviation from which could be fatal, was inappropriate and constituted an aspect of denial of the patient's serious illness.

There seem to be no set rules about what and how much patients should be told about diagnoses of their own terminal illness. Patients deserve thorough assessments of their needs and of their abilities to cope with this knowledge. Becker and Weisman (1967) suggest that in talking with patients about a fatal illness: "The central question is not whether or not to tell a patient about his dim outlook, but who shall tell, how much to tell, how to tell, when to tell, and how often to tell" (p. 647).

FEAR OF DEATH AND DYING

The literature about death frequently employs the phrases "fear of death" and "death anxiety" interchangeably. The word *fear* ordinarily connotes that one is afraid of something or someone; for example, a person may fear loud thunder or airplanes. *Anxiety*, on the other hand, conjures up vague, uneasy feelings. We are not specifically sure what is making us uncomfortable, but we know we are uneasy. Dumont and Foss (1972) suggest that death is sufficiently concrete for fear, sufficiently vague for anxiety (p. 17). Death is specific; we fear it and know it will happen. Yet there are many unknowns associated with death. We are uncertain of how, when, and where we will die; of what will happen to our survivors; and of what it means to be nonexistent. These unknowns can create anxiety. Therefore, we use "fear of death" and "death anxiety" interchangeably, since both feelings are present together.

There is one other distinction to be made in this use of terms before we proceed in our discussion—that is, the difference between the "fear of death" and the "fear of dying." Many people say that they fear dying more than they fear death, for dying connotes weakness, pain, dependency, loss of control, change in body image, and loss of contact with others. The expression of fears of dying may also be seen as defense against the actual expression of fear of death. Fear of death, with its finality of ceasing to be, may be intensely frightening. Of course, both fears may be present. As Collett and Lester (1969) point out, there can be potential usefullness in helping people express what their actual fears are for the fear of death of self, the fear of death of others, and the fear of dying of others can be different fears with different specific origins and, thus, with different avenues open for possible relief (p. 181). If we can be in tune with the messages dying people are giving us, and if we can listen to the fears they are expressing, we may be able to offer them some comfort.

Kastenbaum and Aisenberg (1972) regard the 'fear of extinction, an-

nihilation, obliteration, or ceasing to be as the basic fear of death"
(p. 44). It is their premise that other fears about death are not that dis-
similar from fears we have in life. For example, fear of dying often
involves feelings of becoming weak and dependent, but we have these
feelings in our day-to-day existence. We are fearful of what may happen to us in the moment after death, but often we are fearful in life
about what is going to happen tomorrow, or next year. Ceasing to be,
however, is a difficult concept to consider. Along with this fear of extinction, we are concerned about the loss of those things we enjoy in
life. When we contemplate death, it is difficult to "give up" those individuals and things in life that we enjoy and with which we identify our
"selves." Perhaps, too, we are fearful of what we will miss, of not knowing how life will progress. Many people may fear growing old for similar reasons.

Fear of the unknown can be part of our fear of death and dying. We
simply do not know what happens after death. There is no TV camera
crew to tape "After Death—What?" for the 6 P.M. news. Death evokes
in us a feeling of ultimate powerlessness since, for most, the time and
cause of death are unpredictable.

Another reason for fearing death may be that in death, we can no
longer achieve. Part of this fear may lie within our goal-oriented culture and in the fact that our self-esteem is related to what we produce,
what projects we complete, how much money we make. One research
study demonstrated that those who have attained most of their goals
fear death the least (Diggory & Rothman, 1961). Booth (1975) hypothesized that when individuals feel they have completed their life's work,
they are ready to die.

Fear of death may be related to our dread of isolation or separation.
One of our basic human needs, according to Sullivan (1953), is for intimacy, or relating to other human beings. Death, of course, is the ultimate separation and may be seen as total isolation and aloneness,
states of being that are intolerable to us in life. In Tolstoy's *Death of
Ivan Ilych* (1896), we can sense the anguish of Ivan's fear of the unknown and of separation when he says,

Yes, life was there and now it is going, going and I cannot stop it. Yes.
Why deceive myself? Isn't it obvious to everyone but me that I'm dying,
and that it's only a question of weeks, days, . . . it may happen this moment. There was light and now there is darkness. I was here and now I'm
going there! Where? (pp. 129–130)

Changes in our religious beliefs and ideas about sinfulness of the body and an afterlife have influenced our perceptions and fears of death. According to Feifel (1969), "fear of death no longer reveals fear of judgment as much as fear of total annihilation and loss of identity; death no longer signals salvation and atonement as much as the threat of loneliness" (p. 126).

Our society's emphasis on independence and control of our own destinies may also contribute to our fear of death and dying. We fear losing consciousness because this symbolizes loss of self-mastery. Along with this, we fear disrespect and humiliation. We may no longer even be in control of our bodily functions. For example, many dying patients become incontinent and must rely on others to clean them.

We are often reluctant to make out a will for equitable distribution of our material accumulations, although another fear we have of death is what will become of our dependents; who will take care of our children, our spouse, and our aged parents? Perhaps writing a will forces us to take one step farther in contemplating our own death, and we are reluctant to do this.

Could part of our fear of death be related to our fear of growing older? We have no place for older people in our youth-oriented society. Fulton states we will have 25 million people over age 65 at the end of the decade, and we don't know what to do with them (Symposium on death and attitudes toward death, 1972, p. 54). The thought of joining this group of people may be part of our death fear. In attempting to discover how old people themselves feel about death and dying, Butler (1964) and others questioned old people on their attitudes toward death. Many of the poeple in Butler's study stated their wish to avoid a painful death and to avoid being a burden to their families. The researchers also found that questioning old people about death was not as disturbing as they had expected. It seemed a source of some relief for the old people to have the question openly discussed. Thus, the process of conducting this study itself presented a new hypothesis—that the fear of death may be related to the lack of opportunity to discuss one's fear of death.

STIGMA AND THE DYING PERSON

It may well be that we see a dying person as a person with a stigma, because the dying person represents what we fear in and of our own deaths. Goffman's (1963) discussion about stigma seems applicable here:

> By definition, of course, we believe the person with a stigma is not quite human. On this assumption we exercise varieties of discrimination, through which we effectively, if often unthinkingly, reduce his life chances. We construct a stigma ideology to explain his inferiority and account for the danger he represents, sometimes by rationalizing an animosity based on other differences, such as those of social class. (p. 5)

Epley and McCaghey (1977–78), in their study on attitudes toward the terminally ill, found the existence of more negative attitudes toward the dying than are generally found expressed toward the ill or healthy. Our practices of isolating people who are dying and of not speaking openly about dying support the idea of death as a stigma and the feeling that certain diseases are more feared than others.

The stigma of death can also be transferred to a specific disease entity. Many people believe that the diagnosis of cancer is synonymous with death; and the word *cancer* is so powerful that a patient's knowledge of this diagnosis can actually hasten death. Relatives and friends often request that a patient not be told because "it will kill him," as if the knowledge and not the disease would be the cause of death. Once a patient is told, he or she must cope not only with personal fears but with those of relatives, friends, health care professionals, and society at large. This manifests itself in a variety of ways, and the cancer patient is often confronted with isolation from friends ("I don't know what to say"); loss of employment ("How can a dying person work?); withdrawal of loved ones ("I feel as if she's dead already"); and neglect or indifference by the medical staff ("Why bother, he's full of it"). The diagnosis so alters the image of individuals, both to themselves and others, that they become "different."

On the other hand, the cardiac patient faces none of these dilemmas. It would seem foolish not to inform a patient of a cardiac condition. Family and friends don't worry about what to say to cardiac patients about their disease. To the contrary, what led to the heart attack, course of treatment, and so on are frequent topics of conversation in visits with these patients. Employers often encourage their employees "to take it easy" and arrange for less stressful assignments upon return to work. Yet heart disease accounts for nearly 50 percent of all deaths in the United States, and cancer accounts for less that 17 percent (American Cancer Society, 1974). Recent figures provided by the

American Cancer Society indicate that one out of five patients will be without evidence of disease five years after diagnosis and treatment. Statistics do not seem to support the public's view of cancer. Based on these facts and figures, we should be less cancer phobic and more cardiac phobic. Why is this not so? Sontag (1979) suggests that the labels, notions, and myths around an illness create a metaphor that transforms the illness and gives it special meaning. She postulates that cancer lends itself to metaphor because it is "intractable and capricious—that is, a disease not understood—in an era in which medicine's central premise is that all diseases can be cured" (p. 5). Richards (1972) provides a similar description: "Cancer is one of the most intractable, variable, and incomprehensible forms of cellular derangement. A cancer is a crab as its name indicates. It claws at us, it hides in the sands of our flesh; like a crab it ignores straight walking, progresses sideways both in its refusal to behave in an honest, purposeful manner and in its need to invade neighboring tissues" (p. 74).

The metaphor will continue until the cause and cure of cancer are found. Sontag points out that terms used to describe the disease and treatment are military in nature: "cancer victim," "evasive," "colonizing cells," "bombarded," "chemical warfare," "kill the cells," Nixon's "War on Cancer." Everyone becomes involved in "fighting the unknown enemy." Fear of the unknown is universal and takes on special meaning for cancer patients. They have the image of "something" unknown growing within their bodies. They search for a meaning—"Why me?" Since the disease appears so irrational, it evokes irrational responses. Frequently patients view the disease as a punishment and experience feelings of shame and disgust.

Also connected with the unknown etiology is a fear of contagion. Although we consider ourselves a sophisticated society, many people worry that being around a cancer patient may be dangerous. One relative, a successful, prominent lawyer, spoke about his feelings regarding his mother: "I know this sounds foolish, but I found myself not wanting to touch her. I became worried. We really don't know the cause of cancer. My solution was to hire someone to care for her."

A cancer patient also faces a rigorous treatment regime that temporarily or permanently affects the body image. Surgery often results in physical disfigurement. This disfigurement can be hidden from view but remains a frequent source of anxiety. The colostomy patient worries about offensive odors and having "accidents." Postmastectomy patients are reassured that a prosthesis will be so "lifelike" that they will escape detection by the outside world. These reassurances are a double-edged sword, for the implicit message is that one has something to hide. Sontag (1979) also notes that we assign a hierarchy to our organs. Cancer frequently occurs in parts of the body—for example, colon, bladder, rectum, breast, and sex organs—that we are embarassed to acknowledge. She suggests that leukemia is a more "romantic" form of cancer since it is a nontumor malignancy and involves no specific organ and no surgical treatment. Cancer patients also fear they are no longer sexually attractive. Treatment often results in hair loss, weight loss, and diminished energy. Unlike cancer patients, cardiac patients know the etiology of their disease—they have a malfunctioning heart. It is organ specific and not the result of "cellular derangement." They experience more control over the progress and treatment of the disease. The malfunctioning heart can be "fixed" by medication, surgery, diet, and modification of lifestyle. Cardiac patients rarely are worried that they are no longer sexually attractive. Anxiety is related to the idea that sexual activity may "cause" another attack.

In recent years more attention has been focused on the "cancer personality." Hutschnecker (1965) describes the cancer patient as "a passive, dependent personality whose predominant attitude was a deep sense of futility and hopelessness" (p. 241). The work of LeShan (1977) suggests that there is a personality configuration that includes a childhood or adolescence marked by feelings of isolation, loss of a meaningful relationship in adulthood, and a belief that life holds no meaning. Simonton et al. (1978) describe the cancer personality as a person with a tendency toward self-pity and an inability to form and maintain meaningful relationships. Sontag (1979) objects to this psychologizing of a disease: "Psychological theories of illness are a powerful means of placing the blame on the ill" (p. 56). The psychosomatic component of any illness remains a controversial issue within the medical profession. In this discussion we are simply drawing attention to the negative multiple constructs placed on the "cancer personality." In contrast, the "cardiac personality," the executive Type A, has many more positive features. Hutschnecker (1965) describes cardiac patients "as persons striving for success, capable of postponing actions to achieve long-term goals" (p. 243). The public has a general image of a busy, successful, dynamic individual whose major "problem" is that he works too hard—a positive attribute in a society that traces its roots to the Puritan work ethic.

The type of death associated with each of these diseases is very different. Cancer is associated with protracted illness; increasing debilitation and dependency; intensive, unrelieved pain; and the knowledge that one is dying. Cardiac death suggests a fast, relatively painless death that comes without warning.

COPING WITH DEATH AND DYING

One way of dealing with the inevitability of death is by developing some sense of continuity of life. Lifton's (1964) concept of achieving a sense of immortality through the ideology of a life after death, as discussed in Chapter 1, has been prevalent in many religious beliefs. Often, dying patients who have been atheists seek out clergy, wishing to be united with a god or a belief that will offer them some promise of continued existence. We are again dealing with our fear of the unknown, of not knowing what death is, and of not knowing what, if anything, occurs after death. Jung (1969) has said that "the fact that we are totally unable to imagine a form of existence without space and time by no means proves that such an existence is in itself impossible" (p. 414).

Other ways of coping may be inferred from Dr. Raymond Moody's (1975) book *Life After Life*. He reports numerous case studies of "survival of bodily death." Actually the title of the book is somewhat misleading, as Dr. Moody discusses conscious awareness during the death experience rather than an ongoing existence after death. The people reporting death experiences relate events such as being met by dead relatives or friends and feeling the presence of a loving, warm spirit. They view a panoramic, instantaneous playback of major events in their lives, and reach some kind of border indicating a dividing line between earthly life and the next life. Not all people experienced all these events. In his review of cross-cultural literary sources, Holck (1978–79) found that the contemporary experiences of death described by Moody resembled the experiences of other people in different cultures in the past. This correlation raises the question of "whether these experiences are archetypal in nature in the sense of Jungian symbolism or whether they are to be understood as statements of factual events" (p. 10). We also raise the question of whether some of the components of these near-death experiences are being used on some level to mitigate the fears of death, and are therefore being utilized as defense mechanisms to cope with these fears. Certainly the experience of not being alone, of being met by dead relatives or dead friends, could help one to cope with the fears of loneliness and of nonexistence.

How do people feel who know that their death is imminent, whose death is not vaguely in the future but very soon? Hinton (1963), a British psychiatrist, interviewed 102 patients who were expected to die within six months. He also utilized a matched control group of "nondying" patients. He found that at least three-fourths of his dying patients knew their prognosis. Both groups were depressed and anxious, but the dying patients were more so than the control group. Interesting data about depression were revealed, in that differences between the groups were greater for depression than for anxiety. We see from Hinton's study that anxiety can be found in people who are facing death but that this need not be overwhelming, and that depression may be a more common expression of feelings. Kübler-Ross's work also indicates that people confronting their dying have varying feelings and may not be overwhelmed with fear for the remainder of their lives.

Pattison (1977a) analyzed the types of ego-coping mechanisms used by the dying. Table 2.1 summarizes his work. He cautions that he has summarized "typical mechanisms during the living–dying interval" (p. 314).

If we can come to terms with our fears of death, we may begin to focus on ourselves and review how we are living. Time becomes more precious. We ask ourselves, If I knew I had one more week, month, year to live, how would I spend my time? Some of us may well feel that we are living our lives to our fullest satisfaction and would not change our routines and schedules. Others may start thinking more of the quality of our actual lifestyles and routines. Nadine Stair (as quoted in Burnside et al., 1979), an 85-year-old woman living in Louisville, Kentucky, wrote the following:

If I had my life to live over, I'd dare to make more mistakes next time. I'd relax. I would limber up. I would be sillier than I have been this trip. I would take fewer things seriously. I would take more chances. I would take more trips. I would climb more mountains and swim more rivers. I would eat more ice cream and less beans. I would perhaps have more actual troubles, but I'd have fewer imaginary ones.

You see, I'm one of those people who live sensibly and sanely hour after hour, day after day. Oh, I've had my moments and if I had it to do over again, I'd have more of them. In fact, I'd try to have nothing else. Just moments, one after another, instead of living so many years ahead of each day. I've been one of those persons who never goes anywhere without a thermometer, a hot water bottle, a raincoat, and a parachute.

If I had it to do again, I would travel lighter than I have.

If I had my life to live over, I would start barefoot earlier in the spring and stay that way later in the fall. I would go to more dances. I would ride more merry-go-rounds. I would pick more daisies. (pp. 425–426)

From "The Later Decades of Life: Research and Reflections" by I. Burnside in Irene Burnside, Priscilla Ebersole, & Helen Monea (ed.), *Psychosocial Caring Throughout the Life Span.* Copyright © 1979 McGraw-Hill. Used with the permission of McGraw-Hill Book Company.

SUMMARY

Death has different meanings for all of us, both negative and positive. As we age and mature, our meanings change. It is difficult to say when we enter the dying process. However, once we are defined as dying, according to Kübler-Ross, we experience five stages: denial, anger, bargaining, depression, and acceptance. E. Mansell Pattison sees the patient as going through three phases: the acute crisis phase, the chronic living–dying phase, and the terminal phase. These theories are important because they provide the caregiver with a framework for working with the dying person.

Fears of death may be similar to other fears we have in life: fear of the unknown, fear of no longer achieving, fear of loneliness. One way to cope with our fears is to discuss them. Some diseases, such as cancer, elicit more fear than others, such as cardiac disease.

Ways to cope with death and dying include developing a sense of continuity of life. We may also use a variety of psychological mechanisms. If we can come to terms with our fears, then we can live more fully.

LEARNING EXERCISES

1. Discuss with your family and/or friends the idea of making a will and/or having life insurance. What does the discussion indicate about their thoughts and fears of death?

Table 2.1. Typical Ego-Coping Mechanisms of the Dying Throughout the Life Cycle[a]

Ego-coping Mechanisms	Early Childhood	School-age Child	Adolescence	Young Adult	Middle Age	Aged
Level 1: Primitive						
Delusions	+	+				
Perceptual hallucination	+	+				
Depersonalization	+	+				
Reality-distorting denial	+	+				
Level 2: Immature						
Projection	+ +	+ + +	+		+	
Denial through fantasy	+ +	+	+			
Hypochondriasis		+ +	+ +	+ +	+ +	+ + +
Passive-aggressiveness		+ + +	+ +	+ + +	+ +	+ +
Acting-out behavior		+ + +	+ +	+ + +		
Level 3: Neurotic						
Intellectualization			+ + +	+	+ + +	+
Displacement			+ +	+ +	+	
Reaction formation			+ + +	+ + +	+	
Emotional dissociation			+ + +	+	+	+

Level 4: Mature

Altruism	+		+	+ +
Humor	+	+	+	+
Suppression	+ +	+ + +	+ + +	+
Anticipatory thought	+ + +	+ + +	+ + +	+ + +
Sublimation	+	+	+ +	+ + +

^a + = occasional use
  + + = moderate use
  + + + = considerable use

E. Mansell Pattison (Ed.), *The Experience of Dying*, © 1977. Reprinted by permission of Prentice-Hall, Inc., Englewood Cliffs, N.J.

2. Visit a cemetery. By reading the epitaphs, can you make inferences about people's ideas about death?
3. Read *Death of Ivan Ilych* by Leo Tolstoy. What was Ivan Ilych's process of dying?
4. Role play physician and patient. The physician tells the patient that he or she is dying. Is the physician able to do this? Discuss the feelings and reactions of the physician and of the patient.

AUDIOVISUAL MATERIALS

How Could I Not Be Among You? 28 min/color/1970. Spectrum Motion Picture Laboratory.
A sensitive poet, Ted Rosenthal, depicts through poetry and visual accompaniment his feelings about having leukemia.

Dying. 97 min/color/1976. WGBH-TV.
Four different family groups respond to the death of a family member; a young widow, a single woman, a wife and her dying husband, and a black minister are represented in these groups.

Confrontation of Death. 35 min/color/1972. University of Oregon or University of Iowa.
People's perceptions of death are explored through the use of music, role playing, poetry, visual aids, and discussion.

To Die Today. 50 min/black and white/film or videotape/1971. Filmmakers Library.
Dr. Elisabeth Kübler-Ross discusses her theory of the dying process.

Facing Death. 20 min/color/1968. National Medical Audiovisual Center.
A panel discussion in which four physicians discuss the problem of telling a patient and family about a terminal illness.

REFERENCES

American Cancer Society. *Cancer facts and figures*. New York: ACS Publishers, 1974.

Becker, A. H., & Weisman, A. D. The patient with a fatal illness—To tell or not to tell. *Journal of the American Medical Association*, August 21, 1967, *201*, 646–648.

Benoliel, J. Talking to patients about death. *Nursing Forum*, 1970, *9*(3), 254–268.

Booth, G., M. D. Personal communication, 1975.

Brauer, P. H. Should the patient be told the truth? In J. Skipper & R. Leonard (Eds.), *Social interaction and patient care*. Philadelphia: Lippincott,1965.

Burnside, P. E., Ebersole, P., & Monea, H. *Psychosocial caring throughout the life span*. New York: McGraw-Hill, 1979.

Butler, R. N. Attitudes toward death, an interview. *Geriatrics*, February 1964, *19*, 58A.

Collett, L., & Lester, D. The fear of death and the fear of dying. *Journal of Psychology*, 1969, *72*, 179–181.

Diggory, J. C., & Rothman, D. Z. Values destroyed by death. *Journal of Abnormal and Social Psychology*, July 1961, *63*, 205–209.

Dumont, R. G., & Foss, D. C. *The American view of death: Acceptance or denial?* Cambridge, Mass.: Schenkman, 1972.

Epley, R. J., & McCaghey, C. H. The stigma of dying: Attitudes toward the terminally ill. *Omega*, 1977–78, *8*(4), 379–393.

Erikson, E. *Childhood and society*. New York: Norton, 1963.

Feifel, H. The problem of death. In H. M. Ruitenbeck (Ed.), *Death: Interpretations*. New York: Delta, 1969.

Fitts, W. T., Jr., & Ravdin, I. S. What Philadelphia physicians tell patients with cancer. *Journal of the American Medical Assocation*, 1953, *153*, 901–904.

Fletcher, J. *Morals and medicine*. Boston: Beacon Press, 1960.

Freud, S. Thoughts for the times on war and death. *Standard edition, Vol, XIV*. London: The Hogarth Press and the Institute of Psychoanalysis, 1957.

Garfield, C. *Psychosocial care of the dying patient*. New York: McGraw-Hill, 1978.

Glaser, B., & Strauss, A. *Time for dying*. Chicago: Aldine, 1968.

Goffman, E. *Stigma*. Englewood Cliffs, N.J.: Prentice-Hall, 1963.

Goldstein, A. M. The subjective experience of denial in an objective investigation of chronically ill patients. *Psychosomatics*, January–February 1972, *13*, 20–22.

Hinton, J. The physical and mental distress of the dying. *Quarterly Journal of Medicine*, 1963, *32*, 1–21.

Hinton, J. Facing death. *Journal of Psychosomatic Research*, July 1966, *10*, 22–28.

Holck, F. H. Life revisited (Parallels in death experiences). *Omega*, 1978–79, *9*(1), 1–11.

Hutschnecher, A. Personality factors in dying patients. In H. Feifel (Ed.), *The meaning of death*. New York: McGraw-Hill, 1965.

Jung, C. The soul and death. In *Collected Works*, Vol 8, ed 2. The structure and dynamics of the psyche. Bollingen Series XX, Princeton, N.J., Princeton University Press, 1969.

Kastenbaum, R. Death and development through the life span. In H. Feifel (Ed.), *New meanings of death*. New York: McGraw-Hill, 1977.

Kastenbaum, R. J. *Death, society, and human experience*. St. Louis, Mo.: C. V. Mosby, 1977.

Kastenbaum, R., & Aisenberg, R. *The psychology of death*. New York: Springer, 1972.

Kastenbaum, R., & Weisman, A. The psychological autopsy as a research procedure in gerontology. In D. Kent, R. Kastenbaum, & S. Sherwood (Eds.), *Research, planning and action for the elderly*. New York: Behavioral Publications, 1972.

Kelly, W. D., & Friesen, S. R. Do cancer patients want to be told? *Surgery*, June 1950, *27*, 822–826.

Kübler-Ross, E. *On death and dying*. New York: Macmillan, 1972.

LeShan, E. *The wonderful crisis of middle age*. New York: D. McKay, 1973.

LeShan, L. *You can fight for your life*. New York: Harcourt Brace Jovanovich, 1977.

Lifton, R. J. On death and death symbolism: The Hiroshima disaster. *Psychiatry*, August 1964, *27*(3), 191–210.

Moody, R. A. *Life after life*. Covington, Ga.: Mockingbird Publishing, 1975.

Oken, D. What to tell cancer patients. *Journal of the American Medical Association*, April 1961, *175*, 1120–1128.

Pattison, E. M. The dying experience, retrospective analyses. In E. M. Pattison (Ed.), *The experience of dying*. Englewood Cliffs, N.J.: Prentice-Hall, 1977.

Pattison, E. M. The experience of dying. In E. M. Pattison (Ed.), *The experience of dying*. Englewood Cliffs, N.J.: Prentice-Hall, 1977.

Pellegrino, E. D. Protection of patients' rights and the doctor–patient relationship. *Preventive Medicine*, December 1975, *4*, 398–403.

Richards, V. *Cancer: The wayward cell*. Berkeley: University of California Press, 1972.

Shneidman, E. *Deaths of man*. New York: Quadrangle, 1973.

Shneidman, E., & Farberow, N. *The cry for help*. New York: McGraw-Hill, 1961.

Simonton, O. C., Mathews-Simonton, S., & Creighton, J. *Getting well again*. New York: J. P. Tarcher, 1978.

Sontag, S. *Illness as metaphor*. New York: Vintage Books, 1979.

Sullivan, H. S. *The interpersonal theory of psychiatry*. New York: Norton, 1953.

Symposium on death and attitudes toward death. *Geriatrics*, August 1972, *27*, 52–60.

Tolstoy, L. *The death of Ivan Ilych and other stories*. New York: New American Library, 1960.

Ufema, J. Do you have what it takes to be a nurse-thanatologist? *Nursing*, May 1977, *77*, 96–99.

Weisman, A. D. *On dying and denying*. New York: Behavioral Publications, 1972.

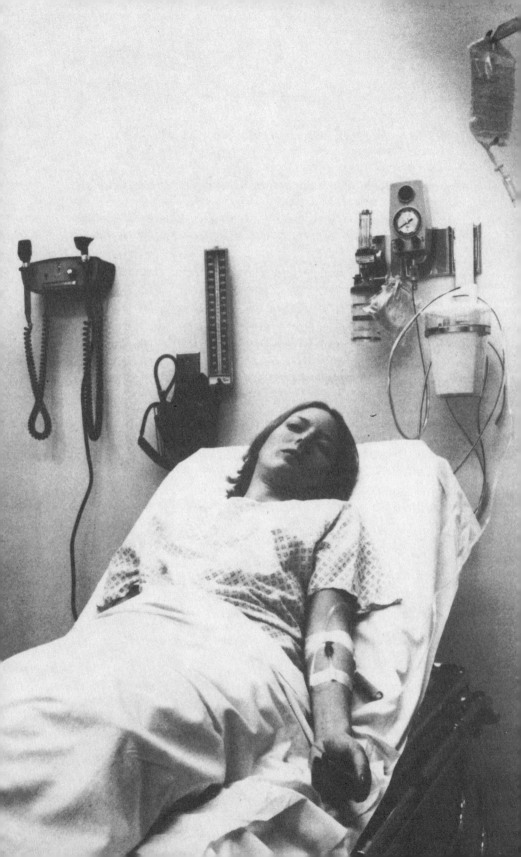

3
The Hospital and the Dying Patient

The central goal of hospitals today is patient care, with an emphasis on the cure aspect of that care. Many specialized procedures supported by complex equipment and drugs are performed in hospitals to accomplish this goal. Although these procedures are indeed awesome and at times miraculous, the hospital primarily is an organization of human beings, of both staff and patients; and without these human beings working together, technological, scientific, and medical knowledge cannot be utilized to their fullest extent. Curing and caring are thus affected by human values, emotions, and thoughts.

EVOLUTION OF HOSPITAL CARE

The earliest hospitals existed as the healing temples of ancient Egypt, along with the public hospitals of Buddhist India and the Muslim East. The modern hospital of the Western world has evolved from European medieval institutions of the same name but with different functions (Burling et al., 1956). In their origin, these hospitals did not have client cure as their primary goal; in actuality they were not concerned with the care of the sick at all. During the religious pilgrimages in the Age of Faith, many travelers were in need of overnight lodgings, but there were no commercial inns or hotels. Religious organizations, supported by gifts of wealthy parishioners, met this need by establishing inns and lodging houses called *hospitals,* this name being derived from the Latin *hospes,* meaning "host." Gradually these hospitals began to take in the homeless and the poor within the cities and provide more permanent lodging for them. The original hospitals, then, were not for the practice of medicine, nor were they even concerned with the care of the sick. However, as many of the poor and homeless seeking refuge in the hospitals were physically ill, some kind of nursing care, and eventually medical care, was provided. The provision of such care was minimal and haphazard, and the hospitals were crowded and unsanitary. The hazards to health were usually greater in the hospital than in the home, and admission to these institutions was frequently regarded as a disgrace (Commission on Hospital Care, 1957, p. 424). Religion and religious orders continued to have an influence on the development of hospital care. Wars also contributed to this development, as care was needed for those who became sick or wounded in battle.

In the eighteenth century, there were still many people who believed that the only possible place for recovery from disease was in the natural environment of social life, the family. The ill person at home was freely exposed to all the natural curative and caring aspects of family life—the benevolence, the comfort, the consolation. Doctors made home visits and family members nursed the ill person. Added benefits of this "home care" were that the cost of sickness to the nation was reduced to a minimum, and the risk of the disease spreading to a large hospital population was avoided. Our current "modern" ideas of home care and the hospice movement, which are discussed later in this chapter, had already been practiced 200 years ago.

> Generally speaking, it might be said that up to the end of the eighteenth century medicine related much more to health than to normality; it did not begin by analyzing a "regular" functioning of the organism and go on to seek where it had deviated, what it was disturbed by, and how it could be brought back into normal working order; it referred, rather, to qualities of vigour, suppleness, and fluidity, which were lost in illness and which it was the task of medicine to restore. To this extent, medical practice could accord an important place to regimen and diet, in short, to a whole rule of life and nutrition that the subject had imposed upon himself. This privileged relation between medicine and health involved the possibility of being one's own physician. (Foucault, 1973, p. 35)

Nineteenth-century medicine, on the other hand, was regulated more in accordance with normality than with health (Foucault, 1973, p. 35). Pathological anatomy—utilization of autopsies to ascertain the focal point of disease—and scientific and technological advances focused the experience of medicine on pathological reactions, physiological knowledge, and on diagnosis and intervention. Florence Nightingale's recognition of the relationship between filth and hospital death rates, Pasteur's work with bacteria, Lister's work with antisepsis, and the introduction of the clinical thermometer, ophthalmoscope, sphygmomanometer, and diagnostic instruments were among the innovations that helped the hospital to become a safer place.

Hospitals were used for teaching medical practice during the nineteenth century, and during the last few years of that century, a new medicine and teaching developed, based on careful observation of patients and broader theoretical teaching. For clinical experience for students, and for the advancement of medical and scientific knowledge, it was necessary for hospitals to reorganize their structure to include teaching and research functions. Hospitals thus have evolved from being providers of lodging for travelers and a last resort for the poor, helpless, and dying to being centers that serve the entire community for both minor and major illnesses. They also serve as sources of private initiative, teaching, research, and, for many communities, employment.

We might say that the turning point in medical knowledge that influenced the goals of the hospital came during the last years of the eighteenth century. The new structure of medicine could be seen by the difference in a basic question: "What is the matter with you?" was what the eighteenth-century doctor asked the patient; it was now replaced by the other question: "Where does it hurt?" (Foucault, 1973, p. xviii). The latter question focuses on the idea of a cause-and-effect relationship of disease, with the implication that once these are determined, intervention can proceed. The "cure" orientation was established. What, then, is the structure of a health care system with a cure orientation, and how does a dying person, someone who cannot be "cured," fit into such a system? We shall look at hospital norms and values as a reflection of our current health care orientation, since hospitals are a primary provider of health services and since consumers are increasingly utilizing them for all types of care.

GOALS OF HOSPITAL CARE

The curing goal of hospital care today reflects our culture's contemporary concepts of illness. In the United States we have a general belief that health and physical well-being are ends worth pursuing, and that they are possible to attain (Mumford, 1967, p. 32). We regard illness as a mishap, something that can be overcome, and we expect professional medical people to help us get well when we are sick. As a people, we believe that there should be a new and better way for doing every-thing, and that there must be a way to solve each problem. We do not tolerate ambiguity well; we are sure we can find an answer to conflict-ing situations. Our beliefs about life, health, and illness have stimu-lated many people in the United States to concentrate their energies and attention on the healing arts and sciences. These efforts are re-flected in the tremendous increases in technological and scientific knowledge we are consistently experiencing. Hospitals, as organiza-tions of people in this culture, also reflect these beliefs and values.

Many hospitals, because of their increases in size as well as the quan-tity and quality of services offered, high client turnover, and tenden-cies toward increased specialization, have become formal bureaucra-cies. Merton (1957) defines a bureaucracy as a "formal, rationally organized social structure which involves clearly defined patterns of ac-tivity in which, ideally, every series of actions is functionally related to the purposes of the organization" (p. 195).

A bureaucracy is based upon rationality; that is, it is an organization that is set up so that the goals of the organization will be met effi-ciently. If the goal of the hospital bureaucracy is to cure people, then what happens to those who cannot be cured? Mauksch (1975) points out:

> The dying patient represents a series of human events where the needs of the patient cease to be translatable into routines and rituals. It is in this fundamental sense that the dying patient threatens the hospital and its personnel. The routine orders, the predictable activities, when applied to the dying patient, cease to be meaningful, cease to be effective, and above all, cease to be satisfying either to the people doing them or to the patients who receive them. (pp. 9–10)

Professional caregivers working within a hospital bureaucratic system are exposed to two lines of authority—professional and bureaucratic—both of which are important to the hospital's functioning but that may also lead to conflicts for the caregivers. Professional authority lies within the person who has the freedom and responsibility to make judgments and decisions based on professional skill and knowledge. The professional person has basic authority from outside the bureau-cracy, and uses this authority on behalf of the individual client. The bureaucracy emphasizes conformity to rules and regulations and to "getting things done." The professional caregiver utilizes means to achieve an end; in a bureaucracy, with emphasis on procedures and tasks, the means may often *become* the end. This difference in goals can lead to a dichotomy between loyalties—one to the organization and one to the patient. A nurse working in a hospital unit may have six or seven seriously ill patients to care for on a certain day. One of these patients is dying and needs the nurse for much physical care as well as for time to spend talking. The routine of the unit is to have all patient care completed by 11 A.M. If the nurse takes the time to administer the complete care this dying patient needs, she or he will not be finished at the prescribed time. Evaluations of nursing performance may be made on how quickly and efficiently nurses complete their assignments; their promotions, salary, and, often, days off are based on these evaluations. The conflict is real, the frustration great, the solution not easily found. For caregivers to find the balance between adherence to rules and regulations and the important flexibility often indicated in providing professional care is difficult but necessary if patients are to receive the individualized treatment they need.

We can thus begin to understand some of the conflicts and problems that arise for hospitalized dying patients, both within themselves and within the people who provide care for them. Relating within a bureaucratic organization, with cultural beliefs that something can be done about illness, and with expectations that the modern hospital— with all its advanced knowledge—can diagnose and cure, staff and dying patients are now confronted with the uncomfortable ambiguity of death, and often with a disease that cannot be cured. There frequently are no definitive answers to offer dying patients about the time and manner of death, what it will be like, and why this is happening to this particular person. Caregivers, who are used to providing answers, may find this vagueness unacceptable to their professional identities. Caregivers may also feel that they have failed in that they did not do enough for the patient. They may ask themselves whether they explored every possible avenue of treatment for this person, whether there could have been any new procedures just developed that might have helped. Caregivers may carefully review everything they did with the patient, for there can often be a haunting doubt that an error was committed that may have contributed to the death (Mauksch, 1975).

Clients may feel angry because their expectations for help are not being met.

> Generally, in our culture, the explicit goal of medical treatment is that of partial or complete recovery of the patient. This tends to be the most valued goal in an achievement-oriented society ... (Coser, 1963, pp. 232– 233)

However, not all patients can get well. The task of the hospital's caregivers is not only to get the patients better but also to care for them if their illness or disability is irreversible. In Catholic cultures, taking care of the suffering tends to be considered a "good deed" in itself, and nuns who engage in this activity are highly esteemed in the community. On the other hand, in our achievement-oriented culture, not much prestige is associated with the task per se of *caring* for patients (Coser, 1963). We can look to the number and qualifications of staff in nursing homes and mental institutions as compared to those of teams in hospital intensive care units as examples of this.

In a study that included observations of staff behavior in a hospital defined as one that "only" cares for patients who cannot get better, Coser (1963) found that the abandonment of the culturally approved goal of "curing the sick" had several significant consequences (p. 233). The scaled-down goal of caring rather than curing had a direct effect on staff: it encouraged either ritualistic or retreatest behavior. Ritualistic behavior was seen as behavior in which active striving was given up but institutional norms were still carried out, and retreatest behavior was an escape from active involvement in either goals or means. This study indicates that by its definition of organizational needs, an institution can evolve a social structure that will help form a socially established pattern of behavior for its members.

In analyzing the goals and power structures in complex organizations, Perrow (1963) hypothesizes that

> over the long run, an organization will be controlled by those individuals or groups who peform the most difficult and critical tasks. The characteristics of this dominant group (social background, career, ideology or point of view, personal interests, and so on) will determine major operating policies and thus organization goals. (p. 113)

If patients come to a hospital expecting a cure, and if physicians are seen and portrayed as the group providing this cure, then cure is the critical task to be accomplished, and physicians' ideology of cure will prevail as a major institutional goal. And if hospitals are organized and perceived as acute treatment centers and the primary goal is cure, the caregivers' behavior will reflect this goal. In our thinking about health care in hospitals and about other health services, we must begin to work through the implications of illnesses that cannot, in general, be cured but only "managed" and lived with; this thinking must include the needs and care of dying people. Care and cure are not mutually exclusive, but as long as the cure aspects assume higher priority, status, and rewards, this will be the main organizational emphasis and goal for patients and staff. Consumers of health care, as much as the caregivers, must provide the impetus and demand for health services that provide adequate care and assistance in "living with" an illness.

ROLE EXPECTATIONS

In order to understand further the goals of hospitals and how these goals influence staff and patients, it is important to consider the roles people assume in hospitals. For each position (patient, nurse, doctor, aide, social worker) in a social organization such as a hospital, there are some expectations about what the person in that position is supposed to do. "These include the rights and privileges that go with the position and also the obligations and duties" (Mumford, 1967, p. 57). The combination of expectations about what one is supposed to do in such a position is called the *role*. Examples of role expectations in a hospital setting are that patients follow doctors' orders; nurses administer medications; aides make beds; social workers talk to families and assist in aftercare planning.

Conflicts may arise among role partners when their ideas of fulfilling their roles do not coincide; patients may disagree with doctors' orders, and nurses may ask patients to administer their own medications. Such conflicts can lead to further understanding and development of roles, or they can result in an impasse among participants, with a possible detriment to patient care. We have created a special position for sick people in our society. Role expectations for being ill include the right to be dependent, to accept help from strangers, and to expect to be helped. Patients must also conform to the rules and regulations of bureaucratic structure. In their study of a large medical center's functioning, Duff and Hollingshead (1968) state:

> Between admission to and discharge from the hospital, the patients were subject to the orders of the staff. They were separated from their families. Their street clothes were shed. They were assigned to beds, given numbers, and dressed in bedroom apparel. They had to permit strangers access to the most intimate parts of their bodies. Their diet was controlled, as were the hours of their days and nights, the people they saw, and the times they saw them. They were bathed, fed, and questioned; they were ordered or forbidden to do specified things. As long as they were in the hospital they were not considered self-sufficient adults. (p. 269)

People who do not comply with these role expectations cause much annoyance within the health professions. Patients who come from different cultural backgrounds have not learned these role concepts and hence may not know this sick role as we define it. Patients of our own culture who are dying may not fit into this sick role; they may refuse certain treatments, and they may wish to remain as independent as possible, seeking as much living in each day as possible. Caregivers who expect these patients to assume the usual sick-role behaviors may often consider them malingerers, complainers, obstreperous, or attention seekers if they do not conform.

Ill and/or dying people who are at home still have some control over their environment. They may decide when they will eat and sleep and may be responsible for taking their own medicine. They may still retain their family roles of parent, child, grandparent, and so on, and are still usually included in family decision making and planning. On the other hand, once people enter the hospital as patients, they lose their normal social roles and must learn to interact in a totally new and alien environment. Patients need to learn what questions to ask of whom; in order to do this, they must understand the division of labor in the hospital and the staff status hierarchy. Questions about prognosis will most likely be answered by doctors; nurses will respond to questions about hospital policy and rules; and nurses' aides are the people who will give the most realistic information about the ward routine. Patients will need to learn the jargon of the hospital before they can know what is expected of them in this new role. A patient was asked each day for three days if she had voided; the patient responded no each day. On the fourth day a nurse came into the patient's room with catheterization equipment. The nurse explained to the patient that she was going to help her pass her water since she had not done so in three days. The patient exclaimed, "So that's what they were asking me—of coure I've peed—why didn't they just ask me that?"

How we perceive patients as they enter the hospital system greatly influences our care of them. Do we see patients as being at the top of the totem pole, as important people for whom we will mobilize our resources and those of the hospital to assist them physically and emotionally? Or do we see patients at the bottom of the system's hierarchy, as people who should do as we dictate and who will receive our services at our convenience? Coser (1962) points out that "as an ideology, hospital staff adhere to the belief that concern for the Patient (with a capital "P"), as a total person, is the mainstay of their practice but that in reality, the individual patient tends to remain an object or a 'case'" (p. 34). With this latter orientation, the patient is seen, not as a person

in a strange environment who is ill and struggling to maintain autonomy, identify, and respect, frequently in a state of physical and mental
powerlessness, but as someone to be "managed"—as one would manage a thing, rather than a human being.

Excerpts from a letter written by a patient to hospital staff summarize the foregoing statements quite candidly.

2:00 A.M.

12 December 79

To all who care about patients

1979, for me, was a year filled with much pain and agony, trauma and
shock, sadness and hurt, setbacks, recoveries, happiness, and hope. I've
overdone my time here at the hospital. . . . I was admitted with lower body
pains and as a result of an overactive spinal tumor and many complications I'm now a paraplegic. I spent a wonderful month of October at
home for the first time since November '78 only to have to return to the
hospital again. Hopefully I'll be honorably and permanently discharged
next week and with some home physical therapy and outpatient chemotherapy, I aim to stay there for a while.

Enough history, though I hope just the right amount to sufficiently prove
that I've had ample experience in the role of patient. Speaking medically,
I was well taken care of by many competent doctors and outstanding
nurses, though many isolated incidents irreparably tarnished the view of
doctor as omnipotent and patient (me) as blind obeyer. I started asking
many questions, getting unsatisfactory or evasive answers, and then finally
learning the truth, which generally was not pleasant. . . .

I still question; I still complain; and I grieve over what I think is one of
the WORST problems in this hospital and probably in other large institutions . . . that patients are looked at and treated by many just as Case
#16, Disease #12, Temperature 99.2° Do you know what it feels like to
wake up to 12 pairs of eyes (rounds) staring at you in the morning, or one
pair shaking you awake at 2:00 A.M. and in both cases, "and how are you
today?" In one case, I don't know yet as I was sleeping; in the other, it
had taken me an hour to finally fall asleep and what am I supposed to say
now?!? Ever have a hematoma (black and blue in street language) on your
arm, a foot long, and they still insist on taking blood from the same place?
Ever been emotionally upset, drained, about surgery, and then going
through ups and downs of rescheduling and cancelling? not to mention
the anxiety of the families too? It's all happened, that and more, again

and again, to me!! There's a problem here that many forget, that PA-
TIENTS ARE PEOPLE, TOO! . . . like any other people, except we're
suffering in some way and that makes us oversensitive and less tolerant.
We've no privacy of body or soul; closed curtains don't often stop the un-
invited from entering. How many patients know that there is a document
stating patient rights? How about some compassion; a smile? Just sacrifice
some mechanical performance and call me by my name! Show concern for
me and not just for my liver!

Staff and patients may have different perceptions of the purposes of
the hospital and, hence, different expectations about their roles and
hospital functions. In her study of doctor–client relationships in a
medical center, Roberts (1977) found that medical students, interns,
and residents felt that the first purpose for their being in that setting
was education; patients, on the other hand, felt that since this was a
hospital, its obvious purpose was the care and cure of patients (pp. 45–
46).

Although the hospital does follow a bureaucratic structure in terms
of rules and regulations, there is some leeway in how these are interpreted. Staff and patients are involved in ongoing negotiation processes within this structure. For example, physicians seeking hospital admission for their clients may be told by admissions personnel that no
beds are available. The doctors may then negotiate: if they discharge
one of their patients the next morning, the new patient may be admitted now. A doctor and a nurse may negotiate regarding treatment
plans for a particular patient, each having a different plan and both
trying to arrive at a unified approach. Patients enter the negotiating
process also; they may negotiate for certain privileges, such as smok-
ing, and also for information that is important to their own understanding of their illness.

Patients who are dying may have to negotiate a great deal with staff
in order to be treated the way they so much want. Negotiations between dying patients and hospital staff are difficult at best and, at
times, nonexistent. Why does this occur?

CAREGIVERS' RESPONSES TO DYING PATIENTS

In the hospital the idea of dying in a sense labels a patient, places a
frame of interpretation around a person (Sudnow, 1967). Dying patients may be assigned a private room at the end of the corridor, away

from other patients and the nurses' station. This is ostensibly for the patient's peace, quiet, and privacy, but a closer analysis could indicate the staff's unwillingness to be in contact with that patient. Once the patient is admitted, staff may find many reasons not to go into that room at the end of the hall unless absolutely necessary; these may be "Too busy," "Other clients are more sick," "I'll spend time there tomorrow." "We speak often of the loneliness of dying patients and they are indeed lonely, for not only are they going where no one wants to follow but also the people around them prefer to pretend that the journey is not really going to happen" (Morison, 1973, p. 57).

In working with dying patients, we often function within a network of ambiguous definitions of what might be done, what should be done, what must be done (Duff & Hollingshead, 1968, p. 307). Caregivers consider such conflicting questions as to what extent evasions, misrepresentations, or untruths should be used to "protect" the patient and the family, and to what extent a disease should be treated. Patients also deal with conflicting questions, such as: "Is the physician telling me all I need to know, or should I ask about my illness? If I ask, will I be realistically answered? If I get an answer, should I tell my family? Will the physician tell my family?" Family members may ask the physician not to disclose information to the patient for fear of emotional upset. Pretenses about the fatality of an illness are not so easy to maintain as the illness advances in severity. Patients begin to question the more frequent, longer visits of family and their increased kindness and solicitude. Patients ask further questions about their illnesses that often evoke even greater pretenses on the part of family and staff. Eventually patients may tire of trying to get answers, and live out the rest of their lives without discussing their impending death with any other person. The result of such situations is isolation among all people involved, and the most isolated person is the patient.

To understand the difficulty caregivers have in providing care rather than cure, and in not informing patients of their dying, we must again go back to our cultural expectations of the helping professions and of hospitals. We expect treatment of disease; we expect caregivers "to do" something; we look for miracles instead of death. We must also again understand that, as caregivers, we are part of our death-denying society, and unless a conscious effort is made to look at our attitudes toward death and dying, we may be unaware of how these attitudes influence our care of dying patients. As part of a study of geriatric clients in an intensive care unit, Kastenbaum (1967) asked attending personnel (attendants and LPNs) to report what they said to patients who spoke about their own prospective deaths. Their comments could be divided into the following five general categories:

Reassurance: "You're doing so well now. You don't have to feel this way." "You're going to be feeling better soon, then you won't be thinking this way. You'll be feeling more like your old self again."

Denial: "You don't really mean that." "You are not going to die." "Oh, you're going to live to be a hundred."

Changing the Subject: "Let's think of something more cheerful." "You shouldn't say things like that; there are better things to talk about."

Fatalism: "We are all going to die sometime, and it's a good thing we don't know when." "When God wants you, He will take you. It's a sin to say that you want to die."

Discussion: "What makes you feel that way today? Is that something that happened, something somebody said?" "You do? Could you tell me why? I'd like to know." (p. 25)

This study revealed that the most frequently employed tactics used by staff were changing the subject or making a fatalistic statement. Discussion was used more frequently by LPNs than by attendants, but was not a top-priority response. Most of us have used these responses at one time or another with patients; will we continue to use them or attempt to change?

Effects of Who Knows What

Whether or not patients have been told about their dying, and who knows what about the matter, has a definite effect on interactions between staff and patients in hospitals. In their book *Awareness of Dying*, Glaser and Strauss (1965) discuss "awareness context," a term that "refers to who, in the dying situation, knows what about the probabilities of death for the dying patient" (p. ix). Their research suggests that depending upon who knows what, there are discernible and predictable patterns of interaction between dying patients, families, and staff. Glaser and Strauss identified four typical awareness contexts: closed, suspected, mutual pretense, and open (p. 11).

In *closed awareness*, patients do not know they are going to die, even though everyone else does. Various factors may contribute to this closed awareness, including the patient's need to use denial as a defense mechanism, the physician's reluctance to tell the patient, the family's need not to have the patient know, and the general collusion of

hospital staff to avoid discussing patients' illnesses with them specifically. Staff interactional patterns in this awareness context are based on
a fictitious approach to patients, in that patients must be led to believe
that their illnesses are not fatal and that things will turn out "all right."
Patients who remain in a closed awareness context until they die have
little chance to say good-bye to their lives, their friends, their families.
They do not have a chance to put their business and personal affairs
in order and may make future plans that have to be undone after they
die. Family members cannot share their grief with their dying loved
ones. On the other hand, hospital staff may prefer the closed awareness context in that they do not have to talk about death. Patients who
are unaware of their dying may die without much emotional turmoil,
and the routine of the ward will thus be less disturbed.

In *suspected awareness*, the patient suspects what others know and tries
to confirm or negate that suspicion. Patients in this awareness context
seem always to be on the offensive in trying to get realistic information
from a defensive staff. Factors that may contribute to this awareness
context are the patient's recognition of new and changing physical
signs and symptoms and hints and cues provided by staff, such as nam-
ing the patient's illness as cancer but disclaiming its fatality, or moving
the patient to an intensive care unit. However, if patients try direct
questions to staff, direct avoidance is the result. This is a very uncomfortable and unstable state for patients, as there is no consensual validation of their perceptions with staff, and vagueness and insecurity
persist. The possible consequences of suspected awareness are evident.
As in closed awareness, patients do not have a chance to say good-bye
or to arrange their business and personal affairs. Family members may
be under a great strain to remain silent about the patient's prognosis.
Nursing staff may also feel the strain of trying to maintain a guard
against the patient's questions. As staff, client, and family continue to
interact, suspected awareness may change into a mutual pretense game
or open awareness.

The *mutual pretense* context exists when all people involved know that
the patient is dying but all in some way tacitly agree to act as if this is
not so. There are various rules to follow in playing the mutual pretense game. Dangerous topics, such as the patient's death, are avoided.
Safe topics are permissible for discussion; these may include chatter
about the events on the ward, sleeping and eating habits, the weather,
social and political events. Safe topics are those that signify that life is
proceeding as usual. This awareness context may change to open
awareness as the patient nears death and physical changes, such as

pain, occur that make it evident that the patient is dying. One of the consequences of the mutual pretense context is that patients may have some privacy and dignity in their dying. However, as in the other awareness contexts, isolation and loneliness can occur. Hospital ward organization and mood may be less tense than in suspected awareness. Staff may feel more comfortable in that they do not have to work "psychologically" with a dying client.

The context of *open awareness* exists when all people involved acknowledge openly their knowledge that the patient is dying. Staff and patients may have different expectations of each other in terms of the dying process, but one of the positive aspects of open awareness is that these discrepancies can be discussed. Awareness of impending death gives patients a chance to close their lives with some control. They can plan for their family, finish projects, say farewell to friends. They can play a part in managing their own death. On the other hand, some patients may have great difficulty in accepting the knowledge of their impending death. With these people, open awareness may bring much fear and unresolved despair. Staff is more likely to become emotionally involved with patients when open awareness exists. A nurse may be the person to whom the patient talks about fears, reminisces about past experiences, shares dreams and fantasies.

DETERMINANTS OF THE CARE OF DYING PATIENTS

Staff perceptions of, and responses to, dying patient; the goals of the hospital; whether or not patients are told their diagnoses; and staff–patient interaction all affect the care of dying patients in hospitals. Patients' social class and status may also influence not only their care but also how and when they die.

Sudnow (1967) discusses the rather strong relationship between the age, social background, and perceived moral character of clients brought into an emergency room and the amount of effort that is made to attempt revival when "clinical death signs" are detected (p. 103). If you should become critically ill at home or suddenly collapse while working or shopping, the initial evaluation of your state of health will most likely not be that of a doctor but of a police person, ambulance driver, or passerby. Those who find you may regard you as an emergency "case" and attempt to resuscitate you and rush you to a hospital; or you may be assumed to be dead already, in which case your trip to the hospital may take a longer time. Once you arrive at the hospital, the older you are, the more likely it is that tentative death will be accepted without resuscitation. Sudnow's study at a county hospital revealed that efforts at revival of patients brought into the emergency room were admittedly superficial with the exception of attempts on very young or occasionally wealthier patients who by some accident were brought to the county Emergency Room (p. 103). Sudnow also found that at private, wealthier hospitals, the overall attention given to patients "initially dead" was greater than that given to patients in the public county hospital.

Caregivers also may often provide different types of care to dying patients based on prejudged moral character and on perceptions of the patient's social value. Thus:

> The moribund patient who appears to be of low social class, is shabbily dressed, unwashed, or smells of alcohol, seems to be less likely to receive vigorous attempts at resuscitation, as will the patient with perceived social deviancy—the addict, the suicide, and the vagrant. On the other hand, the great and powerful—like Generalissimo Franco—may be denied the possibility of an unharassed death and may receive bizarrely prolonged and desperate resuscitation attempts. (Simpson, 1979, p. 111)

Lasagna (1970) also found that the treatment of patients varies according to the social acceptability of the patient as defined by the staff: wealthier people are treated better than poor people; young people better than old people; nonalcoholics better than alcoholics.

Patients' dying trajectories may influence care given to them in a hospital. Dying trajectories (as discussed in Chapter 2) are perceived courses of dying rather than the actual courses themselves. This definition will, to a large extent, determine where and how a patient will be treated in a hospital. If the patient is admitted via the emergency room, the dying trajectory will be defined there. Patients who are near death may either be treated there, sent to surgery, or sent to an intensive care unit. If the evaluation is that the person may live, care in these areas is concentrated, quick, and efficient, and staff is geared to providing heroic measures to save lives.

Patients who enter the hospital with chronic illnesses, or with problems that are not yet diagnosed, have more uncertain dying trajectories, and very often are sent to medical units where staff and organization of work allow for many different types of dying trajectories. These units allow time for changing definitions of diagnoses and for changing definitions of dying trajectories. Staff and work organization are more closely geared to providing long-term care for the dying than in the emergency and intensive care units, yet staff may still have difficulty in providing this care. Long-term care of dying patients is seen by some as monotonous and routine. Staff may feel helpless when there is nothing more they can do in terms of life-saving treatments; they may begin to avoid seeing and being with these patients. Physicians may lose their interest in the patient as palliative care becomes essentially a nursing prerogative. Nurses may feel that they must carry alone the responsibility of caring for dying patients. Few rewards are given in terms of status and prestige for providing that care and fulfilling these patients' needs, and staff may delegate work to aides because of this, with the thought that professional service is more effectively invested in patients who have a chance for recovery.

ALTERNATIVES TO HOSPITAL CARE

The preceding provides a pretty grim description of the situation the dying individual faces. Are there alternatives? Where does the dying patient go? Is there a place for the dying in the cure-oriented milieu? One obvious solution has been the increasing trend toward placement in nursing homes. This, however, represents an incomplete, value-weighted solution. As discussed in Chapter 2, the infirm 89-year-old is not labeled "dying." Often the patient is told that nursing home transfer is necessary because "you are too sick to go home, but not sick enough to be in a hospital." This statement is not inaccurate. It simply avoids and evades the real issue. Benoliel (1979) describes nursing homes as "custodial institutions for the prolonged dying of individuals with low social value" (p. 146). Each year approximately 30 percent of people in nursing homes die. While the nursing home ostensibly does not provide terminal care, it does provide a place to die!

Terminal Care Facilities

A few charitable organizations established institutions to provide care for the terminally ill in the late 1800s. These include the seven facilities run by the Order of Hawthorne, Dominicans, and Youville Hospital in Massachusetts. Wald (1979) notes that these institutions have not "challenged or involved the existing care system" (p. 174). For example, none of these institutions accept reimbursement from Medicare, Medicaid, or private insurance carriers, and thus do not have to address the issue of "appropriate use of hospital beds." They also provide access to only small numbers of people in the areas they serve. St. Rose's, one of the Hawthorne facilities in New York City, has 28 male and 15 female beds. Admission to the home for women "takes a very long time"; for men, "maybe it's about a month" (N. Russell, personal communication, 1980).

A notable exception is Calvary Hospital in New York City. Founded in 1899 by several Catholic women, Calvary is a fully accredited, 111-bed hospital with more than 300 full-time employees. This staff includes physicians, nurses, social workers, dietitians, recreational therapists, and chaplains. In its brochure, Calvary declares its philosophy: "It is recognized that people in the final stages of terminal disease require a specialized approach to care. The overriding concern is for a personalized and humanistic presentation of patient care services recognizing at all times the singular dignity of the individual" (no page). Calvary Hospital is in the unique position of attempting to function within the existing reimbursement structure of our health care system while espousing a philosophy that does not lead to the regular definition of services. In 1979, the hospital was given "acute care" status, which increased its rate of reimbursement per bed. Although this offset the spiraling costs of delivering medical services, Calvary Hospital must now comply with the Professional Standards Review Organization's (PSROs) standards and with the subsequent utilization review related to appropriate use of an acute care bed, which includes documenting "active" treatment. How Calvary will reconcile "active" and "the singular human dignity of the individual" remains to be seen.

Home Care

If a patient cannot stay in the hospital, is care in the home possible? Our current health care delivery system is extremely inadequate. Medicare provides for 100 home care visits that include skilled nursing visits, a home health aid attendant for four to six hours a day, five days per week, and physical and speech therapy. Most private carriers follow this model, although individual policies vary a great deal. Some policies provide no home health aid coverage; others provide for unlimited private duty nurses if the need is justified by a physician. Reimbursement for equipment, supplies, and medication is also variable. Medicaid coverage of services varies from state to state and by locality within each state. In New York City, Medicaid will provide a home health aide for 24 hours, seven days a week. Unfortunately, patients need to wait for establishment of services for three to six months. The patient wishing to return home can also appeal to community agencies to supplement their current coverage. The resulting home care plans, however, represent a patchwork of independent systems stitched together to provide a comprehensive home care plan. These systems often break down, and the patient and/or relatives are faced with holding the pieces together.

These deficits have not gone unnoticed by the health care profession. A major obstacle is the lack of adequate documentation that home care can be effective and cost-efficient. Dr. Ida Martinson, Professor of Nursing at the University of Minnesota, received a National Cancer Institute grant to demonstrate the feasibility and desirability of home care for the dying child. Her project was based on the premise that parents could be primary caregivers when given appropriate support from their physicians and nursing staff. The nurse served as the primary consultant to the family and assisted in setting up care in the home and procuring equipment, taught about procedures and the dying process, and offered emotional support. Contact with family consisted of home visits and frequent phone calls. Bereavement follow-up was also part of the program. This model of care has become part of the health care delivery system in Milwaukee. Similar programs have been established at Children's Hospital in Los Angeles, California, and at Children's Hospital in Seattle, Washington.

Hospice Care

The increasing inability of large medical institutions to provide the humanistic and individualized care required by the terminally ill has also created the impetus for individuals to seek alternate forms of care. The pendulum appears to be swinging back across the centuries, and twentieth-century humanity is echoing the words of the citizenry of sixteenth-century England in petitioning Henry VIII to provide "for the ayde and comforte of the poore, sykke, blynde, aged and impotient persons . . . wherein they may be lodged, cherysshed and refreshed" (Stoddard, 1978, p. 1). Indeed the concept of hospice care, one of the most rapidly growing trends in terminal care, traces its origins to medieval Europe and England. The reawakening and translating into modern medical terms of this concept is largely the result of the pioneering and exhaustive work of Dr. Cicely Saunders at St. Christopher's Hospice in London.

St. Christopher's Hospice

St. Christopher's Hospice in London was founded in 1967 and, according to Saunders (1977), "was planned to be something between a hospital and the patient's own home: combining the skills of one with the warmth and welcome, the time available, and the beds without invisible parking meters beside them" (p. 160). Dr. Saunders identifies the aims of hospice as (1) to understand, properly diagnose, and treat pain associated with terminal illness and (2) to establish a standard for terminal care. The major focus at St. Christopher's is to assure that each patient is free from pain and the memory of pain. This is accomplished by the sophisticated use of polypharmacy, including what is now referred to as Brompton's mixture or Hospice mix—a combination of heroin, gin, cocaine, chlorpromazine, and sugar. This is often given in combination with antidepressants and tranquilizers. Each patient's dosage is carefully titrated and tailored to provide adequate pain control. Although relatively high doses are given, patients remain alert, and drug addiction has not been a problem.

St. Christopher's has 54 beds divided into four- and six-bed bays. This floor plan was developed to encourage patient interaction and to prevent the isolation terminally ill patients often experience. Patients are encouraged to bring personal effects, including pets; and visitors, particularly children, are welcome 12 hours a day. The average length of stay is only 10 days (Saunders, 1977, p. 166). This may seem surprisingly low, but it is in large part due to the extensive home care program that is part of the service provided by St. Christopher's. The home care team continues to maintain support in the home as long as it is possible and desired. Frequently, patients enter St. Christopher's for a few days' "rest period" and then return home again.

Each week an interdisciplinary team of physicians, nurses, psychiatrists, pharmacists, clergy, social workers, and volunteers meet to discuss inpatients and outpatients and to evaluate individual care plans. Care of the patient is very family centered. Staff often spends as much time with relatives as with patients, and contact is maintained after the death of a patient to assist relatives in their bereavement. A sense of community is encouraged, and relatives often return to volunteer or to attend Sunday chapel service. One wing of St. Christopher's, the Draper wing, contains living arrangements for 16 elderly people who live there as permanent residents. Although this wing is separate from the main building, residents are encouraged to visit patients. St. Christopher's also has a playgroup and school club for the children of staff and of the nearby community. Children play and mingle with patients on a regular basis. This provides a blending of all ages and encourages the concept that death is a normal, natural life event.

A discussion of St. Christopher's would be incomplete if no mention were made of the sense of spirituality and community among its staff and patients. Although no effort is made to foster faith or philosophy, Saunders (1977) explains: "At any time some may be finding their way through doubt to faith, while others feel they can only go on waiting for the answer, all find the strength of being with others who are also searching" (p. 176).

People erroneously assume that England's National Health Service substantially contributed to the development of St. Christopher's Hospice. This is only partially true. The idea for St. Christopher's began in 1948 with a £500 gift from a dying man. Dr. Saunders, then a medical social worker, worked with the man during the last two months of his life. During this period they discussed what "place" could meet his needs. A charity was established 13 years later; finally, in 1967 the necessary £500,000 for land, building, and equipment had been donated (Saunders, 1977, p. 160). Today capital needs are still met by gifts. The National Health Service subsidy is two-thirds of the hospice's annual budget; the rest is provided by donations ("For the Terminally-Ill," 1974).

Hospice in America

Although hospice in the United States has used St. Christopher's as a prototype, the form it has taken here is a reflection of the diverse needs of our country and of the compromise required to dovetail an innovative health care service into our current delivery system. Wald, Foster, and Wald (1980) state, "Today hospice is broadly conceived as referring to a kind of care for terminally ill and their families that can be given in a variety of ways and under different auspices" (p. 174). It is presumed that each approach will adhere to the "Assumptions and Principles Underlying Standards for Terminal Care" formulated by the International Work Group on Death, Dying, and Bereavement (see "Appendix" at the end of the chapter). Five forms of hospice care now exist in the United States: (1) free-standing institutions, (2) hospice teams within an existing institution, (3) palliative care units within an existing institution, (4) home care services, and (5) voluntary programs.

Free-Standing Institutions

Connecticut Hospice was the first hospice program organized and operated in the United States. It began in 1974 as a demonstration project funded by the National Cancer Institute. The initial program design had the following components: (1) coordinated home care/

inpatient beds under a central, autonomous hospice administration; (2) skilled symptom control (physical, sociological, psychological, and spiritual); (3) physician-directed services; (4) provision by an interdisciplinary team; (5) service available 24 hours, seven days a week; an on-call basis with emphasis on the availability of medical and nursing skills; (6) the patient/family regarded as the unit of care; (7) bereavement follow-up; (8) use of volunteers as an integral part of the team; (9) structured staff support and communication systems; and (10) acceptance of patients into the program on the basis of health needs, not ability to pay (Wald et al., 1980, p. 42).

Hospice Connecticut has been operating for six years without meeting its first criterion—being an autonomous inpatient facility. Wald eloquently outlines the torturous route the organization had to traverse to comply with local, state, and federal regulations in its attempt to build this facility. In the interim, its home care program has served 888 patients as of January 1980, and the principals are hopeful that the inpatient facility finally opened in June 1980 (p. 176).

A similar program was instituted in Tucson, Arizona, and serves a population of approximately 500,000. Hillhaven has a comprehensive program modeled on St. Christopher's. It has a 39-bed inpatient facility; an outpatient day- or night-care program; home care; supportive services, including physical therapy, social services, occupational therapy, dietary services; a chaplain and counseling services; and a one-year bereavement program. Hillhaven is of special interest because it is the first hospice program implemented by a proprietary nursing-home chain—Hillhaven, Inc. The hospice recently was successful in obtaining licensure from the state under a special designation—"special hospital/hospice." Blue Cross and Medicare have covered the costs of inpatient services, and it is hoped that, with this new designation, hospice services will be eligible for coverage by private insurers.

Hospice Team within an Existing Institution

St. Luke's Hospital Center in New York City developed a hospice program in 1975 and provides inpatient services in addition to home care. It has no identified unit within the hospital; the hospice team circulates throughout the institution. An interdisciplinary team consisting of a full-time nurse-clinical specialist and coordinator of the program and a part-time medical director, two nurse-clinical specialists, a chaplain, a social worker, and volunteers provide hospice care for patients referred to the program. The program is limited to 20 to 25 adult terminal cancer patients and has been financed by a private foundation. In 1980 it was designated a Demonstration Project by New York State, but funding still is a crucial issue.

A Palliative Care Unit within a Hospital

Patients are accepted into a special unit of an acute care hospital. This model is similar to the St. Luke's model, but patients remain in a special unit and are not scattered throughout the hospital. This type of unit is available at Mercy Hospital, Rockville Center, New York, or at the Royal Victoria Hospital, Montreal, Canada. Home care staff members provide services on a 24-hour basis. Since the unit usually cannot accommodate all referrals, consultation is provided by a physician and a nurse to regular hospital personnel to develop comprehensive care, and with the hope of educating all staff about palliative care skills. Bereavement services are offered to key family members by telephone contact, home visits, and letters.

Home Care Services

Hospice of Marin, Marin County, California, was founded in 1974 and began providing home care services in 1976, when it obtained licensure as a home health agency. The team at Hospice of Marin includes physicians, nurses, counselors, an art therapist, licensed home health aides, a chaplain, a home care secretary, a director of volunteers, and volunetters. Home care is familycentered, and the agency offers bereavement service.

Another example of home care services is a project funded by the National Cancer Institute at the Ephraim McDowell Cancer Center. This project involves three modesl of home care: (1) a public home health agency, (2) a private home health agency, and (3) a hospital-based home health agency. The project is located in Kentucky and serves a largely rural area in the Appalachian Mountain region.

Voluntary Programs

There are multiple programs throughout the United States. They can be as large as Haven of North Virginia, which was established in 1976 and has a staff of over 170 volunteers who undergo training, orientation, and ongoing in-service educational programs to provide home care services, counseling, financial and legal aid, and bereavement follow-up; or as small as five people struggling to develop a project. It is extremely difficult to assess the extent or quality of services they provide, and they represent a stopgap measure because funding is so difficult.

The future of the hospice movement remains uncertain. It is a phenomenon that is challenging the current system, but like any reform, it is facing the complex task of maintaining its basic integrity while remaining elastic enough to accommodate change. Many of the first-generation reformers are experiencing burnout, questioning: Will it ever happen? Perhaps this is a reflection of our culture and our "fast-food generation." Each project must negotiate the intricate system of local, state, and federal regulations regarding delivery of health care. The first step is application for a Certificate of Need. This process it time-consuming (often taking six months to two years) and involves public hearings, testimonials, and bureaucratic red tape. Once this Certificate of Need is granted, the state and/or county must grant licensure. Another major obstacle is reimbursement. The Department of Health and Welfare announced its intent to underwrite 26 hospice programs in a two-year demonstration project. These projects are under the supervision of the Health Care Financing Administration (HCFA). Many states have simultaneously undertaken demonstration projects. For example, New York State, via the Public Health Council and the Office of Hospital Systems Management, requested proposals for hospice programs within New York State. Of the 37 proposals received, 15 were granted Demonstration Project Status. Unfortunately, HCFA is refusing to grant Medicare or Medicaid reimbursement to these projects until after the evaluation of the 26 projects they have sponsored. Janet Lunceford, R.N., M.S.N., Project Director of Hospice, NCI (1980), comments: "Without Medicaid and Medicare reimbursement, hospice staff would not be fully paid for their services and consequently the hospice program would not remain solvent for long" (no page).

The reluctance of the federal government to underwrite another health care program is well founded. Prior to Medicaid and Medicare in 1965, the federal government spent 4.8 percent of its budget, or $5.2 billion, on health care. In 1977 health expenditures represented 12.4 percent of the federal budget (Feder et al. 1980, p. 10). The Sub-Committee on Aging, headed by Senator Moss, found that spending on nursing homes had risen 1400 percent from 1960 to 1973 (NASW: *A Report of the Task Force on Nursing Homes,* 1977, p. 12). Caution and care in planning new programs are justified. The dilemma facing the health care professional involves how much caution can be exercised in the face of the overwhelming needs of the terminally ill.

SUMMARY

For most of the history of medicine, caring—not curing—was the focus of practice; practitioners sustained people through distress, attempting to alleviate pain if possible and offering hope. Nursing has continued this emphasis on helping people live with and through illness and maintain health, while contemporary medicine has moved to a "cure" orientation, around which the bureaucracy of the hospital is organized. Determinants of the care of dying patients in hospitals include the goals of the hospital; staff perceptions of, and responses to, dying patients; whether or not patients are told of their terminal illness; patients' social class and status; and patients' dying trajectories.

We once more need to concentrate on the human aspects of medical and nursing care. The delivery of sophisticated care involves new forms of institutional organizations, which can lead to further separation of care and cure. We need to increase our psychological understanding of each of our dying patients, but this must not supplant the equally important goal of evaluating the system of caring for patients. Emerging new models that provide alternatives to institutional care for dying patients include the hospice movement and home care.

APPENDIX: ASSUMPTIONS AND PRINCIPLES UNDERLYING STANDARDS FOR TERMINAL CARE (Formulated by The International Work Group on Death, Dying, and Bereavement)

There is agreement that patients with life-threatening illnesses, including progressive malignancies, need appropriate therapy and treatment throughout the course of illness. At one stage, therapy is directed toward investigation and intervention in order to control and/or cure such illness and alleviate associated symptoms. For some persons, however, the time comes when cure and remission are beyond the capacity of current curative treatment. It is then that the intervention must shift to what is now often termed "palliative treatment," which is designed to control pain in the broadest sense and provide personal support for patient and family during the terminal phase of illness. In general, palliative care requires limited use of apparatus and technology, extensive personal care, and an ordering of the physical and social environment to be therapeutic in itself.

There are two complementary systems of treatment, which may often overlap. One system is concerned with eliminating a curable disease and the other with relieving the symptoms resulting from the relentless progress of an incurable illness. There must be openness, interchange, and overlap between the two systems so that the patient receives continuous appropriate care. The patient should not be subjected to aggressive treatment that offers no real hope of being effective in curing or controlling the disease and may only cause the patient further distress. Obviously, the clinician must be on the alert for any shifts that may occur in the course of a terminal illness that make the patient a candidate for active treatment again. Patients suffer not only from inappropriate active care but also from inept terminal care. This is well documented by studies that only confirm what dying patients and their families know firsthand. The following principles have been prepared as an aid in delineating standards of care for those who have initiated or are planning programs for the terminally ill.

General Assumptions and Principles

Assumptions

1. The care of the dying is a process involving the patient, family, and care-givers.

2. The problems of the patient and family facing terminal illness include a wide variety of issues—psychological, legal, social, spiritual, economic, and interpersonal.

3. Dying tends to produce a feeling of isolation.

4. It has been the tradition to train care-givers not to become emotionally involved, but in terminal illness the patient and family need to experience the personal concern of those

Principles

1. The interaction of these three groups of individuals must constantly be assessed with the aim being the best possible care of the patient. This cannot be accomplished if the needs of family and/or care-giver are negated.

2. Care requires collaboration of many disciplines working as an integrated clinical team, meeting for frequent discussions with a common purpose.

3. All that counteracts unwanted isolation should be encouraged. Social events and shared work that include all involved should be arranged so that meaningful relations can be sustained and developed.

4. Profound involvement without loss of objectivity should be allowed and fostered, with the realization that this may present certain risks to the care-giver.

taking care of them.

5. Health care services customarily lack coordination.

6. A supportive physical environment contributes to the sense of well-being of patients, of families, and of care-givers.

5. The organizational structure must provide links with health care professionals in the community.

6. The environment should provide adequate space, furnishings that put people at ease, the reassuring presence of personal belongings, and symbols of life cycles.

Patient-oriented Assumptions and Principles

Assumptions

1. There are patients for whom aggressive curative treatment becomes increasingly inappropriate.

2. The symptoms of terminal disease can be controlled.

3. Patients' needs may change over time.

4. Care is most effective when the patient's lifestyle is maintained and philosophy of life is respected.

5. Patients are often treated as if incapable of understanding or of making decisions.

Principles

1. These patients need highly competent professionals, skilled in terminal care.

2. The patient should be kept as symptom free as possible. Pain should be controlled in all its aspects. The patient must remain alert and comfortable.

3. Staff must recognize that other services may have to be involved but that continuity of care should be provided.

4. The terminally ill patient's own framework of values, preferences, and outlook on life must be taken into account in planning and conducting treatment.

5. Patients' wishes for information about their condition should be respected. They should be allowed full participation in their care and a continuing sense of self-determination and self-control.

6. Dying patients often suffer from helplessness, weakness, isolation, and loneliness.

7. The varied problems and anxieties associated with terminal illness can occur at any time of day or night.

6. The patients should have a sense of security and protection. Involvement of family and friends should be encouraged.

7. Twenty-four-hour care must be available seven days a week for the patient and family where and when it is needed.

Family-oriented Assumptions and Principles

Assumptions

1. Care is usually directed toward the patient. In terminal illness the family must be the unit of care.

2. The course of the terminal illness involves a series of clinical and personal decisions.

3. Many people do not know what the process of dying involves.

4. The patient and family need the opportunity for privacy and being together.

5. Complexity of treatment and time-consuming procedures can cause disruption for the patient and family.

Principles

1. Help should be available to all those involved—whether patient, relation, or friend—to sustain communication and involvement.

2. Interchange between the patient and family and the clinical team is essential to enable an informed decision to be made.

3. The family should be given time and opportunity to discuss all aspects of dying and death and related emotional needs with the staff.

4. The patient and family should have privacy and time alone, both while the patient is living and after death occurs. A special space may have to be provided.

5. Procedures must be arranged so as not to interfere with adequate time for patient, family, and friends to be together.

6. Patients and families facing death frequently experience a search for the meaning of their life, making the provision of spiritual support essential.

7. Survivors are at risk emotionally and physically during bereavement.

6. The religious, philosophical, and emotional components of care are as essential as the medical, nursing, and social components, and must be available as part of the team approach.

7. The provision of appropriate care for survivors is the responsibility of the team who gave care and support to the deceased.

Staff-oriented Assumptions and Principles

Assumptions

1. The growing body of knowledge in symptom control, patient- and family-centered care, and other aspects of the care of the terminally ill is now readily available.

2. Good terminal care presupposes emotional investment on the part of the staff.

3. Emotional commitment to good terminal care will often produce emotional exhaustion.

Principles

1. Institutions and organizations providing terminal care must orient and educate new staff and keep all staff informed about developments as they occur.

2. Staff needs time and encouragement to develop and maintain relationships with patients and relatives.

3. Effective staff support systems must be readily available.

"Standards for Hospice Care: Assumptions and Principles" by Zelda Foster. Copyright © 1979 National Association of Social Workers, Inc. Reprinted with permission *Health and Social Work*, Vol. 4, No. 1 (February 1979), pp. 124–127.

LEARNING EXERCISES

1. Role play a patient and a nurse, a doctor, or a social worker interacting in each of Glaser and Strauss's awareness states.
2. Imagine where you would like to go to die. Design this place architecturally, and decide how you would staff it and how it would be structured in terms of organization.

3. Eight deaths:
   a. *Mary*—age 87—at home, after 15 years of feeling more or less "useless" due to aging condition and disabilities.
   b. *George*—age 69—suddenly, of a heart attack, still active in his job.
   c. *Carl*—age 57—after four weeks in the hospital, having experienced a lot of pain, but having taken the opportunity to prepare family and close friends.
   d. *Sam*—age 72—in a nursing home, six months after his wife died.
   e. *Henry*—age 48—shot in the street by a random bullet from a madman upon coming out of a restaurant.
   f. *Betty*—age 37—in an auto accident, leaving husband and two small children.
   g. *Carrie*—age 30—from a drug overdose.
   h. *Keith*—age 23—after a kidney transplant and a long, heroic struggle in the hospital, where everybody on the staff loved him.

   Choose the "best" death and the "worst" death from the preceding examples. Discuss the reasons for your choice.

AUDIOVISUAL MATERIAL

Death. 43 min/black and white/1969. Filmmakers Library, University of Michigan, University of Iowa, University of California.
This film, by focusing on a dying, 52-year-old man is an institution for the terminally ill, depicts the problems of communication between him and relatives and hospital staff.

The Dignity of Death. 30 min/color/1973. ABC News.
A news documentary filmed at St. Christopher's Hospice in London, which includes interviews with Dr. Cicely Saunders, patients, and others.

The Detour. 13 min/color/1977. Phoenix Films, Viewfinders.
An elderly woman who is dying in a hospital presents her views on the care being given to her.

The Final Proud Days of Elsie Wurster. 30 min/black and white/1975. Penn State University: Audio-visual Services.
The film depicts Elsie's life in a nursing home before she dies.

The Street. 10 min/color/1976. National Film Board of Canada.
An animated film based on a story by Mordecai Richler shows the death of a grandmother at home.

REFERENCES

Benoliel, J. Q. Dying in an institution. In H. Wass (Ed.), *Dying: Facing the facts.* New York: McGraw-Hill, 1979.

Burling, T., Lentz, E. M., & Wilson, R. N. *The give and take in hospitals.* New York: Putnam's, 1956.

Calvary Hospital. *Calvary Hospital: Staffed by people who care!* New York: Author, brochure, no date.

Commission on Hospital Care. *Hospital care in the United States.* Cambridge, Mass.: Harvard University Press, 1957.

Coser, R. T. *Life in the ward.* East Lansing: Michigan State University Press, 1962.

Coser, R. T. Alienation and the social structure. In E. Freedson (Ed.), *The hospital in modern society.* London: The Free Press of Glencoe, Collier-Macmillan, 1963.

Duff, R. S., & Hollingshead, A. B. *Sickness and society.* New York: Harper & Row, 1968.

Feder, J., Holahan, J., & Marmon, T. (Eds.). *National health insurance: Conflicting goals and policy choices.* Washington, D.C.: The Urban Institute, 1980.

For the terminally-ill, a hospital that cares. *Medical World News,* July 19, 1974, *15,* 46–47.

Foster, Z. Standards for hospice care: assumptions and principles. *Health & Social Work 4* (1), February 1979, 124–127.

Foucault, M. *The birth of the clinic.* New York: Pantheon Books, 1973.

Glaser, B. G., & Strauss, A. L. *Awareness of dying.* Chicago: Aldine, 1965.

Hackley, J. A., Farr, W. C., & McIntier, S. Tuscon 1977—Hill Haven Hospice. In G. Davidson (Ed.), *The hospice development and administration.* Washington, D.C.: Hemisphere, 1978.

Kastenbaum, R. Multiple perspectives on a geriatric "Death Valley." *Community Mental Health Journal,* 1967, *3,* 21–29.

Lasagna, L. Physicians' behavior toward the dying patient. In O. Brim, H. Freeman, S. Levine, & N. Scotch (Eds.), *The dying patient.* New York: Russell Sage Foundation, 1970.

Lunceford, J. *Hospice in America.* Paper presented at St. Christopher's Hospice, London, June 1980.

Mauksch, H. O. The organizational content of dying. In E. Kübler-

Ross (Ed.), *Death: The final stage of growth.* Englewood Cliffs, N.J.: Prentice-Hall, 1975.

Merton, R. Bureaucratic structure and personality. In *Social theory and social structure.* Glencoe, Ill.: Free Press, 1957.

Morison, R. S. Dying. *Scientific American,* September 1973, *229,* 55–62.

Mumford, E. *Sociology in hospital care.* New York: Harper & Row, 1967.

National Association of Social Work. *A report of the task force on nursing homes.* February 1977.

Perrow, C. Goals and power structures: A historical case study. In E. Freedson (Ed.), *The hospital in modern society.* London: The Free Press of Glencoe, Collier-Macmillan, 1963.

Roberts, C. M. *Doctor and patient in the teaching hospital.* Lexington, Mass.: Heath, 1977.

Russell, N. Personal communication, 1980.

Saunders, C. Dying they live: St. Christopher's Hospice. In H. Feifel (Ed.), *New meanings of death.* New York: McGraw-Hill, 1977.

Simpson, M. A. Social and psychological aspects of dying. In H. Wass (Ed.), *Dying: Facing the facts.* Washington, D.C.: Hemisphere; McGraw-Hill, 1979.

Stoddard, S. *The hospice movement: A better way of caring for the dying.* New York: Vintage Books, 1978.

Sudnow, D. *Passing on: The social organization of dying.* Englewood Cliffs, N.J.: Prentice-Hall, 1967.

Wald, F., Foster, Z., & Wald, H. The hospice movement as a health care reform. *Nursing Outlook,* March 1980, *28*(13), 173–178.

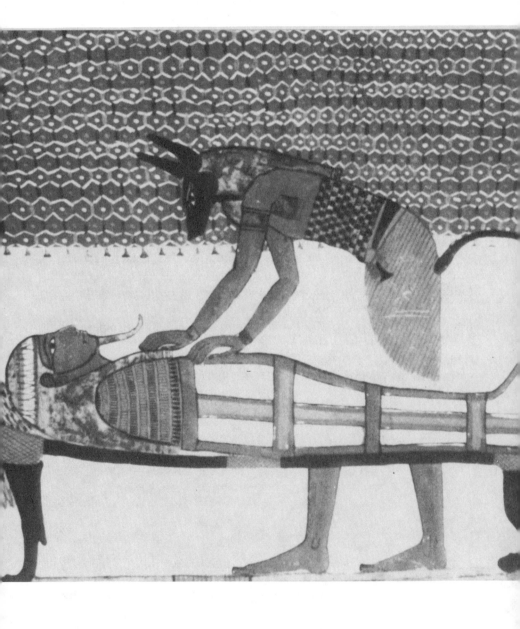

4

The Helping Professions and the Terminally Ill

Caregivers, as members of our society, have many of the death fears and anxieties of our culture as discussed in Chapter 2. What happens in interactional processes between caregivers and patients? How do caregivers deal with their own death fears, and how do they help patients deal with feelings about dying? Are caregivers prepared educationally to work with dying patients? In the following discussion we attempt to look at these questions and issues.

NURSES

Nurses are the caregivers who are in the most continuous contact with dying patients in institutions and who provide them with the most direct care. How do nurses learn to provide this care, and are these educational experiences influential in changing their attitudes about death?

Quint and Strauss (1964) reported on their findings of a survey of how students are taught about death and dying in schools of nursing. They found, in general, that relatively little teaching focused on death. Several reasons for this were rapid rotation of students, clinical experiences, and frequent change of instructors. Also, teaching students about caring for dying patients is quite complex; each dying patient presents a unique and different experience, and each student brings to that experience different perceptions, attitudes, feelings, and cultural responses. Given these variables and the fears and inexperience of some nursing faculties in dealing with this content, we can begin to understand why curriculum development in death and dying is a difficult task.

A further review of the nursing literature through the sixties and seventies indicates that although nursing education has begun to address itself to the teaching of death content, curricula in this area are still being developed and advanced. The survey of Schoenberg et al. (1972) of 97 nursing schools in which death content was studied revealed that more than 95 percent of the schools specifically prepared students to deal with the patient's response to dying, the role of denial, the dying patient's grief, and the family's grief (p. 7). However, this study also revealed that 72 percent of the schools did not have a specific person who taught the care of the dying patient, and that 44.6 percent of the students reported being displeased about teaching efforts to prepare them to care for dying patients (p. 8). Research is indicated to continue to develop nursing education that will be relevant to patients, students, and faculty.

A significant factor that has developed in nursing curricula and workshops on death and dying is the emphasis on becoming aware of one's own feelings and reactions. Self-involvement in the course content is an important motivation for learning (Sanford & Deloughery, 1973, p. 24). In an effort to provide more empirical evidence that an individual's ability to face death is related to providing better care, C.W. Ross (1978) investigated the concept that a professional's awareness of concerns about his or her own death is helpful in the treatment of dying clients (p. 64). He found that exploration of personal concerns about death does increase one's ability to respond more openly and to interact more congruently with dying patients' statements (p. 67). Robinson (1974) describes a course on death and dying she offered to senior nursing students in which one of the requirements was that each student maintain a relationship with a dying patient. She emphasizes that it is extremely important that students in such a course have every opportunity to discuss their experiences. Students do need support and help in coping with these painful episodes and in learning from them. Such support can help them not to fear experiences with patients that evolve deep feelings, and to learn that these very experiences that seem so painful can help them become more humane, compassionate people. Herein lies a major area for change in better preparing nursing students in caring for dying patients. Faculty must have a commitment to this care not only in the form of curriculum change but in their own nursing practices. Faculty themselves need to feel comfortable in caring for dying patients. They need to be available to listen to students' experiences and to support and sustain them. With the pressures of current faculty teaching hours, this is not an easy responsibility to assume. Faculty themselves need support and supervision in assisting students to learn how to function effectively in caring for dying patients. Peer supervision and inservice programs might be effective methods for helping faculty members in this area of teaching.

We may well ask ourselves at this point if these efforts in curriculum change are actually effective in changing attitudes toward death and dying and in providing more appropriate care for dying patients. Several research studies in attitude change indicate an answer in a positive direction (Golub & Reznikoff, 1971; Yeaworth et al. 1974). Lester et al. (1974) hypothesized that fear of death and dying will decrease with increased academic preparation. The researchers sampled the attitudes of undergraduates, graduate nursing students, and nursing faculty at a university school of nursing. In general the findings of the study supported their hypothesis. A major exception to this was that the mean scores of first-year graduate students on several death attitude subscales were greater than those of senior undergraduate students, and approached the scores of junior undergraduate students. The researchers suggest that these findings could indicate that an intervening period of clinical involvement between educational experiences may promote one's fears of death and dying (p. 52). If this is so, graduate nurses will need continued support and supervision in caring for dying patients.

While these research studies suggest that important changes in nurses' attitudes toward death can occur from education, the question also arises of whether involvement with a death experience should be included to influence an attitude change. At present, educational programs designed to deal with death anxiety among nurses and nursing students are based to some extent on an untested assumption that high death anxiety and aversive reactions to death result from nonexperience with death (Denton & Wisenbaker, 1977, p. 61). The complication for education arising from this assumption is that in order to decrease the anxiety of persons caring for the dying, it is necessary for them to be in contact with dying people. There are several research studies whose findings contradict these assumptions, suggesting that increased experience with death may lead to increased death anxiety (Feifel et al. 1967; Lester et al., 1974). These studies and assumptions suggest that further research is indicated before we can assume definite relationships between death experience and death anxiety, and before we can determine that death experiences, if any, can be meaningful in helping nurses deal with their own death anxieties. Hopping (1977) suggests that in nursing education, we may not necessarily need to try to change students' attitudes about death but rather, more realistically, to help prepare students to meet the death of a significant other in a more positive manner (p. 447).

The research studies reviewed in this discussion indicate that death and dying content in a nursing curriculum may influence students' attitudes in this area. A major factor in influencing a positive attitude change seems to be the amount of support and supervision that faculty, students, and graduate nurses need in order to continue to provide appropriate, humanistic care to dying patients. Further research is needed to determine more specifically what educational content and what clinical experiences are most helpful in assisting nurses to care for dying patients.

Nurse/Patient Interaction

In caring for dying patients, nurses confront several conflicts in terms of personal and professional identity. If nurses themselves have not come to terms with death, caring for a dying patient can present many problems. Defending against one's own death anxieties may take the energy and focus away from the dying patient's needs. A discussion of death can evoke fear, sadness, and anger about one's own mortality and powerlessness. These are personally uncomfortable feelings as well as being disturbing ones in a society and a profession where keeping one's emotions in control is emphasized. Defenses commonly used by nurses to avoid interacting with dying patients are behaviors such as evading conversation, avoiding patients, briskness and efficiency in providing physical care, speaking only when spoken to by the patient, and talking only about topics that are comfortable for the nurse. One nurse checked out her avoidance techniques in relation to dying patients and found herself saying: "I'm too busy," "Someone else can profit more from my care," "He needs the rest," or "He prefers to be alone" (Speer, 1974, p. 70). On realization of this avoidance, she discovered that she could indeed schedule 20 to 30 minutes of each working day to spend with a dying patient.

Caring for dying patients may be viewed as being in conflict with the nursing goals of promoting health and maintaining wellness. Death would seem to have no part in these professional goals. However, at that point when death becomes a certainty for a patient, whether it be months or days, the treatment plan and goals change from recovery to comfort. The nursing staff assumes the major responsibility for providing this comfort, and this is indeed a significant part of nursing interaction with a dying patient. A person who is dying may increasingly become dependent upon others for personal care—for assistance in bathing and hygiene, nutrition, and elimination. How nurses provide this assistance is critically important for the patient, not only physiologically but also because such care can convey basic respect or disrespect for the patient as a human being. A very simple example of this display of respect is for a nurse to ask a patient having a bed bath whether he or she would prefer being washed with soap or just plain water on the face. Patients and nurses can collaborate in planning this physical care assistance; even when patients are totally dependent on staff for care, they can take part in decision making as to when they will have a bath, a dressing change, a pain medication, or whether or not they want visitors that day.

The actual touching involved in providing this physical care is also critical. Patients often need this direct expression of human contact. When we were children, a parent might have kissed away our bruises and scrapes. A child in pain in a hospital once said to a nurse, "Touch me where it hurts." As an adult in our Western society, it is difficult to ask anyone to "hold me" or "touch me." It is easier to ask for a pill for the pain. Dying people, besides often experiencing pain, may feel unclean or repulsive, or that there is an unpleasant odor about them that will keep people away. Therefore, how nurses touch patients in providing physical care can convey caring, acceptance, and respect.

Caring for patients who are dying and who are dependent on others is a difficult part of nursing. The day-to-day total physical care and psychological support required by such people unceasingly taps nurses' energy levels. Nurses do not have the mobility on hospital units, as doctors and social workers do, to come and go throughout an eight-hour shift; nurses remain on the unit with the patients. Although this can be problematic at times, in terms of nurses' own needs to get away from the situation for a short time, it also provides them with a unique experience—being there when patients need someone. Nurses are also in a position to influence the social milieu of dying patients. Nurses, along with social workers, coordinate the care and decisions made by the various people involved in caring for the dying person; they often serve as the patient's support and advocate in conveying the individual's wishes to these many caregivers about how he or she is deciding to live and to die. Nurses' provision of comfort to dying patients, then, involves not only physical and psychological care but also collaboration with the patients in deciding upon their plan of care, facilitating their decisions about day-to-day living, encouraging open communication between them and those close to them, and sustaining them in the maintenance of their dignity, self-worth, and self-respect throughout their dying (Benoliel, 1977, p. 135).

Effects of Institutional Practices on Nurse/Patient Interaction

There are various factors that can influence the provision of this kind of nursing care. As mentioned earlier in this chapter, it is important for nurses to face their own feelings about death and their involvement with dying patients. Systems theory explains another factor that influences nursing care. Nurses function interdependently as well as independently in the hospital/health care system and thus are affected by the values and changes in this system. Quint (1966) found that in a comparative analysis of two "high death" wards—one, an intensive care unit stressing recovery, and the other, a cancer unit stressing comfort until death—"emphasis on recovery goals can quite successfully mask the presence of death and protect the staff much of the time from the impact of dying" (p. 55). If nurses do not define patients as dying, they do not have to deal with them on that basis. Hence nurses may see and hear only those aspects of patient care and communication that indicate that the patient may get well; since most hospital units value curing more than caring, institutional values support these perceptions.

Dying patients are often fearful of death, but they also may be experiencing fear of loneliness, of isolation, and of abandonment (Kneisl, 1968, p. 550). The dying patient's feeling of abandonment may be enhanced if a different nurse is assigned to provide care every day. It is not easy for dying people to establish relationships with new people. Can we really expect patients to talk about their dying to a different person each day? A system of primary nursing care where one person is responsible for planning and implementing care for a certain number of patients throughout their hospital stay is perhaps one way to alleviate a patient's feelings of abandonment.

One of the procedures probably most revealing of society's and nurses' attitudes toward death is the institutional practice of postmortem care, which is the preparation of the dead person's body for the morgue and the funeral director. This is indeed a direct confrontation with death. It is often very difficult to deal with the two images of this patient—one, an individual patient whom one has known as a person, with feelings, experiences, and hopes, and with whom one has collaborated in plans of care; the other, a motionless, cold body. In some religions and cultures, preparing the body for burial has been and is a ritual for family members, conveying love and respect for the dead person and perhaps serving as a final way of saying good-bye. Today this task is usually relegated to the nursing staff of the institution in which the patient dies.

Aasterud (1962) presents another view on the ritual of postmortem care and describes it in terms of its demonstrating our strong, primitive feelings of denial and fear of death; our reactions to the dead, though we term them "respect," could more accurately be labeled a "taboo" of the dead (p. 48).

> Should only one person be free to care for the body, that person will invariably wait for another to "help" her, although the task, in fact, could be done by one person. And, although the deceased may have been bathed but a few hours before death, the nurses are seen to don gowns over their uniforms. (Primitive cultures render "unclean" the person who has touched a corpse, and that person is segregated from society for a period of time.)
>
> The voices are lowered as the body is prepared, and if we listen carefully, we note that the deceased's name is seldom mentioned; it has become "he" or "she" or "the body," . . . even though shortly before death he was talked of and addressed by his given name. In primitive races there is widespread prohibition of pronouncing the name of the deceased. (p. 48)

Nurses quite often say that they do not talk about a patient's death with other patients because they do not want to upset them. However, again we may consider the consequences that might result from contact with the dead. Patients could associate a nurse as having had contact with the dead patient and thus unconsciously become reluctant to have that nurse touch or care for them (p. 49). We see this same taboo operating in society in regard to funeral directors. People may hesitate to shake a funeral directors' hand, or to invite one to a social function.

It is important to consider these taboos as possibly functioning among nurses and patients in order to provide the support necessary for all involved. For example, if indeed there is an unconscious taboo about touching a dead person, more than one person may be assigned to postmortem care; after this is completed, they may be given a short time off from the unit.

When a patient on a hospital unit dies, what happens to the other patients? Do they have a chance to discuss this death if they so desire? How ready are we as staff to discuss this with them? Usually after a death on a unit, patients' doors are closed and the dead person is swiftly wheeled away. Some institutions have been known to have linen

carts with false bottoms. The body is "hidden" here and wheeled off
the unit. It is the rare patient who does not know that someone on a
unit has died, even though staff does not verbalize it. Some staff, when
asked what has happened to roommate Mr. Jones, will say that the
dead Mr. Jones was transferred to another unit. By these not-so-
indirect methods, staff are conveying the message, "We do not talk
about death here." This seems unfair, for one patient's death on a unit
is significant. Patients who ask questions about the death of another
patient, or who have known the dead patient, need to be given the opportunity to talk about their feelings if they so desire.

Conveyance of Hope

Nurses, as caregivers prepared to help patients regain and maintain
health, have a basic orientation of hopefulness. Dying patients need to
have some hope, not an unrealistic hope of cure or of future events,
but hope that will allow them to face the remainder of their lives con-
structively. Can we in all honesty convey hopefulness to dying patients
who may be feeling both hopeless and helpless? If patients feel there
is no way, and no one with whom, they can communicate about their
dying, their feelings of hopelessness and helplessness may well increase. If we are open and ready to listen to dying patients, we may at
least give them a sense of coping with their own deaths. This openness
and listening do not convey a false sense of hope but can help patients
feel in some control of their dying.

Another way of facilitating hope is to help patients think of their
lives in the here and now, of the next few weeks, of current sources of
satisfaction and contentment rather than overlooking these in favor of
future prospects (Verwoerdt, 1966, p. 50). Alcoholics Anonymous utilizes a similar concept for maintaining hope—"getting through one day
at a time." In fostering hope in patients, we need to emphasize what
they still are capable of doing and what their strengths are as people.
Too often dying patients are told of restrictions on diet, activity, and
recreation, with little acknowledgment given to their abilities still present. It is also helpful to encourage patients to maintain their regular
daily living patterns if this is possible. This provides a sense of continuity in life for patients, helps them to maintain their self-esteem, and
helps them stay oriented to the here and now (p. 51)

Patients who are attempting to deal with all these feelings—hopelessness, separation, isolation, abandonment—and with threats to the self-
system "may regress in their interpersonal relationships and seek to re-

establish some of the comforts of earlier infantile situations, in which the benevolent idealized parents provided the nurture and comfort for existence" (Muskin et al. 1974, p. 308). Some patients may need to see and use caregivers as surrogate parental figures to help them cope with their impending death. If patients do have this need, they are often labeled "demanding"; hostile behavior by patients can be regarded as what it indicates—a plea for us to provide, as real parents once did, the admiration, approval, and tender care that is needed for comfort and nurturance (p. 310). We must accept this plea and provide this care, keeping in mind, however, that the person is not a child but an adult who has lived an important life and who still has strengths and integrity.

Nurse/Family Interaction

During the living–dying interval, nurses often involve family members in the direct care of the patient. This seems to help a spouse or son or daughter cope with feelings of helplessness and powerlessness; they are "doing" for their loved one. If a patient is at home, family members may need nurses not only to teach them directly and to help them care for the patient but also for much support and encouragement in their ability to provide this care. An elderly woman who was living alone at home needed frequent injections for pain. Another equally elderly woman who was her neighbor volunteered to give her these injections if the public health nurse would teach her how. The elderly neighbor arrived for the first teaching session dressed in a starched white uniform, explaining that she thought this would help the nurse to feel that she really wanted to learn how to care for her friend!

Family members assisting in the care of their relatives may need to be reminded of their own needs for rest, relaxation, and some time of their own. A wife who is with her dying husband in the hospital all day, every day, may need a nurse to talk with her and say: "We'll be here with him and call you if you're needed—why don't you go home and try to relax for a while?" Family members who are caring for patients at home may need to know what alternatives are available when they feel they need some help in this care. They will also need support so as not to feel they have failed as caregivers if they do ask for help.

Nurses are involved in keeping communication open and direct among patients, family, friends, and home and hospital situations so that patients do not become the recipients of possibly confused and emotionally upsetting messages. People who are dying who choose to maintain open communications about their deaths with friends and family have a chance to use tremendous amounts of energy, which would otherwise be invested in the pretense of covering up their dying, to live life as fully as possible (Jaffee & Jaffee, 1976, p. 1939). However, this kind of open communication about dying is not without its problems. The dying person may at a given time want to discuss his or her impending death. The listener, a family member or friend, may feel at this particular time that the discussion is unbearable. As one husband replied to his wife's talking about her dying, "I feel I'm a victim of terminal candor" (p. 1938). Nurses may help families get in closer touch with each other's feelings about discussing a family member's dying. The dying person is going in life in one direction, whereas the other family members must prepare to move in a different direction. These directions, which have different foci in terms of immediate and future planning, will influence how people interact with one another.

When a patient dies in a hospital, nurses may spend some time in the immediate period after the death with the family, but very often that is the end of their contact with them. Follow-up family care should be available and offered if indicated; the family needs to grieve as a unit over the death of its member, in addition to grieving as individuals. We might ask at this point if family members of dying patients have any expectations of nursing care for themselves. Freihofer and Felton (1976) conducted a study to identify those nursing behaviors that provided the most support and comfort to loved ones of a fatally ill, hospitalized adult patient (p. 333). Spouses, relatives, or close friends of a dying patient ranked nursing behaviors that progressed on a continuum from caring for the physical needs of patients, to caring for their emotional needs, to caring for the physical and emotional needs of the bereaved. The data analysis in terms of the total group sample indicated the following four most desired and four least desired behaviors:

Four most deisred behaviors (in order of ranking)
1. Keep the patient well-groomed
2. Allow the patient to do as much for himself/herself as possible
3. Give the pain medication as often as possible (as indicated by doctor's orders)
4. Keep the patient physically comfortable

Four least desired behaviors (in order of ranking)
1. Encourage me to cry

2. Hold my hand
3. Cry with me
4. Remind me that the patient's suffering will be over soon (p. 336)

This study indicated that the grieving needed nursing behaviors to be directed toward the comfort, support, and ease of suffering of the fatally ill patient rather than toward themselves. This indeed has implications for nursing behavior, and further research is indicated to define family needs. The study's finding that the "cry with me" behavior was viewed as least desirable is at variance with thanatology literature (p. 336).

Nurses Need to Grieve

We have been discussing various ideas of "what nurses should do" in death education and in caring for dying patients. However, nurses are not able to accomplish these "shoulds" without having their own responses to caring for dying patients. Nurses also need to go through a grieving process when a person who has been a patient/friend dies. We have stated earlier that patients often fear the process of dying—the loneliness, the isolation, the loss of dignity—more than death itself. Sonstegard, Hansen, Zillman, and Johnston (1976) suggest that nurses working with dying patients fear the same isolation, and wonder who will be available to them to share their feelings of joy and sorrow, anger and acceptance, when patients die (p. 1490). Young adult staff nurses may have special needs to discuss their feelings about dying patients, especially if the patient is another young adult. Older nurses, who are coming to grips more realistically with their own mortality, may also have special needs to talk about death and dying if they are seeing themselves in each dying patient. Such shared discussions among nurses of all age groups may offer much support, learning, and greater appreciation and understanding of feelings and needs. Nurses can provide support for one another through the nursing hierarchy—head nurses, supervisors, and in-service educators. Educational experiences such as conferences and workshops on death and dying to facilitate nurses' understanding and growth in their own feelings about death can be requested and planned. Encouragement of informal peer support, such as giving each other "strokes," especially in times of stress, is important at all levels in nursing. Building in a formal system of dealing with stress—which might involve time off for conferences, rotating different responsibilities on the unit, and mental health days—

may be considered. Nurses who are caring for dying patients may need some time during the day by themselves to examine their own feelings, to think about this experience. They may need a light patient care assignment that day; and if a patient dies, they might need some time off to come to terms with their own feelings and to center themselves to prepare to care for the next patient.

In summary, nurses must assume the responsibility and exercise the power to demand the time needed to nurse dying patients. By "being with" patients, by listening, by touching, nurses can help patients die an appropriate death—a death in which the patient maintains integrity, self-esteem, and control by making choices, by being kept physically comfortable and relatively pain free, and by having human contact when desired.

PHYSICIANS

Studies of physicians' care of the dying show that physicians tend to withdraw once a patient is defined as dying. (For example, see Glaser & Strauss, 1968; Hackett & Weisman, 1964.) The physician may also develop a totally impersonal attitude (Rabin & Rabin, 1970). The following from "The Death of Ivan Ilych" (Tolstoy, 1896) exemplifies the impersonality of the physicians's care:

> The doctor said that so-and-so indicated that there was so-and-so inside the patient, but if the investigation of so-and-so did not confirm this, then he must assume that and that. If he assumed that and that, then . . . and so on. To Ivan Ilych only one question was important: was his case serious or not? But the doctor ignored that inappropriate question. From his point of view it was not the one under consideration. The real question was to decide between a floating kidney, chronic catarrh, or appendicitis. It was not a question of Ivan Ilych's life or death, but one between a floating kidney and appendicitis. (p.121)

One study (Rea et al. 1975) of 151 physicians, however, found that physicians were not likely to withdraw from the terminally ill. Fifty-three percent of the physicians felt that it was their duty to devote additional time "beyond that absolutely necessary" to the dying, and another 38 percent were inclined to accept this. This varied with the age and specialty of the physician. The older the physician, the more likely he or she was to express the willingness to spend extra time with the terminally ill. Oncologists, cardiologists, and neurologists were more likely to devote extra time than internists. These findings do not, however, specify the behavior of the physicians. They only reveal doctors' responses to a questionnaire.

The Role of the Physician

The doctor's role is primarily as a healer of the sick. The ideal doctor is also supposed to show "detached concern." The physician is supposed to be emotionally detached while also responding to the patient's needs. Osler's view of the physician is someone "who must have coolness and presence of mind . . . clearness of judgment in moments of grave peril. The physician who has the misfortune to be without it (imperturbability), who betrays indecision and worry and shows that he is flustered and flurried . . . loses rapidly the confidence of his patients" (as quoted in Hendin, 1974, p. 106). A good doctor must balance being objective with being concerned. However, as Gerber (1972) discusses, the balance is difficult to maintain when the physician is confronted with a dying patient, and the behavior may become weighted in favor of the objective approach.

Doctors also have more power in the doctor–patient relationship because of their ability "to make things better." What happens, however, if the patient is dying? As Benoliel points out (1974), the dying may represent a loss of power and the ability to control, especially as the medical care becomes more and more precarious.

Benoliel discusses other sources of professional loss that may occur when a patient is dying; there is the potential loss of professional demeanor, especially if the patient has become "significant" to the physician. There may be the fear of losing peer respect. A loss of professional competence may be perceived. These last two losses were expressed to Gerber (1972) by a physician during a conversation about autopsies: "The physician indicated that for many house staff members the job of ascertaining consent for an 'autopsy' was 'punishment' for his failure" (p. 3).

Weisman (1974) discusses the four major goals of the physician vis-à-vis patient care: (1) diagnosis, (2) treatment, (3) relief, and (4) safe conduct. Although the goal of diagnosis is the same for the terminal and nonterminal, the other three goals take on different meanings for the care of the dying patient.

Treatment. Treatment is usually considered to lead to curing. When the patient cannot be cured, however, the goal of the treatment changes: it may be to increase the length of the life of the patient, or it may help to relieve the symptoms of the patient's illness; or it may be to satisfy the physician that he or she did everything that was possible. Clinical pathology conferences, or "death rounds," where the medical staff involved discusses all the alternatives that should have been used to avoid death may lead to treatment for treatment's sake. "At stake is not only the patient's life, but also the clinicians's reputation and self-esteem" (Coombs & Powers, 1975, p. 25).

Noyes and Clancy (1977) make the point that one of the major difficulties for physicians in caring for the dying is that they have confused the dying role with the sick role. A person in the sick role must want to get well, and must cooperate with the physician in order to achieve the end of getting better. The duty of dying persons is to desire to live as long as possible; they must also cooperate with their caretakers. Sick people, for the limited time they are sick, are allowed to be dependent, whereas the dying are encouraged to be more independent, to remain active, and to care for themselves as much as possible. The physician may view the patient as if he or she were sick, rather than dying, and both the physician and patient must act as if the patient were improving. One manifestation of this is the continual and active treatment given the patient by the physician.

Relief.   As stated by Weisman (1974): "Adequate relief to pain is mandatory; almost everything is secondary to pain relief." Control of pain for the terminally ill should be the primary goal of treatment. However, the primary goal for many physicians is to extend the patient's life.

Diana Crane (1975), in her extensive study of physicians, found that 43 percent of 660 internists studied were willing to increase their prescription of narcotics even if there was a high risk of respiratory arrest. However, only 29 percent of 750 residents in internal medicine would increase the dosage under the same circumstances. As Crane interprets the findings: for the older physician, the important use of narcotics is to control pain; but younger physicians are afraid that their superiors will perceive their actions as hastening death instead of controlling pain. A more extensive discussion of the ethics of pain medication use appears later in this chapter.

Safe Conduct.   For a patient who recovers, the guarantee of safe conduct is unnecessary. However, for those patients who are dying, who may have to yield control to others, there is a need for safe conduct.

Such patients must trust that they will be taken care of with concern and dignity. Doctors find this particularly hard to do, since death may be conceived as a failure of the physician's skills (Krant & Sheldon, 1971). Since nothing can be done to cure the patient, the physician feels a loss of mastery. The doctor's fantasy of being able to guarantee eternal life to all patients is shattered (White, 1977).

Socialization

The process of socialization is the means by which persons acquire the knowledge and skills to perform in various roles. Medical school education is a primary component in the socialization process of physicians.

Medical schools do not generally provide specific, structured situations in which the student may discuss the area of death and dying. Liston (1975) conducted a survey of all American medical schools to see if they offered courses on death and dying. Of the 83 institutions that responded, only 41 offered such courses. Of these 41 schools, only 22 required the course. In the other 19 schools, only 15 percent of the eligible students enrolled in the course. The composite profile of the courses on death and dying developed by Liston was the following: the course generally utilized interdisciplinary faculty, was part of the preclinical curriculum, included films and patient interviews, and provided on the average 9.5 hours of classroom time per student.

A survey by the Foundation of Thanatology (Schoenberg & Carr, 1972) demonstrates further the lack of medical education concerning the care of the dying (see Table 4.1): Table 4.1 could be interpreted as showing that medical schools do not prepare the student to care for the dying at all.

Samuel Bloom (1958) discusses the three effects of medical education:

1. There is a dehumanization effect implicit in the first two years of medical school (the preclinical years), since the student has no contact with patients while working on cadavers in pathology.

2. There is a compartmentalization or segmentation effect implicit in the whole medical curriculum. During the preclinical years, the students study localized pathology; dissection is stressed, which reduces the whole to its parts. During the clinical years, patients are viewed as disease entities rather than people. Throughout training, the student is overwhelmed by the amount of knowledge that must be learned, which heightens the need for specialization.

3. There is an institutionalization effect implicit in the training in

modern hospitals where students are taught to see patients as hospital cases. The functioning of the institution becomes more important than the individual patient.

These three effects of a medical education lead to a highly technically trained physician who is able to deal with a diseased kidney or liver, but who may not be able to deal with the person containing these diseased organs. For dying patients, when caring is more important than curing, the effects of medical education are dysfunctional for how the patient should be treated.

Table 4.1. Views of Chairmen of Departments in Medical School Regarding Education vis-á-vis Care of the Dying

	Medicine	Surgery	Pediatrics	Psychiatry
Department does not regularly assign students to care for patients suffering from a condition that may lead to death.	9.1%	8.7%	0%	78.1%
Department does not have a policy which defines the division of responsibility among the physician, nurse, social service worker, and the chaplain who are caring for the dying patient.	85.7%	82.6%	78.3%	93.8%
Students are rarely or never asked questions about the specific care of dying patients in examinations.	71.5%	82.6%	84.0%	66.7%
Department does not require reading pertaining to caring for dying patients.	81.8%	95.7%	76.9%	66.7%
Department does not have a specific person who teaches the care of the dying patient.	81.8%	95.7%	50.0%	63.6%
Department does not specifically prepare medical students to understand and deal with:				
a. the patient's emotional response to dying	33.3%	56.6%	34.6%	24.2%
b. the role of denial in the dying patient	33.3%	73.9%	44.0%	18.8%

Table 4.1. (Continued)

	Medicine	Surgery	Pediatrics	Psychiatry
c. the process of patient's separation or disengagement from others	55.0%	77.3%	50.0%	28.1%
d. the dying patient's grief	50.0%	63.6%	52.2%	18.8%
e. the family's anticipatory grief and mourning	55.0%	60.9%	23.1%	28.1%
f. the hospital personnel's emotional reaction to the patient	38.1%	69.6%	28.0%	25.0%
Department does not discuss with students controversial issues that are currently connected with the care of a dying patient, i.e., euthanasia, definitions of death, ethics of organ transplantations, addiction of terminal patients to narcotics.	17.4%	8.7%	37.0%	21.2%

From "Educating the Health Professional in the Psychosocial Care of the Terminally Ill" by B. Schoenberg, A. Carr in B. Schoenberg et al. (eds.), *Psychosocial Aspects of Terminal Care.* Copyright © 1972 by Columbia University Press.

Coombs and Powers (1975) studied the specific stages medical students go through in terms of their socialization for dealing with death. They conducted 229 interviews of a class who entered medical school in 1967 and graduated in 1971. They saw medical students as going through developmental stages:

Stage I Idealizing the Doctor's Role: Freshmen saw the physician as protecting patients from death; they were upset with physicians who did not show compassion over death.

Stage II Desensitizing Death Symbols: In the preclinical years, the students are immediately introduced to a cadaver, which is generally met with initial shock and nausea. They come to cope with their anxieties by losing themselves in the technical details of the work, such as memorizing the scientific names of the bones. In the second year, the students must perform an autopsy. Again, to cope, the students become involved in the technical aspects. A detached scientific attitude is developed, which is reinforced in the basic science courses where illness is discussed on an intellectual, not an emotional, basis.

Stage III   Objectifying and Combating Death: When the student begins to work with patients in the third year, "early experiences with
dying patients make clear the necessity of detaching oneself from the
emotional trauma of death" (p. 22). In order to do this, the students
begin to define patients as scientific entities, and to deal with the pieces
of the organism. (These effects are similar to the effects discussed by
Bloom.)

The following example from Krant and Sheldon (1971) demonstrates this view of the patient.

> A 64-year-old woman died of gastrointestinal carcinoma. Her dying had
> been slow and in many ways difficult because of confusional periods, se-
> vere bed sores that were difficult to control and marked nausea. But,
> through the six weeks that she was a patient on the unit, she was uncom-
> plaining and warm, and several of the nurses involved in her care devel-
> oped strong positive feelings for her. Immediately after the patient was
> pronounced dead, the fourth-year medical student who was involved with
> her care went to the nursing station and asked for an endotracheal tube
> because he wished to practice endotracheal tube placement. The nurse at
> the station, who had been on the unit for five years, refused to give him
> the tube and in the ensuing argument, accused the student of being in-
> human, of using the patient as his plaything. The medical student, a sen-
> sible and capable young man, retreated, bewildered by the outburst.
> (pp. 17–18)

During this stage, death also comes to be viewed as the enemy.

Coombs and Powers see some physicians, after they graduate and
gain more experience, as going through two more stages:

Stage IV   Questioning the Medical Model: Physicians may question
the glorification of the science of medicine (a knowledge of the disease
processes) at the expense of the art of medicine (the interpersonal abilities). They may also come to question whether death is the enemy, especially after seeing the extremes to which some physicians may go in
keeping someone alive.

If the physician does not go through this stage, Coombs and Powers
hypothesize that the individual will develop a "God complex" and try
to control death by demonstrating clinical mastery over it.

Stage V   Dealing with Personal Feelings: This stage comes when physicians realize that in order to deal with patients' feelings, they must
begin to deal with their own feelings. However, little evidence exists
that physicians are likely to reach this stage. Much of the evidence

would lead to the opposite conclusion. For example, Caldwell and Mishara (1972) attempted a study of physicians' feelings concerning dying patients. Seventy-three residents and internists in a private hospital in Detroit agreed to be interviewed. However, when they were approached by the experimenter and told the specific nature of the study, 60 refused to be interviewed. They stated: "They did not want to participate further as soon as they found out that they were to be questioned about how they felt about dying patients" (p. 342). The doctors felt that they would be less effective if they concerned themselves with their feelings.

Personality Factors

Another reason why physicians have difficulty dealing with the terminally ill has been attributed to the personality characteristics of physicians in that they tend to have more fears and anxieties concerning death than others in the population. It has been hypothesized that persons decide to become physicians because of these fears, that by becoming physicians they hope to control death and thereby to lessen their fears.

One psychoanalytic explanation of physicians' behavior vis-à-vis the dying is given by Kasper (1959). He found that physicians tend to grow up with a strong bond with the mother and an ambivalent relationship with the father. They have aspirations of wanting to make others happy. Future doctors are also more likely to have a greater conscious fear of competition and more feelings of physical inadequacy. "Such circumstances, feelings and fantasies always involve worry and puzzlement about the state and fate of one's own body" (p. 263). The doctor needs to care for others and to receive their gratitude. This derives from the physician's ability to cure. Not only is the dying patient an affront to the doctor's ego, but the dying patient may be depressed and/or angry and may not express gratitude to the physician. (It must be noted that Kasper does not cite any specific study that verifies his findings.)

C. W. Wahl (1959) sees the choice of medicine as representing a defense against death, a reaction formation against a fear that could not be conquered in childhood. Supporting this, Feifel et al. (1967) found that physicians were more likely to have had to deal with a threat of death before the age of 5, compared with the lay people studied, who did not face a similar threat until after the age of 6.

Feifel et al. (1967) studied 81 physicians and compared them with control groups of 95 healthy lay persons and 92 critically ill patients

(40 of whom were terminally ill). The physicians were less likely to think about death, but they were more likely to be afraid of death. They showed greater negative imagery concerning death and had more difficulty in answering the questions than did the comparable group.

Livingston and Zimet (1965) studied death anxiety and the authoritarian personality in 114 medical students. The authoritarian personality has repressed certain impulses that have never been integrated into the conscious self-image. The defense mechanisms of reaction formation and compensation are used "to deal with pre- or unconscious tendencies of fear, weakness, passivity, sexuality or aggression" (p. 222). Livingston and Zimet found that there was an inverse relationship between authoritarianism and death anxiety: the higher the authoritarianism, the lower the death anxiety. This finding was expected since a person higher in authoritarianism would be better defended against his or her unconscious. Those students who chose surgery as their specialty were lowest in death anxiety; psychiatrists were highest.

One would have assumed that surgeons, a type of physician likely to deal with death, would have high death anxiety. However, Livingston and Zimet were measuring overt death anxiety. Because of the relationship between death anxiety and authoritarianism, the students choosing surgery were probably highly defended against death anxiety, which would lead to lower death anxiety on Livingston and Zimet's measure.

As medical students become physicians and come into more contact with the dying and death, it may be more difficult to maintain their defenses. As Feifel (1958) says:

> But I would submit that some physicians reject the dying patient because he reactivates or arouses their own fears about dying—that, in some, guilt feelings tied up with death wishes toward one's own parents may play a role, not to speak of the wounded narcissism of the physician, whose function it is to save life, when he is faced with a dying patient who represents a denial of his essential skills.(p. 122)

A further finding by Livingston and Zimet is that although death anxiety increases as the student progresses through medical school, it is largely determined before the student even enters medical school.

A family physician, quoted by Hendin (1974), succinctly states the result of death anxiety in doctors:

> I must admit that when the anxiety, the fear provoked within me as the physician becomes too great, it's very, very comfortable to deal with the dying process on a technical level. Because then there is no real involve-

ment. There have been times when I haven't been able to cope with an individual patient in a terminal situation, and in a cowardly way, I have run to the stereotyped role of myself as a scientist and technical expert, who doesn't concern himself with people's feelings. Certainly, depending upon the individual physician, some may find the anxiety so great that they always deal with it in this way. (p. 116–117)

What Must Be Done

Since there is a recognition of the factors that contribute to the withdrawal of physicians from the dying, these must be examined to see where they could be changed. Although one would not recommend intensive psychoanalysis for physicians, it is certainly important for medical education to be cognizant of the personality factors that may contribute to doctors' withdrawal from the dying. Education for the care of the dying must be included in medical school curricula. As Krant and Sheldon point out, "This education requires discussion of death as a social phenomenon and a personal phenomenon." Doctors should be encouraged to discuss the problems being encountered in the care of the dying. Death should not be perceived as the enemy. Hospitals and doctors must come to believe that "helping a patient die well is a skill unto itself that affords considerable gratification to the physician and others" (Krant & Sheldon, 1971, p. 21).

SOCIAL WORKERS

The bulk of the literature and research regarding attitudes and educational preparation for working with the terminally ill focuses on physicians and nurses. Although the social work profession has a long history in hospitals and other health care settings, it has escaped the scrutiny devoted to these other two professions. This finding is not particularly surprising. Physicians and nurses are the primary caregivers in hospitals. Their behaviors, attitudes, and responses have the greatest impact on patients. The number of social workers in any given institution varies considerably; the social service staff may be limited to one part-time worker or one social worker for every 34-bed unit. The implementation of social service programs for patients is determined by the organizational goals of the institution. Referral systems that determine access to patients, the perception of the social work role, and a broad or narrow definition of patient care are a few of the multiple factors that contribute to the visibility/invisibility of social workers in health care settings.

Social work was introduced into the medical setting by Dr. Richard

Cabot in the beginning of the century. He concluded that physicians "needed a 'helper' to visit the patient's home, to look into his economic situation, to enter into his state of mind, to comprehend or to influence that many-sided psychic, domestic and industrial environment which is often a large part of what ails the patient, and is moreover a necessary avenue to his cure" (Goldstine, 1954, p. 7). Ida Cannon joined his staff in 1908 and, for the next four decades, directed the growth of social work at Massachusetts General Hospital; she is widely recognized as a major contributor to building the profession of social work in a medical setting. Cannon (1923) defined the social work function as seeing "the patient not merely as an isolated, unfortunate person occupying a hospital bed, but as a member belonging to a family or community group that is altered because of his ill health" (p. 14). The task of the social worker was to remove "obstacles either in the patient's surroundings or in his mental attitude that interfere with treatment, thus freeing the patient to aid in his own recovery" (p. 15). The profession has undergone a number of changes as it has continued to grow and develop its knowledge base. The current conceptual model regarding the impact of severe illness includes the individual's capacity for growth throughout the life cycle, crisis intervention theory, systems theory, and an ecosystems approach. This model represents a refinement and an elaboration of Cannon's original statement rather than a departure from the basic tenet of the psychosocial component of illness. Since the social work profession historically espoused the psychosocial aspect of illness long before it became "trendy" among all health care professionals, are there specific personality traits, characteristics, or attitudes that influence the choice of this profession? Does the education and socialization of social work students enable them to deal more effectively with patients coping with chronic and terminal illness? Is their "invisibility" related to status differentials, number relative to other professionals, or lack of interest?

Characteristics and Education of Social Work Students

The social work profession has always been self-conscious and reflective about the selection of students entering the field. In the past 40 years a variety of studies were conducted to assess characteristics and factors influencing career choice. These efforts, however, focused on attempting to perfect the selection process and on assessing the ability of the institution to identify the appropriate candidate (Golden, Pins, & Jones, 1972; Pins, 1963; *Selection of Students for Schools of Social Work,*

1955). While these studies provide specific demographic date and more general information relating to career choice—for example, in 1966, 59.3 percent of the students entered social work for altruistic-personal reasons, which were defined as "one reason based on social work goals and function and one based on monetary and status remuneration" (Golden et al., 1972, p. 38)—they provide little insight into specific personality characteristics. Brigham (1968) suggested that schools of social work were looking for a "seemingly well-balanced, orderly controlled case worker of yore whom one of our students characterized as 'a colorless, dull, middle-aged person of either sex' " (p. 32).

Personality characteristics are generally defined in broad humanistic terms, such as believing in the individual and the democratic process; having good relationship potential, self-awareness, and stability; and being neither exploitative nor overly dedicated and self-effacing. These characteristics do not easily lend themselves to specific measurement criteria. Cryns (1977) points out that the profession has only recently begun research into professional attitudes and ideologies. These include attitudes toward lifestyle and the indigent (Pratt, 1970), ideology and preference of intervention strategies (Epstein, 1968), and workers' positions in the status hierarchy of social work agencies in relation to their political ideologies (Epstein, 1970; Heffernan, 1964).

A literature search has revealed only a few studies specifically related to professional attitudes about death and death anxiety (Brown, 1974; Kirby & Templer, 1975; Weber et al., 1975). In Kirby's study female social work students were found to have a basically average Death Anxiety Scale mean. A two-and-a-half-hour seminar on the matter of death produced no demonstrable effect upon death anxiety. The study revealed positive correlations between death anxiety of the students and that of their parents and siblings. Brown's master's thesis found that social workers did not differ significantly in their attitudes toward death and dying from physicians, nurses, or graduate students in disciplines other than the helping professions. Tull (1975) investigated the stresses of social workers dealing with the terminally ill. She interviewed workers in three medical facilities specializing in service to cancer patients ($n = 14$). Tull noted that the subjects' decision to work with terminal patients produced "nonremarkable results" (p. 147). Respondents' decisions to accept their assignments were based upon "salary, professional and social opportunities" (p. 147).

Since the mid-1950s, social work education has been based on a generic curriculum to provide social workers with a common foundation of knowledge, values, and a beginning competency in the use of a particular social work method (casework, group work, and community organization). As practice issues become more complex in all fields of social work practice, concern about the need for specialization has been expressed (for example, see Briar, 1968; Caroff & Mailich, 1980; Falck, 1978; Piven, 1969; Raymond, 1977; Shulman, 1977). A significant number of social workers are employed in the health care field. Raymond (1977) reports that data from the National Association of Social Workers revealed that about "one-third of its members practice in health settings (16.1%) or mental health settings (14.4%)" (p. 433). Shulman (1977) predicts that this number will increase to 50 percent over the next two decades (p. 439). Perretz (1976) surveyed the programs of schools of social work to "gather data about the investment of schools of social work in the education of social work for the field of health" (p. 358). He received responses from 62 of the 85 institutions contacted. Of the 62 responding, 37 did offer courses in health and medical systems. Many of these have such a broad scope that it is difficult to ascertain specific content, and Perretz concludes that "there were only 11 courses on health care systems offered in all 62 schools of social work in 1972–73, a time when revolutionary changes were taking place" (p. 360). There is no information about specific courses on death and dying. It would be interesting to replicate Schoenberg et al.'s (1972) survey of nursing schools in schools of social work and compare results.

There are several excellent articles by individual practitioners related to teaching death and dying in social work curricula (Cassidy, 1977; Cohen, 1975; Foechler & Mills, 1975; Goldstein, 1977; Jaffee, 1977; Lister & Gachros, 1976; Miller, 1977). All agree on a classroom format to include both a didactic and an experiential component. Emphasis is also placed on the capacity of the instructor to provide an atmosphere of open communication. Miller (1977) suggests that inclusion of death and dying is a slow process, and that "the instructor's conviction about the necessity for teaching death and dying appears to be a greater determining factor for its inclusion than a consensus by teachers that it should be a requirement within a syllabus" (p. 289). She postulates that teachers are often into their middle years or reaching the last maturational stage of their life cycle. "Preoccupation with his own health or that of a spouse, the loss of a mate, assessment of his achievements and feelings of failure" (p. 291) may impede the introduction of death and dying into the classroom discussion. If the instructor is able to maintain open communication, students are provided with the necessary role models to begin to recognize their own fears and anxieties about death.

Social work education emphasizes self-awareness and self-appraising. The social work student is taught to "meet the patient where he is," with "use of self" as a major tool in forming a therapeutic relationship and alliance. Miller underscores the need for the student to reach his or her own feelings. "Only then is he prepared to incorporate the theoretical content" (p. 292). Although this applies to all social work practice, death evokes a particularly strong response. The course module designed by Lister and Gachros (1976) was formulated to address this response. The overall objectives of the course were to (1) open up a potentially charged area for discussion based on information supplied by various media, selected community experiences, and through self-examination; and (2) to prepare students to be responsive and helpful when they work with the terminally ill, those threatened with death, or those who are experiencing recent losses (p. 87). Goldstein (1977) proposes a similar teaching model guiding students through (1) societal values from a highly theoretical discussion to a more emotional discussion, (2) knowledge about dying patients with a redefinition of death as a phase of life, and (3) skills regarding assessments of resources that exist in the patient's life space to determine where to intervene to promote mastery and growth.

A unique course was taught by Lois Jaffee at the University of Pittsburgh Graduate School of Social Work. After she was diagnosed as having acute leukemia, she developed a seminar to provide "an opportunity to interact over a 15-week period with someone who is terminally ill" (Jaffee, 1977, p. 324). Since her teaching was predicated on "cognitive, affective and behavioral approaches" (p. 326), she used herself as a "case example." The course also included interviews with the recently bereaved, several representatives of the clergy, and the head nurse and chief resident from the hematology unit where Jaffee was a patient. She acknowledges that she underanticipated the emotional response to her presence, and modified the course during the second year to provide for earlier appropriate "desensitizing." She no longer teaches the course but appears as a "guest speaker." Dr. Archie Hanlan (1972a, 1972b), an associate professor of social work at the University of Pennsylvania, also participated in an interdisciplinary seminar at that university after he had been diagnosed as having amyotrophic lateral sclerosis, a progressive terminal disease. These are limited examples, however, and it is difficult to determine how much preparation social work students receive for dealing with dying patients. To offer an elective course begs the issue, since it obviously provides limited opportunity and the student body most in need of the course would be able to self-select out.

Death and dying have relevance for social workers wherever they practice. Individuals and families seen not only in hospitals but in family agencies, schools, mental health clinics, settlement houses, nursing homes, geriatric programs, and so forth may be coping with chronic illness, impending death, or feelings of grief related to a recent death. Miller (1977) notes that "it is ironic that social work students are exposed to a wide range of human problems affecting some part of the population but are given very little content about death and dying, the one task that affects everyone" (p. 298). Ginsberg (1977) suggests that the social problems of poverty, disease, crime, loneliness, and interpersonal conflict are responsive to strategies of elimination or amelioration, which are the usual goals of social work. Death does not lend itself to this treatment model and can be viewed as the "ultimate defeat" for both the client and the worker. He further postulates that "social work may be the most optimistic and future oriented of the human service professions" (p. 5), and that social workers have difficulty in distinguishing between social phenomena that are responsive to change and irreversible problems such as death. Thus, the social worker, just as the nurse and the physician, must confront personal and professional conflicts in working with dying patients and their families.

Social Worker/Patient Interaction

How does the social worker, seemingly ill-prepared and professionally ambivalent, interact with dying patients and families? In marked contrast to the limited literature regarding attitudes and curriculum content, there is an abundance of literature regarding direct practice with terminally ill patients. These articles can be categorized as defining (1) basic social work concepts related to the terminally ill; (2) specific therapeutic concepts related to different phases of the life cycle (child, adolescent, middle-aged, geriatric); (3) treatment modalities such as group work and family therapy; and (4) social work's institutional role in program development. In this section we limit review to a few representative articles (see bibliography for additional readings).

As early as 1937, Eleanor Cocherill identified and discussed the needs of the cancer patient that are still relevant today. She noted the avoidance, the fear, the uncertainty about informing a patient of the diagnosis, and the scarcity of environmental supports. Cocherill emphasizes that treatment of a cancer patient requires "awareness by the case-worker of her own feelings as an absolute essential" (p. 192). This belief is a chord consistently reinforced throughout the literature.

She also suggests that cancer is a crisis and that the social work task is to help patients discover and utilize their strength for coping with stress. "The recognition of this concept leads to a realization that there are no special techniques for dealing with the cancer patient, that there can be no uniform approach to him" (p. 193).

Ruth Abrams has numerous publications related to the psychosocial aspects of working with, and the management of, the cancer patient. She (1954) hypothesized that "the patient is usually concerned with, and often aware of the fact that he has cancer and is reacting to it— whether he says so or not" (p. 199). In spite of this, she disagrees with the necessity of soliciting or prompting a patient to talk about dying, and states (1974): "His caregivers must realize that perhaps it is they who wish to talk of death, even though the patient wishes to maintain silence" (p. 77). Abrams identifies the defensive maneuvers of avoidance, suppression, denial, and guilt and the need to understand the dynamics of these defenses to set appropriate treatment goals with patients.

Social workers have recognized that the terminally ill struggle with feelings of rejection and social and emotional isolation, and have applied basic principles of group therapy to this patient population (for example, see Adams, 1976; Goodyear, 1977; Heymann, 1974; Kagen, 1976; Mervis, 1977). This treatment modality provides an opportunity for patients to share and express emotions related to their illness. The purpose of a group, as defined by Goodyear (1977), is to help patients feel less isolated; more free to verbalize questions, anger, and fear; more motivated to explore interpersonal relationships; and to help them establish meaningful relationships with other cancer patients and to be able to call on them for support outside the group (p. 243). Mervis (1977) also emphasizes that the focus of the group is to enhance self-esteem and self-determination, to enable group members to engage in "a dignified meaningful life rather than one characterized by marking time" (p. 240).

The needs of family members are another component of social work intervention. Wijnberg and Schwartz (1977) identify two different sets of tasks that family members must undertake when one member is dying. The first is being able to be helpful to the dying patient with a constellation of behaviors, such as being able to visit, to listen, to allow the patient to maintain an active role with the family, and not to withdraw prematurely. At the same time, the family member must be assisted in coping with the disruption of his or her own personal life. They suggest that social work support should include: (1) stroking, nourishing, and listening; (2) limiting the burden and responsibility;

(3) encouraging role attachments; (4) mobilizing the social network of the family; and (5) helping plan for the future. A number of articles provide specific strategies for families of pediatric cancer patients. J. Ross (1978) identifies critical phases; (a) before the diagnosis; (b) the diagnostic period; (c) remission; (d) relapse; and (e) death and mourning—before and after (p. 258). Social work intervention at each of these stages will require evaluation of family functioning before and at the time of crisis. Ross concludes that "familial response to fatal illness in children is a complicated phase-related process" (p. 271) that requires constant evaluation and shifting of treatment strategies.

In addition to one-to-one interviews, many authors suggest the development of groups for families (Adams, 1978; Borstein & Klein, 1974; Boyd, 1977; Heffron, 1973; Knapp, 1973; Ross, 1979). These groups provide a forum for families to share concerns with others experiencing similar stresses, including enhancing their understanding of the disease and treatment, how to communicate with their ill child and other siblings, the strains placed on the marital dyad, and worry about death. Adams (1978) cautions that "a social worker must have a thorough understanding of growth and development, the effects of hospitalization, response to fatal illness and family and group dynamics" (p. 735) to be an effective leader. In addition to groups for families of pediatric patients, groups have been developed to meet the needs of special patient populations (Bromberg & Donnerstag, 1977; Eustis, 1979; Kagen, 1976; Le Pontois, 1975; Vorgna, 1979; Williams & Race, 1977; Witte & Baber, 1977).

Finally, social work considers within its purview the responsibility for effecting needed social change. Foster (1965) describes the steps and processes required to modify the ward culture on a hematology service from closed, guarded communication that isolated patients and families to a more open communication system between staff, patient, and family that allowed patients a broader range of coping patterns. Koenig (1968) studied the nature and frequency of social problems among patients with terminal cancer. He outlined the social, emotional, financial, and medical care problems encountered by this patient population and strongly recommended a more holistic approach to care: "Stresses arising from problems complicate medical treatment and at times negate the effect of treatment altogether" (p. 90). Articles consistently appear within the professional literature reiterating these themes (Cannon, 1977; Lohmann, 1977; McNamara, 1975; Millet, 1979; Milner, 1980; Wessells, 1949).

What emerges from the literature regarding direct practice is that the social work profession has clearly articulated specific social work tasks and goals regarding the terminally ill. These tasks pervade all of social work and, as outlined by Pilsecher (1979), include: (1) helping patients and their significant others to get in touch with their feelings and to recognize their behavior options; (2) assisting in the development or maintenance of meaningful communication; (3) locating and linking patients to community resources; and (4) helping health professionals whose activities impinge upon the patient to acknowledge their own feelings, to understand the feelings and needs of patients, and to learn effective and sensitive ways of meeting these needs (p. 374). It is difficult, however, to assess how effective the profession has been in carrying out these tasks and in achieving the goals for delivery of services. We could hypothesize that the profession's stress on the psychosocial aspects of illness since the 1900s has contributed to the increasing awareness of all health professionals, but there are no research data to substantiate this hypothesis.

Social Workers' Response to Terminally Ill Patients

Supervision of social work students and beginning social workers has been an essential component in facilitating the education and continuing growth of the entry-level professional. Most agency directors assume that beginning workers will continue to require supervision. The supervisory process offers an opportunity for the worker, with the assistance of a more experienced professional, to enhance and deepen social work skills. Harper (1975) has developed a cognitive/ego-mastery model that she utilized during supervision of workers dealing with patients. During Stage I, which takes from one to three months, the social worker engages in a "conspiracy of silence." During this stage the worker copes by withdrawal and finds talking about death unacceptable. In Stage II (three to six months) the social worker experiences guilt, frustration, and sadness. She or he often is hostile and feels that "nothing can happen therapeutically." The third stage (six to nine months) is characterized by pain, mourning, and grieving. During this period the social worker begins applying experience in a more positive way, and Harper postulates that during this interim the worker will choose to "grow or go elsewhere." By the end of the first year, the social worker enters Stage IV and deals with the dying patient with "moderation, mitigation and accommodation." During this period the worker continues to develop skills to deal with patients and has a deepening sense of self. In the final stage, workers are able to deal with the dying patient with a deep compassion related to their own self-realization, awareness, and actualization. Harper believes the supervisor's role is to provide (1) courage, (2) options (freedom to choose), (3) patience, (4) interest, (5) nurturing, and (6) guidance.

Tull (1975) identified three patterns of coping with the stress of work with terminal patients: (1) constricted defensiveness, (2) active struggle, and (3) integration. The respondents coping with constricted defensiveness displayed "inhibition of positive feelings toward clients; avoidance of contact with the family after a patient died; immediate involvement with other clients; intellectualization of feelings about death and dying and displacement of feelings onto other staff members, the administration and medical profession" (p. 149). The "active struggling" workers had difficulty maintaining appropriate emotional distance with patients and "seemed to experience the losses reported as ego deflating" (p. 152). The third group coped with a "style characterized by an integration of their professional roles and responsibilites, their personalities and their philosophy of life." These workers were able to establish attachment to, and relationships with, clients and allowed themselves to grieve for their clients. Tull points to the need for an individualized supportive program to enable workers to approach the degree of comfort and integration this last group demonstrated, but offers no model for such a program.

In 1978 the Social Work Oncology Group at the Sidney Farber Cancer Institute, Boston, Massachusetts, sponsored a workshop on "Stress and Burn-Out." This workshop identified five major stresses: (1) troublesome symptoms of burnout such as a vague sense of helplessness, progressive apathy, increased minor illness; (2) erosion of belief in the value of one's work; (3) guilt associated with a sense of omnipotence; (4) exclusionary protectionism; and (5) difficult patients. Koocher (1979) reports that the following strategies were suggested: make use of hobbies, work with a variety of patients, share mutual support from colleagues, alternate work assignments, use humor, take time off away from it all, share the sense of helplessness, and limit emotional investment. A supportive network is necessary to utilize these strategies. An oncology social work network has been developed by Marion Stonberg (1977), with membership from Massachusetts, Rhode Island, New Hampshire, Maine, and Vermont. The aims of the network are to increase the level of competence of workers, to identify gaps in services and to develop activities aimed at closing these gaps, and to provide a mechanism for communication between hospitals and community around the problems of cancer patients and their families. A similar network was developed in Brooklyn by Diane Charet, Brooklyn Downstate Medical Center, in 1979. This network now includes groups meeting in every borough in the New York metropolitan area.

INTERDISCIPLINARY CONCERNS:
COMMUNICATION AND PAIN CONTROL

There are many issues of concern to all health caregivers regarding dying people, but there are two specific issues that seem to be highly charged emotionally and that require definite interdisciplinary discussion and consensus if patients are to be offered assistance in coping with their feelings of loneliness, isolation, and fear and with the pain associated with dying. These issues are communication and pain control.

Communication

The situation can arise in which a patient with a terminal illness, whose physician does not want the diagnosis known will bluntly ask another caregiver if he or she is dying. How do these caregivers respond to this? One research study that sampled 15,430 nurses found that most nurses (82 percent) responded by trying to get patients to talk about their feelings (*Dealing With Death and Dying,* 1977, p. 161). Although this is one appropriate answer for the situation, it avoids the basic issue if, indeed, the patient wants a direct answer to the question. Thirteen percent of the respondents in this study said they would first refer the patient to the physician, but that if the patient didn't get a clear answer from the doctor, they would tell the patient the truth (pp. 161–162). Role conflicts may result from such a response since the responsibility among health team members in most institutions for informing patients about terminal illnesses is assumed to be given to the physicians. Nurses, social workers, and physicians may disagree about where this responsibility lies. This may also pose an ethical dilemma for nurses and social workers as to whether such responsibility is within the realm of their professional practice.

A significant part of the issue here is communication among health team members themselves and between caregivers and patients. If the physician discusses the inevitability of the patient's death with other members of the health care team and does not discuss this with the patient, the patient may be aware of a change in staff attitude but cannot understand why. Conversely, the physician may discuss the patient's death with him or her but not relate this to the health care team. Caregivers may then be unclear as to why the patient's behavior has changed. There can be many variations of these interactions between staff and patients when there is uncertainty as to who has been told what by whom!

Current health team practitioners need to talk with each other and plan together what is being communicated to dying patients. Interdisciplinary patient rounds and staff meetings to discuss specific patients may be formal ways of promoting this communication. The coordination of professional education would also seem to be a way to enhance communication among members of the health team. If students in nursing, medicine, and social work could sit together in the core courses for their professional education, they might develop an appreciation of one another's ideas, approaches, values, and goals. Ideally this appreciation and understanding would continue as they assumed more responsibility for patient care. However, Pellegrino (1966) points out a major difficulty in this process of understanding roles;

> The current bias of medical education is strongly toward the physical and biological sciences. Nursing, on the other hand, has tended increasingly to emphasize the social and psychological. As a consequence, medical students and residents are much more anxious about learning disease mechanisms and reductionistic appraisals of patients while nursing leans to the more holistic view and an interest in helping the person through the crisis of ill health. A real factor with medical students (and residents) is that their anxiety is so great, faced with the enormous amount of knowledge for which they are accountable, that there is little time left over for considering those very dimensions the nurse considers the most important and which are important—the social and personal dimensions of illness. (p. 49)

The addition of another discipline, social work, adds to the confusion. Both physicians and nurses often view the social work role as being related to concrete services. Hallowitz (1972) concludes: "She is viewed . . . as a body mover, financial agent and provider of prosthetic devices for individuals" (p. 90). This view conflicts with the social worker's perception of self and with her or his role as a "counselor" with a psychosocial approach. The difficulty rests first in the assumption that several different professions can automatically function as a team because they have an apparent mutual goal—caring for the patient. A health care team needs training to function as a team, but this is consistently overlooked. Rubin in Wise et al. (1974) remarks that

> . . . it is naive to bring together a highly diverse group of people and expect that by calling them a team they will in fact behave as one. It is ironic indeed to realize that a football team spends 40 hours a week practicing teamwork for the 2 hours on Sunday afternoon when their teamwork really counts. Teams in organizations seldom spend 2 hours per year practicing when their ability to function as a team counts 40 hours per week. (p. xviii)

Six characteristics influence and delineate team functioning: (1) goals or tasks, (2) role expectations, (3) decision making, (4) communication patterns, (5) leadership, and (6) norms (Plovnick, Fry, & Rubin, 1977; Rubin & Becknard 1972). Exploration of all of these reveals little congruence between the professional norms, goals, and perceptions of physicians, nurses, and social workers. In discussing these obstacles, Kahn (1974) reports the following:

• Nurses felt that physicians tended to take charge and give orders despite the official emphasis on collegial team relations.

• Social workers insisted on the confidential nature of their records.

• Physicians sought "quick solutions."

• Nurses felt they were willing to do dirty work; whereas social workers offered nothing "tangible" and stirred up feelings.

• Social workers felt nurses sought quick heroic solutions and did not deal with their feelings.

• There is overlapping in nurse–social worker activity.

• Nurses, social workers and doctors have different social class backgrounds, different educational status, different social distance from clientele with resulting conflicts in perceptions and relationships. (p. 19)

Caregivers need to understand these different orientations in one another and together use the best of all their approaches in being with dying people—the knowledge of disease and treatment to provide comfort, and the understanding of fear and anxiety to allow talking and listening. If this is not achieved, the team provides piecemeal service. Lack of mutual respect ultimately leaves the patient as the victim in the battle for professional turf.

Acknowledgment of our own humanity as caregivers is necessary to communicate caring. We often come to an impasse in sharing our feelings and reactions with each other; it is almost as if we negate the human part of our beings. Perhaps we feel that because we have not cured dying patients, we have failed not only them but also ourselves and our colleagues; or perhaps our own fears of death are so frightening to us that we cannot share these feelings. Benoliel (1976) uses the phrase "quality of survival" to designate a system of health care that would shift priorities away from an emphasis on recovery for recovery's sake and toward an emphasis on person-centered goals (p. 10). This system might also permit caregivers to know that it is acceptable to feel, and therefore to grieve for, the loss of a patient. When caregivers are grieving for a patient who dies, it may be helpful if they can get together to talk about the death. Grief work can take many forms— reminiscing about what the patient said or did when on the unit, how people will miss this particular patient, a few minutes of silence. Some people may need to express anger or cry. It is significant that staff share the grief work; its form and expression will vary. As staff members become more comfortable with this sharing of feelings of grief, they in turn may become more comfortable with helping clients and families experience their losses. Our emotional vulnerability is an asset in our care of people; it allows us to be open and receptive to what people are feeling and trying to express. If we realize we have the support of colleagues, this vulnerability need not be feared, but can be used as a vehicle for our own growth as well as for that of our patients.

Pain Control

Pain is a subjective phenomenon, and many factors influence people's reports of this event. Pain is more than simply a bodily response that occurs when tissues are damaged or stressed. According to Chapman (1978), "contemporary theorists stress that pain involves emotional arousal, motivational drive, and cognition in addition to sensory information transmission" (p. 169). McCaffery's (1972) workable definition for nurses presents the idea that pain is whatever the experiencing person says it is and exists when that person says it does. This latter definition, if held by caregivers, supports patients in that their reports of pain are never doubted. Both these definitions include the concept that pain can be of functional and/or organic origin. Management of pain in people who are dying is especially significant, not only in terms of pain relief but also because "one cannot adequately help a man to come to accept his impending death if he remains in severe pain, one cannot give spiritual counsel to a woman who is persistently vomiting, or help a wife and children say their goodbyes to a father who is so drugged that he cannot respond" (Baines, 1980, p.1). Our discussion of pain management is included in this chapter because we believe that such management consists of interactional, interdisciplinary, and organizational processes.

Patients in pain will often put on a "brave face"; they may not appear outwardly to be in any great distress and may state only that they are having a "little" pain. It is therefore important that caregivers assess patients thoroughly to determine the extent and severity of pain. Assessment includes careful history taking and physical examination. History taking includes not only listening to the patient's description of the pain but also asking the patient such questions as: "When did the pain start?" "What makes it worse?" "What makes it less intense?" "Do any medications help?" "Does it stay in one place or move around?"

"Are you in pain all the time, or does it come and go?" It is helpful to have patients describe a normal day's activity pattern and then ask them if pain has interfered in this pattern at all—that is, interrupted sleep, dulled appetite, limited mobility. Interviewing a family member or friend about the patient's pain might also help gain a more accurate picture of what is happening.

Neurophysiological processes may underlie the sensation of pain and should be assessed by physical examination. The results of such an examination may reveal a specific pathology that is causing the sensation of pain and may indicate why the pain is localized in a specific part of the body or why it is perceived as referred pain in another area. However, according to Twycross (1978), "pain is a dual phenomenon, one part being the perception of the sensation and the other the patient's psychological reaction to it" (p. 114). Therefore, a patient's pain threshold may vary according to such nonphysical factors as anxiety, fear, depression, and fatigue. Cultural influences and past life experiences may also affect pain thresholds. These nonphysical factors, which are not generally so readily evident as are physiological elements, must be considered as part of the process of pain assessment and management.

LeShan (1964) suggests that pain may be a communication, perhaps even a cry for help, and that in assessing a person's pain, it may be helpful to ask oneself, Is the person trying to say something by this, is there a message in it? (p. 122). Schmitt (1977) states that "the body does not want pain—it uses it only as a means of telling us that all is not well, that something needs attending to. . . . If the body is speaking to us in the language of pain, it is telling us extremely important truths" (p. 627). The pain may serve a purpose for the patient; it may be a way of dealing with an unresolved conflict or with feelings of guilt. Pain may also be seen as a threat to patients' lives; their lifestyles or their body images might be changed by pain. A caregiver-therapist may work with patients in pain to help them arrive at a meaning, a making sense of what is happening to them; to help such patients act, and react, to their situation; and to help them gain some degree of control over this.

Patients' membership in a particular sociocultural group may also influence pain sensation and behavioral response to it. In a well-known study of pain responses of Irish, Jewish, Italian, and "Old American" patients, Zborowski (1952) found that Jewish and Italian male patients were very emotional in their responses to pain, tending to exaggerate the experience and to be very sensitive to it. However, the research material suggests that in the male Jewish patient, "the function of the pain reaction will be the mobilization of the efforts of the family and the doctors toward a complete cure, while in the male Italian patient, the function of the reaction will be focused upon the mobilization of effort toward relieving the pain sensation" (p. 24). A similar overt behavioral response in two different patients may have two very different meanings. Caregivers assessment of pain should include an evaluation of whether patients are more concerned with immediate, palliative pain relief, or with what the pain means to them, or with finding an ultimate cure for the pain.

Age and sex influence patients' responses to pain. In the United States, women seem to be allowed more freedom for emotional expression of pain than men, although this changes as men grow older and are allowed more freedom in this area. Children's developmental levels need to be considered in assessing pain. Infants and toddlers cannot communicate verbally. Their crying must be interpreted—one must determine whether it is a pain cry or whether it has other meanings, such as expressing hunger, wetness, or wanting to be held. Telling a preschool child that a painful treatment "will be all over soon" does not mean anything, since temporal relationships are not understood (Gilder & Quirk, 1977). Children at this age still utilize a great deal of concrete thinking; a painful procedure just plain hurts, and little relationship is seen between the procedure and getting well. Among school-age children, there is a fear of bodily injury, with anxieties about this frequently submerged. However, these children can understand that pain can be limited. Explaining potentially painful treatments and procedures, letting the children know what to expect, and allowing them to ask questions and to express their anxieties are meaningful for children of this age.

Pain may be alleviated in many patients of all ages if they understand what is causing the pain or that staff members are trying to determine the cause, that caring people are available on an ongoing basis to help them, and that they have a part in planning how to cope with the pain.

Caregivers often have difficulty with understanding a patient's report of pain if there is no physiological reason for it; such pain may not be considered "real." Hackett (1971) identifies several factors that may contribute to physicians assessment of pain: (1) patients with chronic pain are expected by physicians to react to it with the same behaviors as those patients with acute pain; (2) physicians believe that pain must have an organic basis in order for it to hurt; (3) health professionals have a tendency to undermedicate because of their concern about patients becoming addicted. Pain assessment and treatment are not only dependent upon a physical examination and the patient's subjective report but also upon the caregiver's beliefs about the origin of the pain and how people respond to it.

Caregivers may become frustrated in working with patients with chronic pain in that they may feel powerless to relieve the pain and helpless in that they cannot find an organic cause for it. In studying how physicians, social workers, and nurses assess the intensity of pain, Baer et al, (1970) found that social workers tended to infer that patients had the greatest degree of pain whereas physicians and nurses inferred less pain. The author hypothesized that health professionals who are in constant contact with patients in pain may deal with their own feelings of helplessness about what to do about this pain by denying or minimizing it. Nurses, whose education emphasizes relief of suffering, and who are responsible for patient care 24 hours a day, may develop feelings of guilt if they are unable to relieve a patient's pain. Such feelings of guilt and frustration can turn to anger at the person perceived as responsible for the pain or at the person responsible for helping the nurse relieve the pain. This person may be the patient or the doctor. This anger, if directed at the patient, may cause nurses to fell more guilty. They may begin to associate the patient with unpleasant feelings (Doherty, 1979). In order not to experience this, nurses avoid the patient and withdraw. Such withdrawal may not be successful as a coping mechanism, and hence the feelings of guilt may be increased.

Patients are a part of this cycle also. Patients in chronic pain often cannot take care of their own needs and feel dependent upon staff. These feelings of dependency and helplessness may be expressed as anger toward staff. Chronic pain wears people down, and they feel they are losing control of their lives. Such patients may withdraw, and their angry behavior may cause staff to withdraw from them. In order to intervene in this cycle of mutual withdrawal, nurses and other caregivers need to face the reality that it is not always possible to relieve suffering completely, and they need to accept the responsibility of helping patients cope with some pain. Staff members need to acknowledge verbally with patients the existence of pain and the patients' right to feel frustrated and angry and tired about unrelieved pain.

Twycross suggests that relief of pain should have realistic objectives. The ultimate aim is always complete relief from pain, but perhaps graded relief is more realistic—that is, (1) a pain-free, sleep-full night; (2) relief at rest in bed or chair during the day; (3) freedom from pain on movement (Twycross, 1978, p. 115). The latter may be the most difficult to achieve; but if patients can rest comfortably at night and throughout the day, their morale may be able to cope with limited mobility more effectively. The decision upon a course of action for pain relief will be based not only on the patient's requests and needs but also on the caregivers' professional orientation to pain, personal beliefs about pain, political processes, and the organization of health care.

The use of analgesics and other drugs to elevate patients' pain thresholds is a traditional medical model approach to pain control. Other medical model approaches include modification of the pathological process—for example, surgery, radiation, or chemotherapy; interruption of pain pathways, such as chemical neurolysis (nerve blocks); and immobilization, which could include modification of daily living activities (Twycross, 1978). The use of analgesics in pain control bears closer scrutiny at this point not only because of its role in adequate pain relief for patients but also because of its role in influencing the interactional and political processes among staff, patients, and family.

As cited earlier, Hackett (1971) found that health professionals have a tendency to undermedicate because of their concern about patients becoming addicted. Marks and Sachar's (1973) study on narcotic use showed that 32 percent of patients remained in severe distress and that 41 percent remained in moderate distress even though both groups of patients received narcotics for pain. This study revealed that the doctors involved had misconceptions about the danger of patient addiction to narcotics, and thus were reluctant to order medication more frequently and in higher dosages for people with severe pain resulting from a terminal malignant disease. The concern of caregivers about terminally ill patients in pain becoming addicted to narcotics seems overly cautious. Robert G. Twycross (cited in Montgomery, 1978), one of the world's foremost heroin researchers, states:

> When diamorphine [heroin] is given prophylactically to prevent the return of otherwise intractable pain, it is very unusual to encounter true addiction. Most people do not crave the drug when they no longer need relief for their pain. The dangerous situation occurs when diamorphine is given on a p.r.n. (as needed, when necessary) basis and the pain has to return before the next dose is deemed necessary. (p. 1571)

We must also ask whether caregivers' concern about a terminally ill patient becoming addicted is in the best interests of the patient. If the person is dying and is in need of medication for pain relief, is our priority the relief of that pain or a potential addiction?

Caregivers and patients often find themselves in disagreement with one another about the use and administration of narcotics. Patients may feel that they are not obtaining adequate pain relief. Nurses may be reluctant to give regular doses of a narcotic around the clock for fear of the accumulation of side effects that could possibly cause death in some patients. Doctors may be concerned about the origin and reality of the patient's pain. Social workers may feel that no one is listening to the patient's reports of pain.

Along with the fear of addiction, Silman (1978) points out that another common misconception by patients and staff is the expectation that a medication will have an instantaneous onset and an extended duration of action. Drugs have different periods for onset of relief and reach their peak action at different times. Caregivers should be aware of these times of onset and duration to help patients plan their activity and rest throughout the day. A person who needs increased mobility at a certain time may well want to plan that mobility around the time of the drug's peak action, so that pain will be decreased and function improved. In addition, then, to caregivers' beliefs about the origin and quality of a patient's pain influencing pain management, their beliefs (as well as the patients') about how, when, and whether to use analgesics will affect pain control.

The organization of health care itself plays a very significant part in the management of pain, particularly in institutional settings such as hospitals and clinics. Fagerhaugh and Strauss (1977) present three main themes developed from their two-year research study on pain management. The first theme is that pain management occurs within organizational settings that greatly influence the character of the interaction between patients and staff. These interactions, which are extremely important in the management of pain, are affected by the context of the organization itself—its work structure, its goals, its philosophy. An example of this theme may be seen in the difference in pain management in hospices and in acute care centers. In hospices, the philosophy is to help patients on their journey through life. The hospice is considered a place where patients may always come for sustenance. As a result of this philosophy, pain management is collaboratively planned by patients and staff to enhance comfort, alertness, and participation in living. Staff members consistently communicate with one another and with the patient about the effects of pain management—how it is working, what needs to be changed. Pain management in acute care centers may often focus on immediate relief, with the intention of ultimately curing the cause of pain; there is often the expectation that the pain should diminish after intensive treatment. There may be little or no collaboration with patients about how best to relieve their pain. Copp (1974) found that patients who had been fairly successful in managing their pain at home seemed unable to cope with the pain once they were hospitalized. The patients were reluctant to use their own pain-relieving mechanisms because they might be against hospital rules or they might be laughed at as not being scientific enough. The acute care center is also essentially perceived as the home territory of staff; a patient offering suggestions about how to treat his or her individual pain may be seen as intruding upon staff domain. Patients who want some part in their pain management plan may be labeled "difficult," "manipulating," "crocks," or "malingerers." Caregivers may disagree with one another about the reality of the patient's pain and about his or her ability to participate in the treatment plan.

Fagerhaugh and Strauss's (1977) second theme is that political processes influence pain management. Political actions such as persuading, negotiating, appealing to authority, and even threats or use of force may be used by patients and/or staff in the management of pain and in order to get work done. Diagnostic and treatment procedures may involve the necessity of staff inflicting pain upon patients. If patients do not cooperate with these tasks, or if staff's approach does not help patients tolerate the pain involved, force may be used to complete the task. An example of this is restraining a child in order to give an injection. Patients also may use numerous actions to obtain pain relief. If such approaches as cajoling, bargaining, and appeal to rational thinking do not work, patients may forcibly resist staff actions, refuse treatment, seek help from higher authorities in the bureaucratic structure, or even leave the treatment center. Pain management, then, particularly in institutions, may involve patients and staff in political actions that can involve negotiating, agreement, disagreement, withdrawal, physical actions, suppressing of information, and lobbying.

A balancing of decisions is a vital component in the political actions of pain management. "The pain tasks of diagnosing, preventing, minimizing, inflicting, relieving, enduring, and espressing are weighed with the consequences for life and death, carrying-on, interaction, ward work, and personal integrity" (Fagerhaugh & Strauss, 1977, p. 244). For example, a terminally ill patient in an acute care center has morphine ordered for pain relief every four hours *p. r. n.* (as needed). The patient must decide not only when to ask for the medication and how often—but also how requests for medication (a narcotic) will affect his or her interaction with staff and family, whether or not the medication will affect alertness, and how to deal with personal feelings about continually having to ask for help in pain relief. Components of the staff's decision in administering the medication may include their feelings about drug addiction, the reality of the patient's pain, their knowledge of drug action, and their experience in working with terminally ill patients. Organizational and social contexts that are influential in this decision may include the organization of the unit itself— whether it is primarily set up to care for patients with short-term, acute illnesses or for patients with more chronic, long-term illnesses; how busy the unit is; and the unit's ratio of staff to patients. A balancing of factors such as these contribute to the decision on how, if, and when pain control will be utilized.

The third theme development by Fagerhaugh and Strauss (1977) is that the acute care model is inadequate for chronic pain. In Chapter 3 we discussed the implications of the acute care model on the care of terminally ill patients. Again, the disease-oriented ideology of this model, with its emphasis on curing pathological processes in patients, does not leave much room for helping people learn how to manage and live with chronic pain.

Methods of Relieving Pain

As previously discussed, the relief of pain in dying patients is based on preventing the pain rather than waiting for the pain to appear and then trying to treat it. One medication that is effective in this approach is Brompton's cocktail, or Brompton's mixture, long known to the British for use in pain relief with dying patients. (See Chapter 3, St. Christopher's Hospice.) Brompton's cocktail is given regularly every three to four hours around the clock, thus preventing pain. It may provide a pain-free state without such side effects as decreased alertness. Patients no longer fear pain and can therefore engage in social interactions and daily living activities. Living their lives without severe pain and without the anxiety associated with that pain provides many dying people with a sense of freedom and an enhancement of self-esteem. Brompton's cocktail is often given in conjunction with other treatments the patient may be receiving, such as radiation therapy.

Using analgesics as a method of pain control is by no means the only method. Biofeedback is another modality being used in pain management. Biofeedback involves the use of biophysiological instrumentation to provide patients with information about changes in their bodily functioning of which they are not normally aware. This information may enable patients to control voluntarily some aspect of their physiology that is supposedly casually linked to the pain being experienced (Turk, et al., 1979, pp. 1322–1323). Therapeutic touch, hypnosis, acupuncture, relaxation techniques, use of imagery and distraction, behavior therapy, alleviation of anxiety, teaching patients about the nature of pain and its intensity, reduction of stimulus, and the establishment of a trusting relationship between a caregiver and a patient with pain are all being used in pain management. Caregivers and patients often use several of these methods in combination.

Pain centers or clinics have been developed to help people with pain relief. Patients referred to a pain clinic usually have had all the conventional treatments and have seen all the appropriate specialists, but they still have intractable pain. The ideal way to treat pain is, of course, to remove the cause, but patients coming to pain clinics may have pain whose cause is undiscovered or not easily treatable—for example, cancer, amputation stump pain, lumbosciatic syndrome (Swerdlow, 1978, p. 117). Although pain may not be eliminated, it may be reduced or relieved. The staff of a pain clinic is a multidisciplinary one, involving specialists in all areas of medicine, nurses, physiotherapists, and social workers. The clinic offers patients all available methods of treating chronic pain, including physical, pharmacological, and psychological approaches. Research and teaching are also ongoing functions of these centers. It is important when referring patients to pain clinics to prepare them for the possibility of long waiting lists, and to offer confidence without raising undue expectations for immediate relief.

The control of pain is a highly complex process involving interpersonal interactions, political actions, and the organization of health care and its prevailing medical ideology. Caregivers collaborating with patients in pain management need to consider all these factors in arriving at a mutually acceptable treatment plan. Since the use of analgesics, especially narcotics, can evoke so many feelings about dependency and addiction, there is a need for both staff and patients to discuss such usage with one another. Interdisciplinary communication of the pain management plan is extremely important, particularly in institutions where personnel on three different tours of duty are involved. Patients' families also need to be involved in planning and managing treatment. These are all important innovations in pain management that can take place within the health care system as it is currently functioning. However, as consumers utilizing health care continue to legislate for a system based on more equal priorities of caring and curing, it is possible that pain management with dying people will be recognized for what it is—a significant contribution to the enhancement of human life.

SUMMARY

Caregivers and patients share the human fear of death. Professional education that allows practitioners to identify, explore, and come to terms with feelings about death can be influential in enhancing the appropriate care of dying patients. Caregivers need continued support and supervision to maintain professional humanistic values in caring for dying patients in a health care system that currently emphasizes cure rather than care. A major refocus of values in this system needs to be considered; caring functions must be given the same status, prestige, and priority as are life-saving, curing activities. Caregivers also need an opportunity to grieve over the loss of their patients, and must be able to share these feelings with one another, offering support and help as needed. Further research and development of interprofessional curricula are needed to enhance communication skills and understanding of the roles and tasks of each member of the interdisciplinary team.

LEARNING EXERCISES

1. If you were dying, what are the three most desirable behaviors you would want from your physician, nurse, social worker? What are the three least desirable?
2. Discuss whether or not a patient should be given a dose of pain medication that carries a high risk of respiratory arrest. Who should make the decision?
3. In interdisciplinary rounds concerning the care of a dying patient, who should lead the discussion? How did you reach the decision?
4. Given the fact that physicians, nurses, and social workers have difficulty in dealing with dying patients, do you think another profession should be developed? What characteristics would be most helpful?

AUDIOVISUAL MATERIAL

Death and the Doctor. 20 min/videocassette or film/1975. Professional Research Inc.
  Physicians discuss their experiences and responses to dying patients, including their own feelings about life and death and how effective they have been in their relationships with patients.

Counseling the Terminally Ill: Three Lives. 60 min/color. Dr. Charles Garfield.
This film depicts the relationship between the counselor and the dying patient, and how it affects both of them.

Terminal Patients: Their Attitudes and Yours. 16 min/color. Abbott Laboratories.
Professional attitudes can influence and affect the care that terminally ill patients receive. The film explores these attitudes both with professional staff and through the thoughts of two terminal patients.

What Can I Say?. 31 min/black and white/1968. American Journal of Nursing, c/o Association Films.
Discusses how nurses may deal with the questions of dying patients and with their own anxieties.

REFERENCES

Aasterud, M. Defenses against anxiety in the nurse–patient relationship. *Nursing Forum,* Summer 1962, *1*(3), 35–59.

Abrams, R. Social case work with cancer patients. In D. Golstine (Ed.), *Readings in the theory and practice of medical social work.* Chicago: University of Chicago Press, 1954.

Abrams, R. *Not alone with cancer.* Springfield, Ill.: Charles C Thomas, 1974.

Abrams, R., & Finesinger, J. Guilt reactions in patients with cancer. *Cancer,* May 1953, *VI*, 474–482.

Adams, M. A hospital play program: Helping children with serious illness. *American Journal of Orthopsychiatry,* July 1976, *46*(3), 416–424.

Adams, M. Helping the parents of children with malignancy. *Journal of Pediatrics,* 1978, *93*(5), 734–738.

Baer, E., Davitz, L., & Lieb, R. Inferences of physical pain and psychological distress: Part 1. In relation to verbal and nonverbal patient communication. *Nursing Research,* October 1970, *19*, 388–392.

Baines, M. *Principles of symptom control.* Paper presented at St. Christopher's Bar Mitzvah, London, England, June 1–10, 1980.

Benoliel, J. Q. Overview: Care, cure and the challenge of choice. In A. M. Earle, N. T. Argondizzo, & A. H. Kutscher (Eds.), *The nurse as caregiver for the terminal patient and his family.* New York: Columbia University Press, 1976.

Benoliel, J. Q. Nurses and the human experience of dying. In H. Feifel (Ed.), *New meanings of death.* New York: McGraw-Hill, 1977.

Benoliel, J. Q. Anticipatory grief in physicians and nurses. In B. Schoenberg, A. Carr, A. Kutscher, D. Peretz, I. Goldberg (Eds.), *Anticipatory grief.* New York: Columbia University Press, 1974.

Bloom, S. Some implications of studies in the professionalization of the physician. In E. G. Jaco (Ed.), *Patients, physicians, and illness.* New York: Free Press, 1958.

Borstein, I., & Klein, A. Parents of fatally ill children in a parents group. In B. Schoenberg, A. Carr, A. Kutscher, D. Peretz, & I. Goldberg (Eds.) *Anticipatory grief.* New York: Columbia University Press, 1974.

Boyd, R. Developing new norms for parents of fatally ill children to facilitate coping. In E. Pritchard, J. Collard, B. Orcutt, A. Kutscher, I. Seeland, & N. Lekowitz (Eds.), *Social work with the dying patient and the family.* New York: Columbia University Press, 1977.

Briar, S. Flexibility and specialization in social work education. *Social Work Education Reporter,* December 1968, *16*(4), 45–46, 62–63.

Brigham, T. Philosophical issues and trends in student selection today. *Journal of Education for Social Work,* Fall 1968, *4*(2), 27–34.

Bromberg, H., & Donnerstag, E. Counseling heart patients and their families. *Health and Social Work,* August 1977, *2*(3), 159–172.

Brown, T. B. *Attitudes toward death and dying in professionals: A comparative study.* Master's thesis, Louisiana State University, 1974.

Caldwell, D., & Mishara, B. Research attitudes of medical doctors toward the dying patient: A methodological problem. *Omega,* 1972, *3*, 341–346.

Cannon, I. M. *Social work in hospitals: A contribution to progressive medicine.* New York: Russell Sage Foundation, 1923.

Cannon, S. Program development for problems associated with death. In E. Prichard, J. Collard, B. Orcutt, A. Kutscher, I. Seeland, & N. Lekowitz (Eds.), *Social work with the dying patient and the family.* New York: Columbia University Press, 1977.

Caroff, P., & Mailich, M. (Eds.). *Social work in health services: An academic partnership.* New York: N. Watson Academic, 1980.

Cassidy, H. Helping the social work student deal with death and dying. In E. Prichard, J. Collard, B. Orcutt, A. Kutscher, I. Seeland, & N. Lekowitz (Eds.), *Social work with the dying patient and the family*. New York: Columbia University Press, 1977.

Chapman, C. R. Pain: The perception of noxious events. In R. A. Sternbach (Ed.), *The psychology of pain*. New York: Raven Press, 1978.

Cocherill, E. The social worker looks at cancer. In D. Golstine (Ed.), *Readings in the theory and practice of medical social work*. Chicago: University of Chicago Press, 1954.

Cohen, R. *A training seminar for social workers dealing with death and dying*. Paper presented for The Family and Death: A Social Work Symposium, New York City, April 11–12, 1975.

Coombs, R., & Powers, P. Socialization for death: The physician's role. In L. Lofland (Ed.), *Toward a sociology of death and dying*. Beverly Hills, Calif.: Sage Publications, 1975.

Copp, L. A. The spectrum of suffering. *American Journal of Nursing*, March 1974, *74*(3), 491–495.

Crane, D. *The sanctity of social life: Physicians' treatment of critically ill patients*. New York: Russell Sage Foundation, 1975.

Cryns, A. Social work education and student ideology: A multivariate study of professional socialization. *Journal of Education for Social Work*, Winter 1977, *13*(1), 44–51.

Dealing with death and dying (Nursing 77 skillbook series). Jenkintown, Pa.: Intermed Communications, 1977.

Denton, J. A., & Wisenbaker, U. B., Jr. Death experience and death anxiety among nurses and nursing students. *Nursing Research*, January–February 1977, *26*(1), 61–64.

Doherty, G. The patient in pain: Handling the guilt feelings. *The Canadian Nurse*, February 1979, *75*, 31.

Epstein, I. Social workers and social action: Attitudes toward social action strategies. *Social Work*, 1968, *13*(2), 101–108.

Epstein, I. Organizational careers, professionalization, and social-work radicalism. *Social Service Review*, 1970, *44*(2), 123–131.

Eustis, S. Rehabilitation after mastectomy: The group process. *Social Work in Health Care*, Spring 1979, *4*(3), 251–264.

Fagerhaugh, S. Y., & Strauss, A. *Politics of pain management: Staff–patient interaction*. Menlo Park, Calif.: Addison-Wesley, 1977.

Falck, H. Social work in health setting. *Social Work in Health Care*, Summer 1978, *3*(4), 398–403.

Feifel, H. Attitudes toward death in some normal and mentally ill populations. In H. Feifel (Ed.), *The meaning of death.* New York: McGraw-Hill, 1959.

Feifel, H., Hanson, S., Jones, R., & Edwards, L. Physicians consider death. *Proceedings of the 75th Annual Convention of the American Psychological Association,* Washington, D.C.: American Psychological Association, 1967.

Finesinger, J., Shands, H., & Abrams, R. *Problems in clinical cancer research: Managing the emotional problems of the cancer patient.* Published in Sloan-Kettering Seminar Series, Memorial Hospital, New York, 1952.

Foechler, M., & Mills, T. R. *Education for social workers in the care of the dying person and the family.* Paper prepared for The Family and Death: Social Work Symposium, New York City, April 11–12, 1975.

Foster, Z. How social work can influence hospital management of fatal illness. *Social Work,* October 1965, *10*(4), 30–45.

Freihofer, P., & Felton, G. Nursing behaviors in bereavement: An exploratory study. *Nursing Research,* September–October 1976, *25*(5), 332–337.

Gerber, I. *The making of a physician: The socialization process and medical care of the dying patient.* Unpublished working paper, Social Research Unit, Montefiore Hospital, Bronx, N.Y., 1972.

Gilder, J. H., & Quirk, T. R. Assessing the pain experience in children. *Nursing Clinics of North America,* December 1977, *12*(4), 631–637.

Ginsberg, L. The social worker's role. In E. Prichard, J. Collard, B. Orcutt, A. Kutscher, I. Seeland, & N. Lekowitz (Eds.), *Social work with the dying patient and the family.* New York: Columbia University Press, 1977.

Glaser, B., & Strauss, A. *Time for dying.* Chicago: Aldine, 1968.

Golden, D., Pins, A., & Jones, W. *Students in schools of social work.* New York: Council on Social Work Education, 1972.

Goldstein, E. Teaching a social work perspective on the dying patient and his family. In E. Pritchard, B. Orcutt, A. Kutscher, I. Seeland, & N. Lekowitz, (Eds.), *Social work with the dying patient and the family.* New York: Columbia University Press, 1977.

Goldstine, D. *Readings in the theory and practice of medical social work.* Chicago: University of Chicago Press, 1954.

Golub, S., & Reznikoff, M. Attitudes toward death: A comparison of nursing students and graduate nurses. *Nursing Research*, November–December 1971, *20*(6), 503–508.

Goodyear, C. Group therapy with advanced cancer patients. In E. Prichard, J. Collard, B. Orcutt, A. Kutscher, I. Seeland, & N. Lekowitz (Eds.), *Social work with the dying patient and the family*. New York: Columbia University Press, 1977.

Hackett, T. P. Pain and prejudice: Why do we doubt that the patient is in pain? *Medical Times*, February 1971, *99*, 130–141.

Hackett, T., & Weisman, A. Reactions to the imminence of death. In G. Grosser, H. Wechslers, & M. Greenblatt (Eds.), *The threat of an impending disaster*. Cambridge, Mass.: MIT Press, 1964.

Hallowitz, E. Innovations in hospital social work. *Social Work*, July 1972, *17*(4), 89–97.

Hanlan, A. *Notes of a dying professor*. Mimeographed handout from Horizons, Riverside Church, New York, 1972. (a)

Hanlan, A. *More notes of a dying professor*. Mimeographed handout, Horizons, Riverside Church, New York, 1972. (b)

Harper, B. *Professional anxieties about terminal illness*. Paper presented at The Family and Death: A Social Work Symposium, New York City, April 11–12, 1975.

Heffernan, J. Political activity and social work executives. *Social Work*, 1964, *9*(2), 18–23.

Heffron, W. A. Bommelaere, K., & Masters, R. Group discussion with the parents of leukemic children. *Pediatrics*, December 1973, *52*(6), 831–840.

Hendin, D. *Death as a fact of life*. New York: Warner Paperbacks, 1974.

Heymann, D. Discussions meet needs of dying patients. *Hospitals*, 1974, *48*(14), 57–62.

Hopping, B. L. Nursing students' attitudes toward death. *Nursing Research*, November–December 1977, *26*(6), 443–447.

Jaffee, L. The dying professor as death educator in dying. In E. Prichard, J. Collard, B. Orcutt, A. Kotscher, I. Seeland, & N. Lekowitz (Eds.), *Social work with the dying patient and the family*. New York: Columbia University Press, 1977.

Jaffee, L., & Jaffee, A. Terminal candor and the coda syndrome. *American Journal of Nursing*, December 1976, *76*(12), 1938–1940.

Kagen, L. Use of denial in adolescents with bone cancer. *Health and Social Work*, November 1976, *1*(4), 70–87.

Kahn, A. Institutional constraints in interprofessional practice. In H. Rehr (Ed.), *Medicine and social work*. New York: PRODIST, 1974.

Kasper, A. The doctor and death. In H. Feifel (Ed.), *The meaning of death*. New York: McGraw-Hill, 1959.

Kirby, M., & Templer, D. *Death anxiety and social work students*. Paper presented at The Family and Death: A Social Work Symposium, New York City, April 11–12, 1975.

Knapp, V. S., & Hansen, H. Helping the parents of children with leukemia. *Social Work*, July 1973, *18*(4), 70–75.

Kneisl, C. R. Thoughtful care for the dying. *American Journal of Nursing*, March 1968, *68*(3), 550–553.

Koenig, R. Fatal illness: A survey of social service needs. *Social Work*, October 1968, *13*(4), 85–90.

Koocher, G. Adjustments and coping strategies among the caretakers of cancer patients. *Social Work in Health Care*, Winter 1979, *5*(2), 145–150.

Krant, M., & Sheldon, A. The dying patient: Medicine's responsibility. *Journal of Thanatology*, January–February 1971, *1*, 1–21.

Le Pontois, J. Adolescents with sickle-cell anemia deal with life and deal. *Social Work in Health Care*, Fall 1975, *1*(1), 71–80.

LeShan, L. The world of the patient in severe pain of long duration. *Journal of Chronic Diseases*, 1964, *17*, 119–126.

Lester, D., Getty, C., & Kneisl, C. R. Attitudes of nursing students and nursing faculty toward death. *Nursing Research*, January–February 1974, *23*(1), 50–53.

Lister, L., & Gachros, H. Preparing students for effective social work practice related to death. *Journal of Education for Social Work*, Winter 1976, *12*(1), 85–90.

Liston, E. Education on death and dying: A neglected area in the medical curriculum. *Omega*, 1975, *6*, 193–198.

Livingston, P., & Zimet, C. Death anxiety, authoritarianism and choice of specialty in medical students. *Journal of Nervous and Mental Disease*, March 1965, *140*, 222–230.

Lohmann, R. A. Dying and the social responsibility of institutions. *Social Casework*, November 1977, *58*(9), 538–545.

Marks, R. M., & Sachar, E. J. Undertreatment of medical inpatients with narcotic analgesics. *Annals of Internal Medicine*, 1973, *78*, 173–181.

McCaffery, M. *Nursing management of the patient with pain.* Philadelphia: Lippincott, 1972.

McNamara, J. Social work designs a humanistic program to enhance patient care. *Social Work in Health Care,* Winter 1975–76, *1*(2), 145–154.

Mervis, P. Talking about the unmentionable. In E. Prichard, J. Collard, B. Orcutt, A. Kutscher, I. Seeland, & N. Lekowitz (Eds.), *Social work with the dying patient and the family.* New York: Columbia University Press, 1977.

Miller, R. Teaching death and dying content in the social work curriculum. In E. Prichard, J. Collard, B. Orcutt, A. Kutscher, I. Seeland, & N. Lekowitz (Eds.), *Social work with the dying patient and the family.* New York: Columbia University Press, 1977.

Millet, N. Hospice: Challening society's approach to death, *Health and Social Work,* February 1979, *4*(1), 130–150.

Milner, C. J. Compassionate care for the dying person. *Health and Social Work,* May 1980, *5*(2), 5–10.

Montgomery, B. J. Addictive potential of drugs is concern in pain relief. *Medical News, Journal of the American Medical Association,* October 6, 1978, *240*(15), 1571.

Muskin, H. L., Levine, S. P., & Levine, H. Partners in dying. *American Journal of Psychiatry,* March 1974, *131*(3), 308–10.

Noyes, R., & Clancy, J. The dying role: Its relevance to improved patient care. *Psychiatry,* February 1977, *40*, 41–47.

Pellegrino, E. D. The communication crisis in nursing and medical education. *Nursing Forum,* 1966, *5*(1), 45–53.

Perretz, E. Social work education for the field of health: A report of findings from a survey of curricula. *Social Work in Health Care,* Spring 1976, *1*(3), 357–365.

Pilsecher, C. Terminal cancer: A challenge for social work. *Social Work in Health Care,* Summer 1979, *4*(4), 369–379.

Pins, A. *Who chooses social work, when and why: An exploratory study of factors influencing career choices in social work.* New York: Council on Social Work Education, 1963.

Piven, H. The fragmentation of social work. *Social Casework,* February 1969, *50*(2), 84.

Plovnick, M., Fry, R., & Rubin, I. *Managing health care delivery: A training program for primary care physicians.* Cambridge, Mass., Bellinger, 1977.

Pratt, L. Optimism–pessimism about helping the poor with health problems. *Social Work*, 1970, *15*(2), 29–33.

Quint, J. C. Awareness of death and the nurse's composure. *Nursing Research*, 1966, *15*(1), 49–55.

Quint, J. C., & Strauss, A. L. Nursing students, assignments and dying patients. *Nursing Outlook*, January 1964, *12*, 24–27.

Rabin, D., & Rabin, L. H. Consequences of death for physicians, nurses, and hospitals. In O. Brim, H. Freeman, S. Levine, & N. Scotch (Eds.), *The dying patient*, New York: Russell Sage Foundation, 1970.

Raymond, F. Social work education for health care practice. *Social Work in Health Care*, Summer 1977, *2*(4), 429–438.

Rea, M. P., Greenspoon, S., & Spilka, B. Physicians and the terminal patient: Some selected attitudes and behavior. *Omega*, 1975, *6*, 291–302.

Robinson, L. We have no dying patients. *Nursing Research*, October 1974, *22*(10), 651–653.

Ross, C. W. Nurses' personal death concerns and responses to dying patient statements. *Nursing Research*, January–February 1978, *27*(1), 64–68.

Ross, J. Social work intervention with families of children with cancer. *Social Work in Health Care*, Spring 1978, *3*(3), 257–272.

Ross, J. Coping with childhood cancer: Group intervention as an aid to parents in crisis. *Social Work in Health Care*, Summer 1979, *4*(4), 381–391.

Rubin, I. M., & Beckhard, R. Factors influencing the effectiveness of health teams. *Milbank Memorial Fund Quarterly*, 1972, *50*, 317–335.

Sanford, N., & Deloughery, G. L. Teaching nurses to care for the dying patient. *Journal of Psychiatric Nursing and Mental Health Services*, January–February, 1973, *11*(1), 24–26.

Schmitt, M. The nature of pain with some personal notes. *Nursing Clinics of North America*, December 1977, *12*(4), 621–629.

Schoenberg, B., Carr, A., Peretz, D., & Kutscher, A. (Eds.). *Psychosocial aspects of terminal illness*. New York: Columbia University Press, 1972.

Schoenberg, B., & Carr, A. Educating the health professional in the psychosocial care of the terminally ill. In B. Schoenberg, A. Carr, D. Peretz, & A. Kutscher (Eds.), *Psychosocial aspects of terminal care*. New York: Columbia University Press, 1972.

Selection of students for schools of social work. New York: Council on Social Work Education, 1955.

Shands, H., Finesinger, J., Cobb, S., & Abrams, R. Psychological mechanism in patients with cancer. *Cancer,* 1957, *IV*(6), 1159–1170.

Shulman, L. Social work education for health care practice. *Social Work in Health Care,* Summer 1977, *2*(4), 439–444.

Silman, J. Reference guide to analgesics. *American Journal of Nursing,* January 1979, *79*(1), 74–78.

Sonstegard, L., Hansen, N., Zillman, L., & Johnston, M. K. The grieving nurse. *American Journal of Nursing,* September 1976, *76*(9), 1490–1492.

Speer, G. M. Learning about death. *Perspectives in Psychiatric Nursing,* April–May–June 1974, *12*(2), 70–73.

Stonberg, M. A social work oncology group. *Health and Social Work,* August 1977, *2*(3), 173–180.

Swerdlow, M. The value of clinics for the relief of chronic pain. *Journal of Medical Ethics,* September 1978, *4*(3), 117–118.

Tolstoy, L. The death of Ivan Ilych. In L. Tolstoy, *The death of Ivan Ilych and other stories.* New York: New American Library, 1960.

Tull, A. The stresses of clinical social work with the terminally ill. *Smith College Studies in Social Work,* 1975, *45*(2), 137–158.

Turk, D. C., Meichenbaum, D. H., & Berman, W. H. Application of biofeedback for the regulation of pain: A critical review. *Psychological Bulletin,* November 1979, *86*(6), 1322–1338.

Twycross, R. G. The assessment of pain in advanced cancer. *Journal of Medical Ethics,* September 1978, *4*(3), 112–116.

Verwoerdt, A. *Communication with the fatally ill.* Springfield, Ill.: Charles C Thomas, 1966.

Vorgna, D. Group treatment for wives of patients with Alzheimer's disease. *Social Work in Health Care,* Winter 1979, *5*(2), 219–221.

Wahl, C. The fear of death. In H. Feifel (Ed.), *The meaning of death.* New York: McGraw-Hill, 1959.

Weber, R., Jones, M., & Pollane, L. *Attitudes toward death of social service personnel working with the aged.* Paper presented at The Family and Death: A Social Work Symposium, New York City, April 11–12, 1975.

Weisman, A. Care and comfort for the dying. In S. Troup & W.

Green (Eds.), *The patient, death and the family*. New York: Scribner's, 1974.

Wessells, Z. A study of medical social service to tumor patients. *Journal of Social Casework*, November 1949, *30*(9), 375–380.

White, L. Death and physicians. In H. Feifel (Ed.), *New meanings of death*. New York: McGraw-Hill, 1977.

Wijnberg, M., & Schwartz, M. Competency or crisis. In E. Prichard, T. Collard, B. Orcutt, A. Kutscher, I. Seeland, & N. Lekowitz (Eds.), *Social work with the dying patient and the family*. New York: Columbia University Press, 1977.

Williams, C., & Race, D. The intensive care unit: Social work intervention with the families of critically ill patients. *Social Work in Health Care*, Summer 1977, *2*(4), 391–398.

Wise, H., Beckhard, R., Rubin, I., & Kyte, C. *Making health teams work*. Cambridge, Mass.: Ballinger, 1974.

Witte, P., & Baber, L. Group therapy with multiple sclerosis couples. *Health and Social Work*, August 1977, *2*(3), 188–195.

Yeaworth, R. C., Kapp, F. T., & Winget, C. Attitudes of nursing students toward the dying patient. *Nursing Research*, January–February 1974, *23*(1), 20–24.

Zborowski, M. Cultural components in responses to pain. *Journal of Social Issues*, 1952, *8*, 16–30.

5

The Family
and the Dying Child

Often when a child dies, all of our fears, questions, and anxieties about death resurface in our conscious thinking, and our emotional responses reflect our sad and painful feelings of grief. We once again question, Why? Why must a young life be taken? Why this particular child? We feel the impartiality of death and, hence, our own vulnerability to death: if a young child can die, then we too are mortal. We may feel relief for the child whose death has brought an end to pain and suffering; we may also feel relief for ourselves, that we no longer have to invest so much feeling, so much energy, in the dying process. We hurt, and we grieve that this child will never know the joys and sorrows of a human being developing over a life span of years. We take solace in the belief that the child did experience the uniqueness of life, if only for a short time.

The loss of a child has many meanings for parents. A child may be seen as an extension of the adults, a part of their immortality; this is lost when the child dies. The child is also a personal creation of the parents; and this is lost. Parents' hopes and aspirations for the child must be relinquished. Another child born into the family never really replaces the child who has died. Perhaps the most profound of all the losses the death of a child evokes is the loss of love (Ford, 1972).

Children who are dying also experience loss and significant changes in their lifestyles. If they have a fatal illness, they often undergo changes in their actual physical condition and body image. They may feel tired and sick. As a result of different treatments such as radiation or medication, they may have such reactions as itching, loss of hair, and loss or gain of weight. Family reactions and roles may change; parents and relatives may pamper and spoil dying children, and siblings who were once fought with fiercely may become very pleasant. These changes add to the already bewildering questions the child may be wondering about: "What is wrong with me, and why do I feel so badly?"

In the following pages we look at children's awareness of death and dying, family reactions to a dying child, and how caregivers can offer support both to dying children and to their families. It is helpful to begin with a brief review of children's views of death to see what implications these have for dying children's awareness of death and their own dying, and for their care.

CHILDREN'S CONCEPTS OF DEATH

Children experience feelings of loss and separation through their progressive stages of growth, and begin to develop a concept of death. Earlier in this text we discussed our culture's denial of death. The family system incorporates this culture-bound inability to integrate death as a natural part of the process of living (Pattison, 1976). We wonder if, how, and when we should include children in the family's mourning of a dead uncle, parent, grandparent. We may develop various stories or be very vague about what has happened to a family member who has died, telling a child that "Grandma has gone to sleep and you won't see her anymore." We may avoid discussing the death or showing our feelings "in front of children." Children can cope with death but do have difficulties coping with family avoidance about death.

Koocher's (1974) study of well children and their ideas about death lead to some suggestions for discussing death with children who have suffered a loss:

1. Children are interested in the subject of death, seem to want to talk about it, and are capable of discussing this. Silence about death only indicates to them that the subject is taboo and does not help them deal with their loss.
2. Explanations and discussions about death are most helpful if they are simple and direct, especially if children are younger than six or seven years old.
3. It is helpful if explaining about death to a young child to ask the child to explain back to you what has been discussed. Young children often use magical thinking and have many fantasies and misperceptions about death. Having the child explain to you what has been discussed may help clear up some of these distortions. (p. 410)

We often do not know what to say when our children ask, "Mom, Dad, are you going to die?" Our answer should depend upon the age of the child asking the question, but we must remember that children are concerned about being cared for and about what will happen if a loss occurs. Pattison (1976) describes his and his wife's response to their children's question, "Are you going to die?"

> Yes, we will. We are in good health and do not expect to die while you are young and need our help. You can do some things for yourself now, and when you grow older you will not need us to help you. Even if we die when we are old, we will miss each other. It will be sad, but it will be alright because you will be able to take care of yourselves. And if we happen to die while you are growing up, we have made arrangements with Aunt and Uncle for them to become your parents in our place. They cannot replace us, but they can help you as we would want to help you. We would be sorry to die now and not be here to help you and enjoy you. But you will always have our love and that is the most important thing. And because we love you, we have made plans with Aunt and Uncle, who love you too. We cannot predict or prevent our death. We will die someday in your lives. But we can enjoy our family now. And when we die you will have these good days to remember and always be a part of your lives. (p. 678)

Children's views of death may be influenced by such factors as their life experiences, temporal concerns, self-concept at the time they are considering the question of death, age, family attitudes and values, and the social and cultural milieu in which they live.

Nagy's (1959) well-known study presents us with an outline of the developmental levels of children, ages 3 to 10 years, concerning the meaning of death. This study involved 378 children in Budapest in 1948. The children were asked to express their feelings about death in words and pictures. Nagy found that the children's replies about the meaning of death could be categorized into the following developmental stages:

Stage I There is No Definitive Death: Children who are less than 5 years old usually do not recognize death as an irreversible fact; life and consciousness are attributed to the dead. Death may be seen as a departure, or as sleep; or death may be seen as gradual or temporary. Examples of these concepts are cited in Nagy's research:

T.P. (4 years 10 months)

"A dead person is just as if he were asleep. Sleeps in the ground, too."
"How do you know whether someone is asleep or dead?"

"I know if they go to bed at night and don't open their eyes. If somebody goes to bed and doesn't get up, he's dead or ill."
"Will he ever wake up?"
"Never. A dead person only knows if somebody goes out to the grave or something. He feels that somebody is there, or is talking." (pp. 81–82)

T.P. (6 years 6 months)

"My sister's godfather died and I took hold of his hand. His hand was so cold. It was green and blue. His face was all wrinkled together. He can't move. He can't clench his hands because he is dead."
"His face?"
"It has gooseflesh because he is cold. He is cold because he is dead and cold everywhere."
"Does he feel the cold or was it just that his skin was like that?"
"If he is dead he feels too. If he is dead he feels a tiny little bit. When he is quite dead he no longer feels anything." (p. 85)

Children in this group seem to accept death to a certain extent. They do not completely deny the finality of death, as they are thinking of death as a gradual occurrence. At this point, they seem to have arrived at a compromise situation.

Stage II   Personification of Death: Children's personification of death seemed to be most characteristic between the ages of 5 and 9.

B.T. (9 years 11 months)

Death is a skeleton. It is so strong it can overturn a ship. Death can't be seen. Death is in a hidden place. It hides in an island. (p. 89)

We see an increased sense of reality in this second stage. Children accept the existence of death, yet the thought of it is still so frightening that they conceive of it as remote and external in the form of a person.

Stage III   The Cessation of Bodily Activities: Starting at the age of 9 or 10, children reach the point where they recognize that death is universal and signifies a cessation of bodily life.

F.E. (10 years 0 months)

It means the passing of the body. Death is a great squaring of accounts in our lives. It is a thing from which our bodies cannot be resurrected. It is like the withering of flowers. (p. 94)

Nagy's study emphasizes the developmental view of children's concepts of death. The fact that this study was conducted with European children who had experienced the effects of World War II could have influenced the study's conclusions in terms of cultural variables and life experiences.

Meleor (1973) studied 41 children in Colorado who were asked about their concepts of death, and found that their concepts could be classified into four categories:

1. Relative ignorance of the meaning of death. (ages 3–4)
2. Death is a temporary state and is not seen as irreversible. The dead have feelings and biological functions. (ages 4–7)
3. Death is final but the dead can function biologically. (ages 5–6)
4. Death is final and there is cessation of all biological functioning. (ages 6 years and older) (Pp. 359–360)

This study found a progression similar to Nagy's (1959) in children's development of awareness of death as related to age.

Menig-Peterson's and McCabe's (1977–78) study of 96 children's narratives of important experiences in their lives showed that narratives about death were almost nonexistent for 3½- to 5½-year-olds, but that over half of the 5½- to 6½-year-olds produced 14 narratives about death. The most death narratives, 22, were produced by the 7½- to 8½-year-olds (p. 306). The researchers suggested that the older groups of children had a greater conceptual capacity to deal with the topic of death and more curiosity about it than the younger children. Interestingly, the researchers found that children less than approximately 9 years of age had very little if any affective responses to death and dying, whether of animals or people (p. 316). This finding could suggest a developmental progression in being able to cope with death emotionally, and has implications for how, and when, caregivers may want to talk with children about death and dying.

The studies discussed up to this point indicate that children under 4 to 5 years of age have little awareness of death. Rochlin (1968) studied children—aged 3 to 5 years—of urban, well-educated parents whose family life was reasonably stable. The children's parents stated they had not given more than cursory attention to the discussion of death with their children. The researcher found that these children did have a concept of death and that they had developed psychological defenses, such as magical thinking, against the realization that life may end. This study also indicates that the social context in which children learn about death may influence their developing concepts about it. Not discussing the facts of death with children may very well affect how they develop their views; children's exposure to death would seem to be equally influential.

Feelings of loss and separation are very much a part of death awareness. That very young children do experience these feelings is indicated in Bowlby's (1965) studies of infants and young children who
have been separated from their mothers. Behavior changes in these
children such as listlessness, quietness, unresponsiveness to a smile or
a coo, and physical changes, such as weight loss, decrease in activity,
and lack of sleep, indicate that these feelings of loss and separation are
being experienced.

Children's concepts of the universality of death may be related to
age level. The studies by Nagy (1959) and Meleor (1973) cited earlier
indicate this. Childers and Wimmer's (1971) study of children's concepts of death concluded that a moderate relationship exists between
increasing age and an acceptance of the universality of death. The concept of the universality of death was almost unanimously upheld by the
9- to-10-year-olds in this study. However, the irrevocability of death
was found to be much more tenuous. There was no age group that was
clearly sure of death's irrevocability.

In contrast to this finding, Gartley and Bernesconi (1967) studied
the death concepts of 60 Roman Catholic schoolchildren, ages 5½ to
14 years, and found that these children dealt with death in a very mat-
ter-of-fact and realistic way. "All believed in the finality of death rather
than its reversibility as documented in other studies" (p. 83). The researchers suggested that there may have been several influences on this
latter finding: (1) the children mentioned Dr. Kildare and Ben Casey
on TV as sources of information; and (2) religious training was provided in school, and the children had definite concepts of dying and
going to heaven, or hell. Nagy's (1959) findings of children personifying
death between the ages of 5 and 9 years were not substantiated here.
The influence of TV and religious training could be factors in the children's total social context that influenced these findings.

To summarize, children's concepts of death are influenced by their
cognitive and development levels, social and cultural environments,
family and religious attitudes and values, and other factors—some of
which are probably not yet known and all of which interact with one
another to form a concept and awareness of death for each child. We
might begin now to look at how these concepts of death relate to dying
children and to their care.

CHILDREN AND DYING

The infant's world is composed of personal needs only, with hunger,
warmth, and security of major concern. After about 6 months of age,

infants become more aware of their mother as an individual separate from themselves. It is at this time that the infant may exhibit some separation anxiety. Although infants do not conceive of death, they are very much aware of their mother's absence and of the lack of gratification of their needs (Jackson, 1975). Therefore, if a terminally ill infant is hospitalized, it is important that the mother be allowed and encouraged to stay with her child. The mother may also need encouragement to plan her time so she may be with the rest of her family.

Toddlers are very much concerned with themselves and with their ability to do things. They are developing motor mobility, self-awareness, and feelings of power in relation to the environment. However, along with these powerful feelings are fears of body integrity and safety. It is important in caring for toddlers to explain very simply any procedure that may be performed on them. Also, separation continues to be of primary concern, and parents again need support to stay with the child.

The preschool child may have no clear concept of the finality of death. Death is often seen as reversible. Indeed, some of the current life experiences of preschool children seem to confirm this concept: the actor on television is shot dead one day but appears alive and kicking on another program the next day; pets die and are sadly missed but often are immediately replaced (Easson, 1968). At this stage the child's concept of death may involve magical thinking—for example, that thoughts can cause action. Children may feel they have done something "bad" to become ill. Rochlin (1968) points out that the young child "regards death as not due to natural causes but as a result of strife, defiance of authority and retaliation, hostility and the wish to satisfy aggressive, destructive, and sexual impulses . . . morality is introduced very early by the child in the belief that the bad die before the good" (p. 62). Parents and caregivers must listen to cues from dying children since they may feel guilty about something they have "done" that would bring this illness upon them, and must reassure them that they have not done anything "wrong." What dying children of this age also need is reassurance that they are not alone and simple explanations of what is going to happen to them at the time of each procedure and treatment. Much support is likewise needed for the parents, family, *and* treating personnel.

Grade school children are beginning to realize the finality of death. They note that when grandparents or friends die, there is no return. They see death as a separation and a loss. Children may cope with this anxiety-producing realization by developing rituals to ward off these frightening thoughts, such as "always running fast if you have to pass a cemetery" or the rhyme, "If you step on a crack, you break your mother's back." Children of this age may use intellectual coping, trying to find out how things work, or the cause-and-effect nature of an illness. Perhaps by understanding how things happen, one may then prevent one's own death. School-age children are developing their independence and may need time away from parents and staff in the hospital to continue to do this. Maintaining normal daily activities such as school, for even a short period of time, is important to maintain children's self-esteem and to indicate that adults have not given up on them because of their illness. It is also important to answer the children's questions about their illness and to reassure them that someone will be with them when needed.

Adolescents appreciate the meaning of death, but the reality of personal death is difficult to accept. Adolescence is a tumultuous time. Starting with puberty, important physiological changes occur. Peer group approval is important, and peer group pressure and judgment are often harsh. There are strong sexual urges to become intimate with another person, yet these urges are often feared. Self- and parental inhibitions pose further restrictions on their fulfillment. Tension within the family originates from the adolescent's need to separate from parents while still wanting to maintain a closeness. Parents are criticized by their adolescent children; and teenagers often fantasize that these people could not really be their parents, that they indeed must be adopted, that their "real" parents would be more understanding. Adolescents are concerned with their future, with preparing for a career, with becoming "somebody."

Dumont and Foss (1972) state that "adolescents appear to fear death the least because they are too busy to spend much time thinking about it and because they can be reasonably sure of a full life ahead" (p. 21). Indeed, adolescence is a busy time, and death anxiety may be denied and/or used in new ways to affirm the ideals of life, such as relating to meaningful values and goals and developing emotional and intellectual capacities. Denial of mortality may be seen in the adolescent's death-denying involvement with speeding vehicles and experimentation with consciousness-altering substances (Sahler, 1978, p. 19).

Terminally ill older adolescents experience much frustration in that, developmentally, they have decided upon goals they want to accomplish in life but now will not be able to attain them. Adults who are dying have some chance to review what tasks they have completed, what goals they have met; adolescents have not had the chance to try out their newly formed values, beliefs, and dreams.

Glen is a 17 year-old boy with a rapidly progressive neuromuscular disease. Discussions by staff concerning possibilities of tracheostomy, assisted ventilation, and deterioration of his blood gases are continually met with disinterest by him. His parents are concerned by what they interpret as increased anxiety at home. Hospital school teachers and therapists talk about the "strangeness" of Glen's behavior. An invitation to talk with his primary physician about his depression reveals he is not concerned directly with dying but with his virginity. Sexual fulfillment, previously a future goal, has become an immediate one, "before I get hooked up on all that machinery." (Sahler, 1978, pp. 22–23)

Children who are dying are not any different from well children in their abilities and in their need to discuss death. They are extremely perceptive and can see through the smoke screen of "not talking about being sick." Children know from their bodies, if from nothing else, that they are not well: their appetites change, they are tired, and they may not be very interested in anything. Bluebond-Langner (1978), in her study of hospitalized leukemic children, found that the children were very much aware of the social system of the hospital unit—that is, who had what authority and what the pecking order was. Although not all the children knew the name of their disease, acute lymphocytic leukemia, this proved no barrier in their learning as much as any lay adult about it and about its treatment, process, and prognosis (p. 157).

Bluebond-Langner found it quite remarkable that the children were able to find out so much about the hospital, staff, rules, and procedures, as well as about their disease, in a situation in which both parents and staff consciously tried to keep them from learning this information. All the children studied knew their prognosis and that they were dying before death was imminent. However, they did not all express their awareness in the same ways:

Some children said directly, "I am going to die," or "I'm going to die soon." . . . Other children were less direct. They talked about never going back to school, of not being around for someone's birthday, or of burying dolls that they said looked the way they used to look. (p. 165)

In a study designed to ascertain dying children's anxiety about and awareness of their prognosis, Waechter (1977) found that children were significantly knowledgeable about what was happening to them. The study indicated that giving children the opportunity to discuss their fears and prognoses does not heighten death anxiety; on the contrary, allowing children to do this may decrease feelings of isolation and alienation. Waechter concludes that asking whether children should be told that their illnesses are fatal is a meaningless question; what is signficiant is that the questions and concerns that are meaningful to children threatened with death are dealt with in such a way that the children do not feel more alone, different, and alienated from parents and other meaningful adults (p. 27). "If children ask 'Am I going to die?', they are really asking (1) am I safe, (2) will there be a trusted person to keep me from feeling helpless and alone, and to overcome the pain, and (3) will you make me feel all right?" (Vernick & Karon; cited in Ford, 1972, p. 58).

In a pilot study of children who were hospitalized with catastrophic illness, Morrissey (1963) interviewed seven children to determine their emotional reactions to dying, their level of anxiety, and what their attitudes would be toward such interviews if they were offered as a regular service. Findings of the study, although the sample was minimal, indicated that most of the children had much concern and anxiety about their illness and hospitalization. The anxiety was expressed in four different ways:

1. verbally—"I'm worried," "I'm afraid."
2. behaviorally—hyperactive behavior; withdrawal from peers and activities.
3. physiologically—nausea; loss of energy; poor appetite.
4. symbolically—during play for example, saying that a doll had to die, or that a doll's leg was bad and had to be amputated. (p. 344)

The children seemed to welcome a chance to talk about their feelings, their illnesses, and their hospital experiences. Most of the children asked the interviewer to come again. The researcher himself found these interviews to be very difficult experiences, and realized his own needs for support and understanding from staff members.

There are two basic approaches to caring for dying children; one approach emphasizes helping the children discuss their fears and face death, whereas the other focuses on shielding the children from death and protecting them as much as possible from such fears.

Futterman and Hoffman (1973), from the results of their research study, state:

Children, no less than adults, are placed in a dehumanized and isolated position when excluded from discussion of their illness and treatment. Parents, however, strongly asserted their convictions that knowledge might be destructive and that shielding maintains a life orientation. Most parents compromised by encouraging communication of feelings so long as the subject of death was avoided. (p. 140)

In Bluebond-Langner's (1978) study, only two children were able to bring about open awareness (p. 220). Both children initiated this process by similar overt statements about their dying, and their parents were able to acknowledge and respond to them. However, mutual pretense was the dominant mode of interaction between the terminally ill children and staff and parents. (The reader is referred to Chapter 3 of this text for a discussion of open awareness and mutual pretense.) Bluebond-Langner hypothesized that this mutual pretense interaction provided individuals a way to do what society expected of them: children were allowed to act as children, that is, as if they had a future; parents could to some extent continue their roles of nurturing and protecting their children, and caretakers could continue their treatment roles (p. 229).

Although the present trend in literature seems to support the first approach, Evans (1968) lists the following reasons why the second is more favorable:

1. We often deal effectively with fears by suppression or rejection. By open discussion we destroy these defense mechanisms.
2. Parents play a very important role in the management of any ill child and most parents find it very difficult to face the fact that they will not have their children with them in the future. Parents maintain hope for the recovery of their children and are often unable to discuss or share the imminence of their death with them. (p. 138)

We seem to have here a dilemma in providing dying children with what they need in terms of talking about dying and expressing feelings about it. Many professional caregivers feel it is important that children know what is happening to them, yet are reluctant to discuss this with them, ostensibly because the parents want to protect their children from the sorrow of this knowledge. Research indicates that children are aware of their diagnosis and prognosis. The question then arises, Are professionals and parents in reality shielding themselves from discussing death with the children? We need to examine our own feelings about death and children dying as we work with fatally ill children.

Bluebond-Langner (1978) offers some guidelines on what to tell children about their dying. She suggests that we consider the same basic rule of thumb as in deciding what to tell children about sex; tell them only what they want to know, what they are asking about, and on their own terms. Since most children become aware of their prognosis whether or not adults reveal it to them, the more appropriate question might be, "Should I acknowledge the prognosis with the child?" To answer this question, we must take into consideration the needs of the child, the staff, and the parents. We need to be aware of the family's culture, religion, and previous ways of dealing with crisis. The children may need to share their knowledge but also need their parents with them. The parents may need to be with the children, too, but may also need to avoid talking about the prognosis. Staff members need to treat the children and to see them as treatable. It may be possible to help children work out interactions of open awareness with people who can cope with this, while maintaining mutual pretense with people who need this type of interaction. Children are aware that they assume different roles with different people, and can do this very well. The issue, then, is not so much to tell or not to tell but how to tell so that the children's many varied needs, and needs for different interactions, are respected.

Caregivers can offer support to children regarding these needs by careful and attentive listening to what the children are trying to express, especially in dealing with fantasies. Children may have many fears based on their perceptions of what they see in hospitals and on what is not explained to them. For example, such statements as "I'm going to give you a shot now" or "I'm going to take some of your blood," without further explanation, could evoke fears of mutilation and death within a child. Depending on children's developmental levels, simple to more complex explanations can be given as to what procedures they are going to experience, what medications they will receive, what the proposed treatment plan is. The sharing of medical information, especially with older children, is most important in gaining the collaboration of children as well as in dispensing with fantasies. With younger children, who often cannot express their own feelings directly, listening to their "play talk" will give indications of what they really are feeling. A child's comment about a beloved teddy bear hurting or crying or being scared can tell staff much about that child's feelings. Also, children's drawings can be helpful in understanding how they are feeling. A group of children who all were hospitalized with leukemia consistently drew pictures of disasters—fires, accidents, bridges breaking. They were telling us their feelings about their lives ending soon.

Responding to the Dying Child

It is often difficult for parents, siblings, relatives, and friends to know how to respond to dying children, either at home or in the hospital. Children develop their own self-confidence and trust from those closest to them (Miya, 1972, p. 220). Children need large quantities of love and support, but they also need to know the boundaries and limits in which they may live or die. They turn to adults for these needed limits and love, for with both of these, children can feel safe and accepted. Adults may withdraw these needed qualities for children, finding it too painful to continue to love a dying child. Or, in feeling so much sorrow and pity for the dying child they may release all limits and submit to the child's every whim and demand. If this happens, children may feel confused, lost, and without hope, for the source of their feelings of safety and comfort has become inconsistent. They do not know what to expect. It is most helpful if "business as usual" can be carried on as much as possible with dying children. This means the offering of discipline as well as love. "Business as usual" at school as well as home conveys to dying children that there is hope. It also weakens the idea that these children are "different." Special privileges such as inflated grades should not be given, and as normal a school day as possible should be encouraged. If parents can treat the child "normally" during the illness, can refuse special privileges, not be overprotective, and—most important of all—enjoy the child, the child will get more satisfaction for each day he or she lives.

PARENTS OF DYING CHILDREN

As caregivers, we must listen not only to the needs of dying children but also to what their families are saying and needing in this crisis. In Chapter 1, we discussed how death patterns have changed in America. This is particularly relevant in terms of children dying. In the not-too-distant past, adults were quite familiar with the fact of a child's death (Fischhoff & O'Brien, 1976, p. 140). Many parents today, because of improved health care and economic conditions, do not have this experience. Also, the nuclear family often does not have the emotional support of the stable, extended family. Parents therefore may go through the psychic shock and emotional trauma of the death of a child in relative isolation, with little support from the extended family or community. They may need some help with the mourning process in terms of knowing what to expect of their own feelings and reactions after their child dies. They may also need help in coping with their feelings while their child is dying. Koop (1965, p. 557) has commented that families of dying children lose their children twice—once when the diagnosis and prognosis are explained and again when the child actually dies. It is during the time between these two events that caregivers can help families develop the needed supports and coping mechanisms that will enable them to deal with this crisis.

The retrospective study of Binger et al. (1969) of families who had lost a child to acute leukemia indicated that parents felt the most difficult time they experienced was when they first learned their child's diagnosis. "During the first few days or weeks after learning the diagnosis, most parents experienced symptoms and feelings of physical distress, depression, inability to function, anger, hostility, and self-blame" (pp. 414–415). These symptoms gradually subsided, to be followed by a more accepting attitude of the diagnosis and a desire to meet the needs of the ill child.

In their study of hospitalized children with leukemia, Friedman et al. (1963) found that when the parents initially learned of the children's diagnosis, they had what appeared to be an insatiable need to know everything about the disease. Parents not only sought out extensive information from the hospital staff but also compared notes carefully with the parents of other ill children. Such seeking out of information could be seen as a coping behavior for the parents in terms of gaining some control in a situation where they felt so helpless. Another parental coping behavior seen in this study was isolation of affect, in that parents showed very little emotional reaction when initially learning of the child's diagnosis. Only after some hours or days were there expressions of the very painful feelings associated with the diagnosis. Thus, when first explaining the child's diagnosis to parents, it is important to state it simply and directly. More detailed explanations can be discussed later as the parents gradually accept the painful reality.

Bluebond-Langner (1978) found in her study that the most deeply felt parental reactions to the children's hospitalization and terminal prognosis was their loss of authority and control over what was happening to their young. Parents felt powerless before the disease, the hospital staff, the treatment plan, and with their children. They felt they could not care for their children even on a daily basis. Mothers felt that nurses were taking over their nurturing functions. One way of coping with this was to assume a "Why bother?" attitude. Caregivers should be aware of these initial responses, for there is a risk of labeling parents as "cold" or "noncaring" or "intellectual" when, in actuality, they are suffering greatly.

Parents may often feel guilty about something they think they may have done to inflict this fatal illness on their child. A mother may review her pregnancy and wonder whether she took too many vitamins or whether she did not take enough; a father may feel he has not been an adequate provider for the child. Of special significance here is the family whose child is dying of hereditary disease. These parents not only carry the guilt feelings of transmission but are also concerned about future pregnancies and whether siblings will get the disease. Also, in other illnesses as well as in hereditary diseases, parents may blame one another for the child's illness, and grandparents may blame parents for not taking care of the child.

Parents want to hold and cuddle their children, but because of pain from the disease process, the children often do not want to be held or hugged. Also, parents are not able to protect their children from painful procedures. These realities further contribute to their guilt in not being "good parents."

Anger is not an uncommon reaction to the impending loss of a loved person. If someone important to us is dying, we feel angry at losing this person, for he or she is leaving us or is being taken away from us. We are being deprived of a significant relationship in our lives, and we are angry. To express such anger overtly is not acceptable in Western culture, so we may turn to others on whom we can safely displace our anger. In families, parents may turn their anger on each other or may become easily irritated with siblings. Families may vent their anger on doctors, nurses, and the hospital, complaining about the poor care their child is receiving. If caregivers can understand that this anger is part of the grieving process and not take it personally, they may be able to help the family members identify and express their feelings appropriately.

Fear may also be present in the parents' grieving process and may relate not only to what may happen to the child but also to expenses, whether the disease will occur in other children, what other people and relatives will say, and how the family will manage after the child dies. Including the parents in planning the treatment of the child, and in carrying out that treatment can be helpful in reducing parental anxiety. Hamovitch (1964) found that two-thirds of the families he studied involving children with leukemia or cancer were helped by parents' participation in the care of their children. Parents who are active participants in their child's care feel at least some control in the middle of all the uncertainty.

Coping Behavior of Parents

In most instances parents faced with the death of a child will develop some forms of coping behavior. They may first deny the illness, but then they develop ways of meeting the crisis. For example, for some parents, denying their child's illness may be the only way they can function effectively away from the child. From that perspective, such coping behavior may be viewed as good. For those working with the family and the child, this coping mechanism may create problems and therefore be viewed as bad. However, remember that the behavior is not so much to be judged as it is to be viewed as a way that parents respond to their child's dying. Parents are desperately trying to make some sense out of the fact that their child is dying, while simultaneously grieving and attempting to maintain family stability. It is beneficial if those working with parents can help them discuss their feelings and reactions to their child's illness and dying. This is not for the purpose of eliminating the denial, but rather to help the parents express what they are experiencing.

One mother's way of coping with the deteriorating illness of her 11-month-old daughter was to search for information about the cause of the disease and, at the same time, to control the amount and timing of information she received about the child's condition. She elected to call the nursing staff to inquire about her child's condition rather than having the nurses call her on a regular basis. As the child's condition worsened, she began gradually to withdraw and to spend more time with her other child, her home, and her friends. When the baby died, she seemed calm and almost relieved that her daughter's struggle was over (Coddington, 1976, p. 44).

Futterman and Hoffman (1973) found that parents confronted a number of dilemmas in adapting to their children's illnesses. With each adaptive dilemma, parents had to work out a balance between what seemed to be conflicting tasks; for example, "between acknowledging the ultimate loss of the child and maintaining hope; between cherishing the child and allowing him to separate; between maintaining day-to-day functioning and expressing disturbing feelings; between active personal care of the child and delegation of care to medical personnel; between trusting the physician and recognizing his limitations" (p. 130).

Contact with other parents who are experiencing these conflicts and grief can be helpful. It is often useful for parents to participate in group discussions with other parents whose children have died. The sharing of feelings and experiences gives them the opportunity to realize that their grief reactions are not "abnormal," to learn how others are coping with these reactions, and to mourn with others. In the study by Friedman et al. (1963), the primary source of emotional support for most parents during their child's hospitalization was other parents who were going through the same experience. The parents were role models for one another. When a child died, parents could learn that although it was a most painful experience, one did not have "to fall apart" (p. 619). Most parents in the Friedman study also expressed the feeling that religion was of comfort to them.

Heller and Schneider (1977–78) attempted to build on the parental support system described in the Friedman et al. (1963) study by forming a group of parents of dying children and using a peer-oriented, self-help approach called "reevaluation counseling." The authors' basic goal was to establish support through teaching peer counseling— "that is, to have the parents learn to alternate between being counselors and clients with each other" (Heller & Schneider, 1977–78, p. 324). This goal was met, and parents were able to provide mutual support for one another in the setting of these meetings; the groups were very successful. Ordinary families coping with stress need alternatives for help other than the time-consuming and expensive traditional therapy modalities. They need people to listen to them, to reinforce their coping mechanisms, and to "be with" them in their grief. These activities are not the sole prerogative of professionals; indeed, many cannot perform them—perhaps because of time, other commitments, or their own personalities. Peer counseling is one alternative to helping families in stress. Centers such as the MacDonald Houses in New York, Philadelphia, and Chicago, which serve as a home away from home for families of children being treated in city hospitals, are also places where parents can share their feelings with one another.

The study by Binger et al. (1969) found the following to be sources of support to parents: (1) physicians; (2) other parents; (3) clergy—if there had been a meaningful relationship with clergy before the illness; there seemed to be little value in introducing the family to religion at the time of illness if this was not previously present; (4) social workers, who offered practical assistance as well as listening to feelings; (5) parents of other leukemic children; (6) house officers and nursing staffs; and (7) morticians or funeral directors: Fifteen families expressed positive feelings toward the mortician or funeral director for helping them with their grieving (p. 431).

These studies indicate that parents can benefit from the offer of supportive help from peer groups as well as from professionals. To know that their responses are "normal," to have someone available to answer their questions, can help parents a great deal with their anticipatory grief work. Anticipatory mourning is an important concept to consider in reducing the seriousness and duration of psychological reactions in families after a child's death. Anticipatory mourning has been defined as "a set of processes that are directly related to the awareness of the impending loss, to its emotional impact and to the adaptive mechanisms whereby emotional attachment to the dying child is relinquished over time" (Futterman & Hoffman; cited in Tietz et al., 1977, p. 417). These series of processes are interwoven and, as defined by Futterman and Hoffman (1973), consist of:

> Acknowledgment—This involves the parents' growing realization that their child's death is inevitable. The conflict of hope versus despair is evident here and hope gradually narrows in scope as realization of death deepens.
>
> Grieving—Parents experience all of the emotional turmoil involved with the acknowledgment of the child's impending death. Grieving may fluctuate in intensity with exacerbations and remissions of the child's illness but eventually becomes less intense.
>
> Reconciliation—This is a process in which parents develop some perspective about their child's impending death; they feel their child's life has been a worthwhile one and that life will continue to go on for them.
>
> Detachment—Parents begin to withdraw their emotional investment from the child as a growing being with a real future. While still offering love and security to this dying child, they begin to reinvest in relationships which will continue after the child dies.
>
> Memorialization—Here parents develop a mental image of the child which will endure after his death. The parents increasingly think of the child in generalities rather than in terms of specific behaviors. A problem here may be idealization of the child, and perhaps projection of these qualities onto another sibling. (pp. 130–131)

Although anticipatory grief is important, it may cause family members to separate completely from the child before the child has died. This can occur when the dying process extends over a long time. Parents may be upset to find that they have withdrawn from their child before the actual death, both they and the child may need support from staff so that isolation of the child does not occur.

Hope is important for parents of dying children—not hope in the sense of denial of the disease but hope that the child will be comfortable, may have one more remission, may be well enough to stay up that night and watch a TV movie, or may just have one more good day. In a study of a small population of parents of children who died of cancer after prolonged illness, Cobb (1956), found that these parents were grateful for the amount of time—months, weeks, days, even moments—that treatment and experimental therapy gave their children. As long as there was hope and the children's suffering was controlled, these parents wanted to prolong the children's lives. A common wish was that a new experimental treatment would be successful with their child, or that a cure would be discovered.

HOME CARE FOR DYING CHILDREN

Hospices, as discussed in Chapter 3, may offer care for children as well as adults. Home care for the dying child may also be considered as an alternative to hospitalization. Such care at home can greatly enhance and maximize the quality of the family's and child's remaining time together and can make the separation and loss of death easier for all to bear.

The child being cared for at home is part of the family—its happenings, its joys, its arguments. Familiar surroundings, foods, people, toys, and pets enhance feelings of security. Siblings have a chance to participate in the child's care, and some of the mystery of what is happening is removed. The child receives the care/love/discipline from parents that is consistent with his or her view of them. This often does not occur in hospitals, where parents may delegate such parenting functions to caregivers.

"Home care then, puts the child into a comforting environment and gives the parents an active role in care as well as control over the immediate situation" (Martinson, 1979, p. 471). Parents and siblings are able to spend more time with the child. It is easier for many parents to care for the child at home because of transportation, distance, and time involved in commuting from home to the hospital. Parents have talked about the constant conflict they feel about being in one place and feeling responsible for being in another, and about the strains and tensions that can arise in the family because a parent/husband/wife is always at the hospital. Home care can help reduce these types of tensions and conflicts; it is also less costly.

There are some possible drawbacks to home care. Children may sense that family and friends feel uncomfortable about their dying at home. Some children may feel insecure about being away from hospital-level acute care. The commitment of the family to the child's care can cause some physical and emotional strains. Relatives and friends may not approve of the parents' decision for home care and may evoke guilt in the parents for not providing what they consider to be appropriate care for the child.

Martinson et al. (1977) suggest that home care be offered as an alternative to hospitalization when the following conditions are met:

1. Cure-oriented treatment has been discontinued.
2. The child wants to be at home.
3. The parents desire to have the child at home.
4. The parents recognize their ability to care for their ill child.
5. The nurse is willing to be an on-call consultant.
6. The child's physician is willing to be an on-call consultant. (P. 817)

Home care for the dying child may involve various methods of implementation. In Martinson et al.'s project, the parents were the primary caregivers, with the health professionals providing support, teaching, and care suggestions as needed (pp. 815–817). Parents assuming responsibility for the care of their child may need support in maintaining their relationship with the child while dealing with the separation/loss process. They may also need support in their decision to try home care as opposed to hospital care. Nurses may be involved in teaching the family such procedures as giving injections, administering oxygen, and using suction apparatus. Suggestions as to the comfort of the child, including positioning, hygiene, and nutrition, may be needed and helpful. Pain control is a very significant factor in home care. All the people involved—parents, nurses, physicians, and the child—need to understand that pain control is possible and can be effective at home (Martinson, 1978, p. 86). If this is doubted by any of the people involved, the child may experience unnecessary trips to the hospital for pain relief.

Home care may be an alternative choice to hospital care for dying children and their families. Key factors in this choice seems to be family acceptance of the impending death and the child's wish to be at home (Martinson, 1978, p. 88). Caregivers may help people to cope with the death and dying of a family member by providing alternative choices to hospitalization when possible.

MOURNING

After a child dies, listening to the parents express their grief and their concerns is often more important than talking and offering reassurances. If we find ourselves doing more talking than the parents, we must look at our needs to deal with our own helplessness in this situation.

In Western culture, there is a certain pattern of mourning for a dying child that is expected of parents. It is appropriate to be depressed and withdrawn, and for family members to feel alone in their sadness. It is not appropriate for parents to go to a movie or a dance while their child is dying in an effort to gain relief from their sorrow. They are likely to be socially labeled as bad, unfeeling parents (Easson, 1970, p. 81).

Grieving family members may find that they are isolated from the community while their child is dying and for a time after the child's death. In Hamovitch's (1964) study, the critical period of mourning was the first three months after the child's death (p. 117). Parents in this study also stated that friends and relatives avoided them, and certainly avoided any discussion of the child's death. Parents, though, wanted to talk about the child's death, and they wanted company. Isolation may be even more prominent if the child is dying from a disease, such as cancer, that our society fears. Thus, at a time when a family needs the most support from friends and community, the least is offered, and the family mourns alone.

In a small study of five families grieving the death of a child, Wolfe (1977) found that three of the mothers expressed an intense need to talk about the child and the death; their husbands, however, were unable to speak of it and even refused to allow the child's name to be mentioned (p. 77). Each parent reacts to the death of a child in his or her own way. This seems axiomatic, but parents do need to understand that their partners, while experiencing the same feelings of grief and loss, may express their feelings in unique ways. Thus, while one parent talks and cries about the loss, the other may suffer in silence. If parents are told that they may have different responses to the death of their child, they may feel less upset and alone when they find they cannot share their feelings with each other.

Much of the literature on terminally ill children focuses on the grief of mothers (Gyulay, 1977, p. 65). When the child becomes ill, it is usually the mother who spends the most time caring for the child, either at home or in the hospital. The father is often relegated to the background in the dying child's care. Because of traditional roles in our society, he may feel that as a man, he has no choice but to remain stoic and calm since the family is depending on him for strength and stability. Acceptable "manly" emotions for him to display may be anger or acceptance (because of the "strength" either displays) (Gyulay, 1977, p. 65). However, his real feelings may be fear and uncertainty. He may need to cry and talk about his own guilt and sorrow. Often he is left alone with these feelings. He may withdraw from his wife and child. He may take a second job—in many instances, a necessity because of increased medical expenses, but perhaps also to deal with guilt feelings about having failed as a parent, for example, "I may not be such a great father, but I am able to support my family."

Quite often, parents are not in the same stage of grieving at the same time. The mother, because of her usually closer and more continuous contact with the dying child, may reach the stage of acceptance before the father. She may well have worked through her anticipatory mourning feelings of fear, anger, guilt, and sorrow and may see the child's death as an end to suffering. The father, on the other hand, at the time of the child's death, may still be experiencing tremendous feelings of frustration, sorrow, and guilt. In Hamovitch's (1964) study, fathers seemed to suffer more than mothers after the death of the child. Hamovitch speculated that this "is related to the fact that mothers participated more in the care of the child while the child was hospitalized and, therefore, were able to engage in anticipatory grief reaction in a manner not possible for the fathers" (p. 118). Fathers' roles as men in our culture, as mentioned before, could also contribute to this, that is, men are not allowed to show their feelings. Those of us working with families and dying children need to be aware of the roles our culture gives us as men and women and as parents, so that we may try to help our clients talk about what it is they are really experiencing and what alternatives and options they have in coping with the crisis of a dying child. Again, parents' groups for peer support can be very helpful.

Other Family Members

Siblings may pick up very quickly that something is wrong with the sick child other than simply an illness. They may feel jealousy, anger, and fear toward their dying brother or sister. They see their parents leave to visit the child at the hospital with presents; special favors and privileges may be given to the dying child and not to the other children; friends and relatives visit and inquire about the ill child and not about the other children. All these events may be resented by siblings. Siblings also fear that they may have caused the illness. At one time or another, children normally wish their siblings would go away or wish them dead; if a sibling does then actually die, we can imagine how frightening fantasies may develop (Gyulay, 1977, p. 68).

Siblings' behavior often reflects these feelings. Grades may drop, and school attendance may be poor. Frequent visits to the school nurse may indicate the sibling's need for adult attention. In the study done by Binger et al. (1969), it was found that "in half the families one or more previously well siblings showed significant behavioral patterns that indicated difficulty in coping; problems described by parents included an onset of severe enuresis, headaches, poor school performance, school phobia, depression, severe separation anxieties and persistent abdominal pains" (p. 416). Our inability to talk directly about death only enhances children's fears and fantasies. In family-centered care, caregivers need to discuss sibling reactions with parents. Perhaps the relaxing of some hospital visiting regulations, by allowing siblings to visit the ill child, will clear up fantasies and misunderstandings. Children also need a place where they can ask questions, touch, cry, laugh, and act out if need be; they need to know they are accepted and loved, and they need to be told the truth of what is happening. They need to be included in the family grieving process both before and after the ill sibling dies. Some families may be able to do this alone; others may need help, perhaps in the form of family conferences with health care personnel. The significant concept here is that the entire family unit, including siblings, be involved in the total treatment of a dying child.

Once the ill child has died, changes occur that can make quite an impact on the family structure. There is a shift in family dynamics and role relationships. Siblings may have lost a big brother, a protector, or a scapegoat. They are also confronted with a new status in the ordinal structure of the family. In a two-child family, the remaining child is now an only child, and may not understand the concerted parental attention now being focused on him or her. A middle child may become the oldest child, with new privileges and responsibilities that may be both pleasurable and frightening. Parents may have lost an idealized only son or daughter. Family alliances will have to shift and roles be realigned.

In a study by Cain, et al. (1977) of children's disturbed reactions to the death of a sibling, some of the mothers were severely withdrawn, preoccupied, and depressed. They were unable to provide much love or attention to the remaining siblings and were barely able to complete the most basic activities of daily living. The fathers, in convention with their cultural role, were calmer and more stoic outwardly but were actually heartsick, hearing little of what was said to them, constantly forgetting things, and crying to themselves when no one was looking. Parents may not be able to be alert to sibling grief reactions, and may not be able to help their children cope because of their own grieving. Care providers need to be aware of these reactions in siblings and must help both parents and children to grieve.

Grandparents are often the forgotten grievers of a dying grandchild. They are grieving not only for their grandchild; but also for their own daughter or son and for themselves. They feel helpless and out of control in this situation, feeling that they should be able to offer more help in coping and feeling guilt and anger that they were not able to prevent this from happening. Some of the families in the Binger et al. (1969) study reported that grandparents were most supportive, whereas others viewed grandparents' intervention as negative (p. 416). The negative connotations seemed connected to past relations between parent and grandparent, to the grandparents' grief reactions, and to their lack of knowledge of the child's disease. Frequently, grandparents are separated from their children and grandchildren by long distances and this, often coupled with less than the best physical and emotional health, makes it difficult for them to be with their families to provide actual physical care or to help with the emotional strain of the child's illness and dying.

DEATH OF AN INFANT

We question and grieve over the death of any young child, but the death of an infant is particularly difficult to experience. The birth of a baby is seen as a happy event in our culture; very few parents give much thought to the idea that their baby may die. However, although infant mortality is on the decline in the United States, 10 to 20 out of every 1,000 newborns still die in the first few days of life (Helmrath & Steinitz, 1978, p. 785). If their baby dies, parents are usually stunned and cannot believe this is happening to them. Their grieving, contrary to what most people believe, is as intense and as prolonged as that experienced at the death of an older child. The pain, the ache, the sorrow felt over the loss of a longed-for baby is so acute that it can hurt as much as any physical pain. One mother described her feelings about the loss of her 3-day-old son:

> I cannot bear to think that he is gone, that I will never know him as a person, that he will not experience the joys as well as the sorrows of life. I hurt inside—it is like an empty, painful void within me. I long for sleep so I won't feel this loss, and yet it is so difficult to sleep. I wake up and perhaps for a split-second life seems possible but then once more this

overwhelming ache, this pain of his death, engulfs me like a wave and I feel like I cannot go on. I will live, but right now that has little meaning for me.

In their study of couples who had lost newborn babies, Helmrath and Steinitz (1978), found that

... all mothers and fathers had a high degree of mourning and that with all couples, the men and women differed in the characteristics of their grief in that women felt the loss more acutely and tended to grieve for a longer period of time. Guilt was a component of both parents' mourning, with all of the women feeling some degree of responsibility for the death, particularly when the child died as a result of a congenital anomaly. Many of the fathers felt a strong attachment to their newborn babies, having touched and held them before their deaths. However, the fathers felt that they had been socialized with the view of a strong, unemotional male and therefore felt they had to remain "strong" and would not break down and cry. (p. 787)

This study found that parents felt very isolated. Friends and relatives ignored the fact that the couple had had a baby who died; the baby and the death were not discussed. While the parents felt a great need to talk about their feelings about this, friends and family continually avoided it. The couples began to feel that they were behaving inappropriately in grieving, rather than realizing that it was the external system that was inappropriate (p. 788).

The implications for intervention here are clear; couples need support and help in verbalizing their feelings about the death of their babies. They need to be aware of the stages of grief so they will recognize that what they are feeling is appropriate and important. If the parents desire, follow-up visits throughout the grieving period can be arranged to help them with continued support and perhaps guidance in planning for future children.

A particularly shocking and devastating experience for parents is the death of an infant from Sudden Infant Death Syndrome—SIDS. This syndrome, commonly referred to as crib death, is the leading cause of death in infants between the ages of 1 week and 1 year in the United States; it is estimated that between 8,000 and 10,000 infants die each year of SIDS (Weinstein, 1978, p. 831). The cause of SIDS is unknown; an apparently healthy infant dies an unexpected death, and an autopsy does not reveal an adequate cause. Current research into possible causes of SIDS include studies relating to prolonged sleep apnea, chronic oxygen deficiency, and enzyme abnormalities.

Parents' emotional reaction to SIDS is usually very intense because the infant's death is sudden; and without warning. Because the death is totally unexpected, they have had no chance for anticipatory mourning. Guilt may be overwhelming, and parents may feel they are literally going "crazy" with grief. They may ruminate over and over, "If only I had left the window closed that night ... " or "What have I done wrong to deserve this?" Parents may blame themselves for the infant's death, and uninformed friends and relatives may also do so, sometimes even equating the death with child abuse. Parents need to know two important points about SIDS: (1) "Your baby died of a definite disease entity (SIDS)", and (2) "It could not be predicted or prevented; you are in no way responsible for the death" (Loscari, 1978, p. 1286). Other points helpful for parents are that the cause of death is not suffocation; there is no sound or cry of distress from the infant; there is no suffering; and SIDS is not hereditary or contagious.

The crisis nature of this death, coupled with the many questions and feelings arising within the family, creates a need for much support for parents and siblings. If there is not an extended family network that can be utilized as an effective support system, families may need to utilize community resource systems as support networks. Special groups of people who are likely to come in contact with families involved in SIDS may include doctors, nurses, social workers, police, funeral directors, emergency room personnel, ambulance drivers, the clergy, school counselors, and parents' groups. The family's informal network of friends, coworkers, and so on also may provide support. Families may not only need counseling and guidance for their emotional reactions to this crisis, they may also need specific help in such areas as making funeral arrangements and anticipating future crisis points, such as the anniversary of the birth and death of the infant.

The American public needs to be educated about this cause of infant mortality and also about what services are, and should be, available to families who have lost a child to SIDS. The Sudden Infant Death Syndrome Act of 1974 was passed to provide funding for these needs. A source of information about SIDS is the National Foundation for SIDS, Inc., located in New York City.

Dying Children and Caregivers

Easson (1968) states that "in the management of the dying patient, the most difficult treatment problem is frequently not with the patient, not with the family of the patient, but with the treating staff" (p. 203).

Caregivers are part of our culture and hence have the same anxieties and fears about death as any other members of our society. Chapter 4 presented a discussion of how health professionals deal with themselves and death and dying. However, it is helpful here to mention some staff members' reactions to dying children.

Staff may feel that they have failed with dying children. Their goals are to cure the children, and this has not happened. They may even feel the children have failed them, and may become angry with them because they have not responded to their care and treatment. Anger may also be vented upon one another, with doctors and nurses accusing one another of not communicating adequately or of not providing a certain type of care.

Staff members also respond to dying children in terms of their own developmental levels and emotional reactions regarding death. For example, young nurses and interns may respond with youthful rage, feeling that death must be kept away at all costs and initiating all types of treatment procedures to try to accomplish this (Easson, 1968, p. 206). On the other hand, the elderly physician, because of a personal increased acceptance of death as an evolving maturational process, may not understand why the younger members of the treatment team cannot accept suggestions for a palliative course of treatment for the child; he or she may not understand why they are so urgently trying to maintain the dying child's life. Caregivers need to be committed to supporting, and openly communicating with, one another as well as with dying children, for it is within the context of this sharing of feelings, hopes, and goals that we learn how to comfort and sustain our patients, ourselves, and our colleagues.

SUMMARY

Children's concepts of death are influenced by such factors as developmental levels, family attitudes and values, social and cultural environments, and self-concepts. Dying children need to know that they will be cared for and that they will not be left alone. Their questions about their own deaths should be answered on their own terms with regard to what it is they are really asking and with regard to the total family picture of culture, religion, support systems, and past coping with crises.

Children who are dying may be cared for at home and/or in the hospital. It is helpful for parents and siblings to be involved in planning and administering care. Anticipatory mourning may help parents cope with the impending death of their child. Interactions with other parents of dying children may also be an effective coping mechanism.

After the child dies, family members may grieve in different ways, and family roles and relationships may change. Family members need to grieve not only individually but as a family unit, for it is this unit as a whole that is experiencing the changes brought about by the death of one of its members.

A child's death affects each one of us in a different way; we may feel love, hate, relief, anger, impotence, sadness. We may look at ourselves, our own lives, differently. We will not be exactly the same people we were before. For better or worse, this child has touched us, and we cannot go back. Hopefully, we move on, with more awareness for others and for each person's uniqueness and place in life.

ANNOTATED BIBLIOGRAPHY

One way adults can encourage children to discuss and express their feelings about death openly is through children's stories. Parents and teachers may find these stories as comforting and enlightening as the children do. Wass and Shaak (1976) have compiled a selected, annotated bibliography of children's books that have death as their theme (pp. 80–85). This bibliography is listed below.

Preschool Through Age 7

Brown, M.W. *The dead bird.* Glenview, Ill.: Scott, 1965. A group of children find a bird and feel its heart not beating. They have a funeral for it before returning to their play. Life continues.

Buck, P. *The beech tree.* New York: John Day, 1958. The metaphor of a beech tree is used by an elderly man to help explain his impending death.

De Paola, T. *Nana upstairs and Nana downstairs.* New York: Putnam's 1973. Tommy is heartbroken when his bedridden great-grandmother, with whom he has spent many happy hours, dies. He comes to realize that both the Nana that lived upstairs and the Nana that lived downstairs are "upstairs" in Heaven. The hope of life after death brings satisfaction.

Fassler, J. *My grandpa died today.* New York: Behavioral Publications, 1971. A description of Grandpa sleeping away to a peaceful death in his rocking chair is presented. Knowing his Grandpa was not afraid to die, David is able to continue "running and laughing and growing up with only fond memories of Grandpa." Written in simple story-line but with such factual detail that it could be classed as a nonfiction book.

Grollman, E. *Talking about death.* Boston: Beacon, 1970. The finality of death is presented uncompromisingly in simple direct language without softening the blow. Grollman's intent is to protect the child from destructive fantasy and a distorted view of death as well as guilt that often arises when a child is denied information.

Harris, A. *Why did he die?* Minneapolis: Lerner, 1965. A mother's heartfelt effort to speak to her child about death is portrayed. Death is likened to the leaves falling in autumn with new leaves to come in the spring, and to a worn-out motor. Emphasis is on the fact that, no matter what happens, memories of the deceased will never die.

Kantrowitz, M. *When Violet died.* New York: Parents', 1973. A story of the funeral preparations and ceremony for a dead bird, emphasizing the children's reactions, fascination and fun children get out of ceremonies, even funerals, The children are consoled in the continuity of life as shown through their pregnant cat. Life goes on!

Kuskin, K. *The bear who saw the spring.* New York: Harper & Row, 1961. A story of changing seasons and the changes living things go through as they are born, live, and die.

Miles, M. *Annie and the old one.* Boston: Little, Brown, 1971. Annie's Navajo grandmother says she will be ready to die after the new rug is woven. Annie tries to keep the rug from being finished, but her wise grandmother tells her that is wrong, that the "earth from which good things come is where all creatures finally go." Death is a part of life.

Stein, S. B. *About dying.* New York: Walker, 1974. A "shared" and open story about everyday dying, the kind every child meets early in his own life—the death of a pet and a grandparent. Actual photographs accompanying the text of death, funeral, and mourning of Snow, a pet bird, and the Grandpa who had given him to the children. The accompanying adult text serves as a resource for handling the questions and discussion arising from the child's natural curiosity. The book explains reality, guiding a child toward the truth even if it is painful, and gives the children the inner strength to deal with things as they are. Preventive mental health!

Tresselt, A. *The dead tree.* New York: Parents', 1972. The life cycle of a tall oak tree is poetically described, showing that in nature nothing is ever wasted or completely dies.

Viorst, J. *The tenth good thing about Barney.* New York: Atheneum, 1971. The rituals of burial and mourning are observed for Barney, a pet cat. The child is led to understand that dying is as usual as living. Death is a part of life. Some readers may question whether young children will be able to comprehend the abstract idea of Barney's future role as fertilizer.

Warburg, S. S. *Growing time*. Boston: Houghton Mifflin, 1969. Jamie learns to accept the reality and meaning of the death of his dog with the help of his sympathetic and understanding family. He finds out that "death is not easy to bear." Something you love never dies; it lives in your heart.

Zolotow, C. *My grandson Lew*. New York: Harper & Row, 1974. The shared remembrances between a mother and a small child of a sadly missed grandfather keep both mother and son from being lonely. Memories keep the deceased alive in your mind.

Ages 8 Through 11

Cleaver, V. *Grover*. Philadelphia: Lippincott, 1970. Ten-year-old Grover is forced to handle the changes that the suicide of his ailing mother brought about in his own groping ways, as his father is too grief-stricken to help. He finds out that there is no formula for overcoming grief other than time, friends, and maturity.

Cohen, B. *Thank you, Jackie Robinson*. New York: Lothrop, 1974. The story of the slowly deepening friendship between 12-year-old Sam Greene and the elderly black cook in Mrs. Greene's restaurant. After following their "main man"—Jackie Robinson—Sam is bereft when Davy suffers a fatal heart attack. Because their relationship seems solid, readers too will mourn Davy's death and sympathize with an honestly grieving Sam.

Lee, V. *The magic moth*. New York: Seabury, 1972. A very supportive family bravely copes with 10-year-old Maryanne's illness and death from a heart defect. A moth bursting from its cocoon as Maryanne dies and seed sprouting just after her funeral symbolize that "life never ends—it just changes."

Orgel, D. *Mulberry music*. New York: Harper & Row, 1971. The efforts of a young girl's parents to protect her from the knowledge of her adored grandmother's impending death result in turmoil, both within the girl and around her, when in her rash and rebellious actions the girl searches for her beloved grandmother. Keeping the truth of an impending death from a child can cause misunderstanding and fear.

Smith, D. B. *A taste of blackberries*. New York: Crowell, 1973. Jamie dies of a bee sting. His best friend is confronted with grief at the loss and comes to terms with a guilty feeling that somehow he might have saved Jamie. After a period of grief, life goes on.

Zim, H., & Bleeker, S. *Life and death*. New York: Morrow, 1970. This is an answer book for questions young people have about death. The physical facts, customs, and attitudes surrounding life and death are discussed. Death is described as a part of living.

Age 12 And Over

Corburn, J. *Anne and the sand dobbies*. New York: Seabury, 1967. Danny's father tries to answer questions about the death of Danny's sister.

Gunther, J. *Death be not proud*. New York: Harper & Row, 1949. The author writes of the courage of his 17-year-old son while facing death. The book is a celebration of life. It is more difficult for his parents than for Johnnie to accept his death.

Hunter, M. *A sound of chariots*. New York: Harper & Row, 1972. Bridie McShane's happy early childhood during World War I in Scotland is interrupted by the death of her beloved father whose favorite child she was. As she matures, her life is marred by her sorrow, leading her to morbid reflections on time and death, which she finally learns to deal with through her desire to write poetry.

Klein, S. *The final mystery*. New York: Doubleday, 1974. The meaning of death is explored and how people of different religions have coped with it. The on-going war against death is discussed.

Rhodin, E. *The good greenwood*. Philadelphia: Westminister, 1971. A tense and moving story of Mike who lost his good friend, Louie. After time and grief pass, Mike came to realize that Louie was really dead and was not going to reappear around the next corner. He came to remember Louie for the clown and dreamer that he was and for the good times they had together. He was not building another Louie as the grownups were, one that was almost perfect.

From "Helping Children Understand Death through Literature" by Hannelore Wass and Judity Shaak, *Childhood Education*, Nov./Dec. 1976, Vol. 53, No. 2, pp. 83–85. Reprinted by permission of Hannelore Wass and the Association for Childhood Education International, 3615 Wisconsin Avenue, N.W., Washington, D.C. 20016. Copyright © 1976 by the Association.

LEARNING EXERCISES

1. Review children's fairy tales such as "Snow White and the Seven Dwarfs" and "The Sleeping Beauty," and discuss how these relate developmentally to young children's concepts of death.

2. Debate the pros and cons of death education in the public school system.

3. What would you say to a 5-year-old child who asks you, "Where do I go when I die?"

4. Jerry and Beth, a young couple who are your friends, had a 3-month-old baby daughter who died last week of Sudden Infant Death Syndrome (SIDS). You are planning to visit them this evening. Will you bring up the topic of their baby's death, and, if so, what will you say?

5. Explore the resources in your community that could be made available to parents and families who are grieving over the death of a child.

AUDIOVISUAL MATERIAL

Coping. 22 min/color/1974. University of California Extension Media Center.
Through a series of interviews with a terminally ill child, his family, and their physician, this film shows how family support helps all members deal with death.

The Magic Moth. 22 min/color/1977. Centron Educational Films.
Maryanne, one of five children, is in the process of dying. The film depicts the reactions of her family and friends to her illness and death. As Maryanne dies, a beautiful moth emerges from a cocoon that had been a gift to her from her brother.

Very Good Friends. 29 min/color/1977. Learning Corporation of America.
A 13-year-old girl responds to the accidental death of a younger sister. Her parents help her work through her guilt and anger in order for her to come to terms with her feelings about death.

You Are Not Alone. 30 min/color/1976. Bureau of Community Health Services.
This film is a dramatization of couples who have lost a child to SIDS. Advice is given on how and where to get help.

REFERENCES

Binger, C. M., Ablin, A. R., Feverstein, R. C., Kirschrer, J. H., Zoger, S., & Mikkelsen, C. Childhood leukemia: Emotional impact on patient and family. *New England Journal of Medicine*, February 20, 1969, *280*(8), 414–418.

Bluebond-Langner, M. *The private words of dying children.* Princeton, N.J.: Princeton University Press, 1978.

Bowlby, J. *Child care and the growth of love.* Baltimore, Md.: Penguin Books, 1965.

Cain, A., Fast, I., & Erickson, M. Children's disturbed reaction to the death of a sibling. In L. Wilkenfeld (Ed.), *When children die.* Dubuque, Iowa: Kendall/Hunt, 1977.

Childers, P., & Wimmer, M. The concept of death in early childhood. *Child Development,* 1971, *42*(4), 1299–1301.

Cobb, B. Psychological impact of long illness and death of a child on the family circle. *Journal of Pediatrics,* 1956, *49,* 746–751.

Coddington, M. A mother struggles to cope with her child's deteriorating illness. *Maternal Child Nursing Journal,* Spring 1976, *5,* 39–44.

Dumont, R., & Foss, D. *The American view of death.* Cambridge, Mass.: Schenkman, 1972.

Easson, W. Care of the young patient who is dying. *Journal of the American Medical Association,* July 22, 1968, *205*(4), 203–207.

Easson, W. The dying child: The management of the child or adolescent who is dying. Springfield, Ill.: Charles C Thomas, 1970.

Evans, A. If a child must die. . . . *New England Journal of Medicine,* January 18, 1968, *278*(3), 138–142.

Fischhoff, J., & O'Brien, N. After the child dies. *Journal of Pediatrics,* January 1976, *18*(1), 140–146.

Ford, K. I. Dealing with death and dying through family-centered care. *Nursing Clinics of North America,* March 1972, 7, 53–64.

Friedman, S., Chodoff, P., Mason, J., & Hamburg, D. Behavioral observations on parents anticipating the death of a child. *Pediatrics,* October 1963, *32,* 610–625.

Futterman, E., & Hoffman, I. Crisis and adaptation in the families of fatally ill children. In E. J. Anthony & C. Koupernick (Eds.), *The child in his family: The impact of disease and death.* Yearbook of the International Association for Child Psychiatry and Allied Professions (Vol. 2). New York: John Wiley, 1973.

Gartley, W., & Bernosconi, M. The concept of death in children. *Journal of Genetic Psychology,* 1967, *110,* 71–85.

Gyulay, J. E. The forgotton grievers. In L. Wilkenfeld (Ed.), *When children die.* Dubuque, Iowa: Kendall/Hunt, 1977.

Hamovitch, M. *The patient and the fatally ill child.* Duarte, Calif.: City of Hope Medical Center, 1964.

Heller, D. B., & Schneider, C. Interpersonal methods for coping with stress: Helping families of dying children. *Omega,* 1977–78, *8*(4), 319–331.

Helmrath, T., & Steinitz, E. Death of an infant: Parental grieving and the failure of social support. *Journal of Family Practice,* 1978, *6*(4), 785–790.

Jackson, P. The child's developing concept of death: Implications for nursing care of the terminally ill child. *Nursing Forum*, 1975, *14*(2), 204–215.

Koocher, G. Talking with children about death. *American Journal of Orthopsychiatry*, April 1974, *44*(3), 404–411.

Koop, C. E. The seriously ill or dying child: Supporting the patient and the family. *Pediatric Clinics of North America*, August 1965, *16*(3), 555–564.

Loscari, A. The dying child and the family. *Journal of Family Practice*, 1978, *6*(6), 1279–1286.

Martinson, I. M. Alternative environments for care of the dying child: Hospice, hospital, or home. In O. J. Z. Sahler (Ed.), *The child and death*. St. Louis, Mo.: C. V. Mosby, 1978.

Martinson, I. M. Caring for the dying child. *Nursing Clinics of North America*, September 1979, *14*(3), 467–474.

Martinson, I. M., Gees, D., Anglinn, M. A., Peterson, E., Nesbig, M., & Keasey, J. Home care for the child. *American Journal of Nursing*, November 1977, *77*(11), 815–817.

Meleor, J. D. Children's conceptions of death. *Journal of Genetic Psychology*, 1973, *123*(2), 359–360.

Menig-Peterson, C., & McCabe, A. Children talk about death. *Omega*, 1977–78, *8*(4), 305–318.

Miya, T. M. The child's perception of death. *Nursing Forum*, 1972, *11*(2), 214–220.

Morrissey, J. A note on interviews with children facing imminent death. *Social Casework*, June 1963, *44*, 343–345.

Nagy, M. The child's view of death. In H. Feifel (Ed.), *The meaning of death*. New York: McGraw-Hill, 1959.

Pattison, E. M. The fatal myth of death in the family. *American Journal of Psychiatry*, January 1976, *133*(6), 674–678.

Rochlin, G. How younger children view death and themselves. In E. A. Grollman (Ed.), *Explaining death to children*. Boston: Beacon Press, 1968.

Sahler, O. J. (Ed.). *The child and death*. St. Louis, Mo.: C. V. Mosby, 1978.

Tietz, W., McSherry, L., & Britt, B. Family sequelae after a child's death due to cancer. *American Journal of Psychotherapy*, July 1977, *31*(3), 417–424.

Waechter, E. Children's awareness of fatal illness. In L. Wilkenfeld (Ed.), *When children die*. Dubuque, Iowa: Kendall/Hunt, 1977.

Wass, H., & Shaak, J. Helping children understand death through literature. *Childhood Education*, November–December 1976, *53*, 80–85.

Weinstein, S. Sudden infant death syndrome: Impact on families and a direction for change. *American Journal of Psychiatry*, July 1978, *135*(7), 831–834.

Wolfe, M. Families in grief: The question of casework intervention. In L. Wilkenfeld (Ed.), *When children die*. Dubuque, Iowa: Kendall/Hunt, 1977.

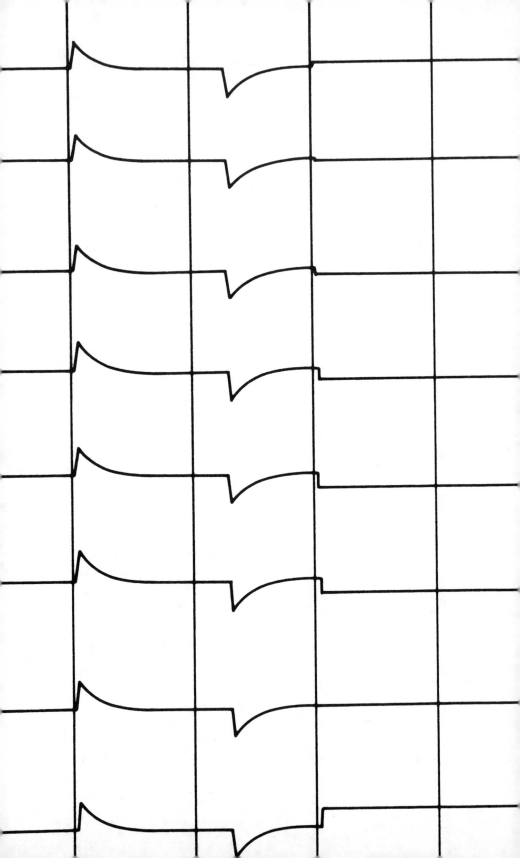

6

Ethical Issues

The ethical issues surrounding death have been discussed throughout history. But because of our advanced medical technology, ethical issues today have become more complex. New machinery, the heart-lung machine, leads us to question the criteria determining death; there are new treatments with painful side effects, and improved forms of treatment maintain the lives of many who would have died in the past without necessarily returning them to a full life. This chapter looks at three major ethical issues surrounding death: the definition of death, the right to refuse treatment, and euthanasia.

THE DEFINITION OF DEATH

John, Joan, and Mary were in an automobile accident. They all became comatose as a result. John was rushed to Northside Hospital; Joan was rushed to Eastside General; and Mary was rushed to Southside Hospital. All three were immediately placed on respirators. For each of them, an electroencephalogram (EEG) was made; all three EEGs were flat. After 24 hours another EEG was made. Again, all three were flat. None of them had any reflex movement; they were totally unresponsive. John, at Northside Hospital, was pronounced dead and then was removed from the respirator. Joan, at Eastside General, was removed from the respirator and then was pronounced dead. Mary was kept on the respirator and was defined as alive.

John, Joan, and Mary are obviously not real people. Yet what occurred in the story does take place: there is confusion over the criteria

171

being used to define death. Death no longer progresses neatly from clinical death, to brain death, to biological death, to cellular death (Hendin, 1974, p. 25). Clinical death occurs when spontaneous respiration and heartbeat cease irreversibly. This should lead to brain death since the brain, at normal body temperature, cannot survive for more than a few minutes. When the brain, which dies in stages, is totally dead, it is known as biological death. Then cellular death sets in, with different cells of the body dying at different times because of their different makeup. For example, hair and nails may continue to grow after biological death has occurred. Today, brain death may occur while heartbeat and respiration continue with mechanical support.

Robert Morison (1971) asserts that death is not an event but a continuous process. Kass (1971), however, disagrees. There is a point at which the human being must be considered dead:

What dies is the organism as a whole. It is this death, the death of the individual human being, that is important for physicians and for the community, not the "death" of organs or cells, which are mere parts. (p. 699)

The question is: At what point is the organism dead?

THE HISTORY OF DEFINING DEATH

Alexander (1980) argues that defining death was not as simple in the past as we tend to believe. In 1740, "The Uncertainty of the Signs of Death and the Danger of Precipitate Interments and Dissections" set off debate on the criteria of death. Putrefaction was considered the only sure sign of death; even this was attacked because putrefaction was found in cases of gangrene. The fear of premature burial and premature cessation of medical care motivated the development of safeguards, which took such forms as the creation of mortuaries and legislation delaying burial for at least one day. These developments enabled people to watch the dead to make sure they actually were dead. The following (Alexander, 1980) is a description of a model mortuary:

The model mortuary contained twenty-three cells for women and the same number for men. Each set of cells was clustered around an observation corridor. The corpse was placed near the cell window through which it could be observed by a guard. The hands of the corpses wore gloves which were attached by strings to an alarm. The slightest movement of a finger caused a large hammer to strike the alarm. The signal was truly frightening, appropriate for the danger it announced. The mortuary also contained a revival room and a pharmacy. On constant duty, guards punched a time-clock every half-hour. A physician directed the mortuary, and physicians made rounds, intervening if necessary. (p. 29)

As the medical profession advanced in terms of developing greater scientific standards, a consensus developed that medical knowledge could lead to the best protection against premature burial. In 1875, an article appeared in the *Dictionnaire Dechambre*, an encyclopedia of medicine, that discussed 27 major signs of death. There began to be agreement among physicians that the major signs of death were the irrevocable cessation of heartbeat, respiration, and consciousness.

THE PUSH TO REDEFINE DEATH

In the late 1950s and early 1960s there was a push to redefine death in terms of the brain rather than the heart-lung definition. The explicit idea of brain death developed from the work of two French neurologists. In 1959, Mallaret and Goulon presented an article concerning grades of coma; the deepest coma was a state without movement, spontaneous breathing, reflex activity, or temperature regulation. "Essentially this was a state approaching conventional death except for the presence of a beating heart kept alive by artificially controlled lungs" (Black, 1978, p. 213).

Simultaneously, transplant operations of organs were being conducted. In December 1954, Dr. Joseph Murray and his colleagues performed the first successful kidney transplant operation. Then, in December 1967, Dr. Christian Barnard performed a heart transplant operation. Today, up to 25 different organs have been transplanted with different degrees of success, including eye corneas, teeth, spleen, and pancreas. Organs became needed for transplantation. If a heart is to be used for transplantation, the donor must be maintained on a heart-lung machine. Other organs would also be of better quality if they were being supplied with oxygen up until removal from the donor. Yet, could a patient be defined as dead if the heart was beating, albeit artificially?

As Glasser (1970) points out, it became imperative to define death in such a way as to protect the "dying patient" and to protect the surgeon from violating the law; and so as not to preclude a potentially life-saving operation for the patient who needed a new organ.

The Definition of Brain Death

In 1968, the Ad Hoc Committee of the Harvard Medical School to Examine the Definition of Brain Death presented their report, in which they presented criteria for determining brain death. The four conditions were as follows:

1. *Unreceptivity and Unresponsivity.* There is a total unawareness to externally applied stimuli and inner need and complete unresponsiveness—our definition of irreversible coma. Even the most intensely painful stimuli evoke no vocal or other response, not even a groan, withdrawal of a limb, or quickening of respiration.

2. *No Movements or Breathing.* Observations covering a period of at least one hour by physicians is adequate to satisfy the criteria of no spontaneous muscular movements or spontaneous respiration or response to stimuli such as pain, touch, sound, or light. After the patient is on a mechanical respirator, the total absence of spontaneous breathing may be established by turning off the respirator for three minutes and observing whether there is any effort on the part of the subject to breath spontaneously. (The respirator may be turned off for this time provided that at the start of the trial period the patient's carbon dioxide tension is within the normal range, and provided also that the patient had been breathing room air for at least ten minutes prior to the trial.)

3. *No Reflexes.* Irreversible coma with abolition of central nervous system activity is evidenced in part by the absence of elicitable reflexes. The pupil will be fixed and dilated and will not respond to a direct source of bright light. Since the establishment of a fixed, dilated pupil is clear-cut in clinical practice, there should be no uncertainty as to its presence. Ocular movement (to head turning and to irrigation of the ears with ice water) and blinking are absent. There is no evidence of postural activity (decerebrate or other). Swallowing, yawning, vocalization are in abeyance. Corneal and pharyngeal reflexes are absent.

As a rule the stretch of tendon reflexes cannot be elicited: i.e., tapping the tendons of the biceps, triceps, and pronator muscles, quadriceps and gastrocnemius muscles with the reflex hammer elicits no contraction of the respective muscles. Plantar and noxious stimulation gives no response.

4. *Flat Electroencephalogram.* Of great confirmatory value is the flat or isoelectric EEG. We must assume that the electrodes have been properly applied, that the apparatus is functioning normally, and that the personnel in charge *is* competent. We consider it prudent to have one channel of the apparatus used for an electrocardiogram. This channel will monitor the ECG so that, if it appears in the electroencephalographic leads because of high resistance, it can be readily identified. It also establishes the presence of the active heart in the absence of the EEG. We recommend

that another channel be used for a noncephalic lead. This will pick up space-borne or vibration-born artifacts and identify them. The simplest form of such a monitoring noncephalic electrode has two leads over the dorsum of the hand, preferably the right hand, so the ECG will be minimal or absent. Since one of the requirements of this state is that there be no muscle activity, these two dorsal hand electrodes will not be bothered by muscle artifact. The apparatus should be run at standard gains 10μV/mm, 50μV/5mm. Also it should be isoelectric at double this standard gain which is 5μV/mm or 25μV/5mm. At least ten full minutes of recording are desirable, but twice that would be better.

It is also suggested that the gains at some point be opened to their full amplitude for a brief period (5 to 100 seconds) to see what is going on. Usually in an intensive care unit artifacts will dominate the picture, but these are readily identifiable. There shall be no electroencephalographic response to noise or to pinch.

All of the above tests shall be repeated at least 24 hours later with no change.

The validity of such date as indications of irreversible cerebral damage depends on the exclusion of two conditions: Hypothermia (temperature below 90° F[32.2° C] or central nervous system depressants, such as barbiturates. (p. 338)

From "A Definition of Irreversible Coma" by Henry K. Beecher et al., *Journal of the American Medical Association*, August 5, 1968, Vol. 205, pp. 337–340. Copyright © 1968 American Medical Association.

The Harvard criteria have become the standard reference point for the definition of death in the United States. Evidence for the validity of the Harvard criteria has come from a study of 2,650 comatose patients with flat EEGs over a 24-hour period. Not one patient who was not excluded by the Harvard criteria because of depressants recovered. Furthermore, 128 consecutive autopsies on people who met the Harvard criteria showed that their brains had been destroyed (Veatch, 1976, p. 48).

In Europe, instead of waiting 24 hours, if the person fulfills the Harvard criteria, including a flat EEG at one point in time, an arteriograph is given that tests brain circulation, which should be nonexistent in brain death. (Blood flow is cut off because of the swelling of the brain cells.) The advantage of this procedure is that it only takes 30 minutes. However, it is a cumbersome procedure, and some American physicians feel the test may harm a brain that is not yet totally dead (Black, 1978).

There are also discussions of viewing brain death solely in terms of the neocortex, which would base the definition of death solely on a flat EEG. Since the brain stem is still alive, the person would have spontaneous respiration and certain brain-stem reflexes. Brierley, Adams, Graham, and Simpson (1971) present two cases in which each patient survived five months after neocortical death. They argue:

> In essence, it seems that a person who resumes spontaneous respiration after cardiac arrest, yet exhibits an isoelectric EEG, is to be regarded as "alive," while another surviving the same accident, also with an isoelectric EEG but whose cardiac function depends upon mechanical ventilation may be regarded as "dead." Clearly, this distinction between "alive" and "dead" attaches cardinal importance to the function of respiration and none to those higher functions of the nervous system that demarcate man from the lower primates and all other vertebrates and invertebrates. (p. 564)

A Framework for Analyzing the Definition of Death

Veatch (1976, pp. 25–54) proposes a framework that would enable us to analyze the various definitions of death. He states that four separate levels must be distinguished:

1. There should be a formal definition of death such as the following: "Death means a complete change in the status of a living entity characterized by the irreversible loss of those characteristics that are essentially significant to it. It would be the point at which the individual is no longer treated as a human being" (p. 25).

2. We must then decide on the concept of death. That is: What is significant about life that when we lose it, there is death? Is life found in the flow of vital fluids, the breath or blood; or in our soul; or in our capacity for bodily integration; or in our capacity for social interaction?

3. Once we have defined our concept of death, we must determine the locus of death. Where should we look to see if death has occurred? If our concept of death concerns the loss of vital fluids, then one must look at the heart and lungs; if one is concerned with bodily integration, then one focuses on the total brain; if the concept is based on social interaction, then death would probably be found in the neocortex. For the soul, one might look for the pineal body, as suggested by Descartes.

4. Then the criteria of death should be decided: What specific tests—for example, the EEG—must be applied at the locus of death to see if death has occurred?

Table 6.1 summarizes the framework presented by Veatch and how it would be applied, depending upon our various concepts of death.

Table 6.1. Levels of the Definition of Death

Formal Definition: Death means a complete change in the status of a living entity characterized by the irreversible loss of those characteristics that are essentially significant to it.

Concept of Death:	*Locus of Death:*	*Criteria of Death:*
Philosophical or theological judgment of the essentially significant change at death.	Place to look to determine if a person has died.	Measurements physicians or other officials use to determine whether a person is dead—to be determined by scientific empirical study.
1. The irreversible stopping of the flow of "vital" body fluids, i.e., the blood and breath	Heart and lungs	1. Visual observation of respiration, perhaps with the use of a mirror. 2. Feeling the pulse, possibly supported by electro-cardiogram
2. The irreversible loss of the soul from the body	The pineal body? (according to Descartes) The respiratory tract?	Observation of breath?
3. The irreversible loss of the capacity for bodily integration and social interaction	The brain	1. Unreceptivity and unresponsivity 2. No movements or breathing 3. No reflexes (except spinal reflexes) 4. Flat electro-encephalogram (to be used as confirmatory evidence) —All tests to be repeated 24 hours later (excluded conditions: hypothermia and central nervous system drug depression)

Table 6.1. (Continued)

Concept of Death:	Locus of Death:	Criteria of Death:
4. Irreversible loss of consciousness or the capacity for social interaction	Probably the neocortex	Electroencephalogram

Note: The possible concepts, loci, and criteria of death are much more complex than the ones given here. These are meant to be simplified models of types of positions being taken in the current debate. It is obvious that those who believe that death means the irreversible loss of the capacity for bodily integration (3) or the irreversible loss of consciousness (4) have no reservations about pronouncing death when the heart and lungs have ceased to function. This is because they are willing to use loss of heart and lung activity as shortcut criteria for death, believing that once heart and lungs have stopped, the brain or neocortex will necessarily stop as well. (P. 53)

Reprinted with permission from *Death, Dying and the Biological Revolution* by Robert Veatch. Copyright © 1976 Yale University Press.

The point in distinguishing the levels of death is that the criteria we use to measure death should come from our concept of death. They should not come from our needs for organs for transplantations, nor from economic considerations. However, when we look at pieces of legislation concerning the definition of death, most are linked up to the need for organs.

Legislation and the Definition of Death

In 1970, Kansas was the first state to legislate a definition of death, as "a result of prodding from the transplanters" (Veatch, 1976, p. 63). The statute reads as follows:

A person will be considered medically and legally dead, if in the opinion of a physician, based on ordinary standards of medical practice, there is the absence of spontaneous respiratory and cardiac function, and because of the disease or condition which caused, directly or indirectly, these functions to cease, or because of the passage of time since these functions ceased, attempts at resuscitation are considered hopeless; and, in this event death will have occurred at the time these functions ceased; or

A person will be considered medically and legally dead if, in the opinion of a physician, based on ordinary standards of medical practice, there is the absence of spontaneous brain function, and if, based on ordinary standards of medical practice, during reasonable attempts to either maintain or restore spontaneous circulatory or respiratory function in the absence of aforesaid brain function, it appears that further attempts at resuscitation or supportive maintenance will not succeed, death will have occurred at the time when these conditions first coincide. Death is to be pronounced before artificial means of supporting respiratory and circulatory function are terminated and before any vital organ is removed for the purpose of transplantation.

These alternative definitions of death are to be utilized for all purposes in this state, including trials of civil and criminal cases, any laws to the contrary notwithstanding. (Kansas Session, Laws of 1970, Ch. 378)

This statute was strongly criticized for four reasons (Kennedy, 1971):

1. The Kansas act was drafted because of transplants, which might be considered "meddling with the donor for purposes of improving the transplant."
2. It has at least two points along the death continuum where someone may be considered dead.
3. It does not require at least two physicians' opinions.
4. No distinction is made between the physician attending to and/or certifying the death and the physician dealing with the transplant.

The law could result in there being two different groups of people— those whose organs are available for transplant and those whose organs are not—people who will be defined as dead in different ways.

Since the Kansas statute, 17 other states have enacted definition of death laws, many of which have taken into consideration the criticisms of the Kansas statute; for example, the California statute includes the provision that "there shall be independent confirmation of the death by another physician" (California Health and Safety Code §7180 [1974]).

A model statute would clearly define death, protect the rights of the dying, and make sure that duties "toward the living would not be exacted toward dead bodies" (Grisez & Boyle, 1979, pp. 78–79).

Capron and Kass (1972) propose a model statute: A person will be considered dead if in the announced opinion of a physician, based on ordinary standards of medical practice, he has experienced an irreversible cessation of spontaneous respiratory and circulatory functions. In the event that artificial means of support preclude a determination that these functions have ceased, a person will be considered dead if in the announced opinion of a physician, based on ordinary standards of medical practice, he has experienced an irreversible cessation of spontaneous brain functions. Death will have occurred at the time when the relevant functions ceased. (p. 111)

Veatch (1976) believes the following should be added in order to avoid any conflict of interest on the part of the physician, and to insure freedom of choice to the patient:

It is provided, however, that no person shall be considered dead even with the announced opinion of a physician solely on the basis of an irreversible cessation of spontaneous cerebral functions if he, while competent to make such a decision has explicitly rejected the use of this standard or, if he has not expressed himself on the matter while competent, his legal guardian or next of kin explicitly expresses such rejection.

It is further provided that no physician shall pronounce the death of any individual in any case where there is significant conflict of interest with his obligation to serve the patient (including commitment to any other patients, research, or teaching programs which might directly benefit from pronouncing the patient dead). (p. 76)

THE RIGHT TO REFUSE TREATMENT

The principle that adults have a right to refuse treatment was stated in 1914 by Judge Cardozo:

Every human being of adult years and sound mind has a right to determine what shall be done with his own body; and a surgeon who performs an operation without his patient's consent commits an assault, for which he is liable in damages. (As quoted in Grisez & Boyle, 1979, p. 88.)

This statement was reinforced in 1960 when the courts acknowledged the right of patients to informed consent (as quoted in Montange, 1974):

Anglo American law starts with the premise of thorough-going self determination. It follows that each man is considered to be master of his own body and he may, if he be of sound mind, expressly prohibit the performance of life-saving surgery, or other medical treatment. A doctor might well believe that an operation or form of treatment is desirable or necessary, but the law does not permit him to substitute his own judgment for that of the patient by any form of artifice or deception. (p. 1634)

Informed consent means that the patient must be told the risks involved in any treatment and that he or she must consent to the treatment for it to be implemented. Implicit in the principle of informed consent is the principle of informed refusal.

"The fact is that no competent patients have ever been forced to undergo medical treatment for their own good no matter how misguided their refusal may have appeared" (Veatch, 1976, pp. 117–118), except for the following reasons:

1. When medical treatment is required by law in the interests of public safety; for example, children must have a smallpox vaccination before beginning school.

2. When refusal to be treated would harm a patient's ability to care for his or her minor children. For example, in the *Application of the President and Directors of Georgetown College*, a 25-year-old female Jehovah's Witness, mother of a 7-month-old baby, was ordered to have a blood transfusion although the patient and her husband refused to authorize the treatment. The judge authorized the transfusion since the state was preventing the "ultimate abandonment" of a child by its parents (Cantor, 1972).

3. When a patient is "willing to be coerced"; that is, although the patient's religion may forbid a treatment, the patient would not resist treatment. This occurred in the case of *Powell v. Columbian* [sic] *Presbyterian Medical Center*. Mrs. Willie Mae Powell, a Jehovah's Witness, needed a blood transfusion after having a cesarean section. She did not object to the transfusion, but because of her religious beliefs she could not sign a consent form. The judge ordered the transfusion (Veatch, 1976, p. 156).

The loophole in the right to refuse treatment is that the adult must be "competent." Courts tended to rely on physicians' judgments as to what constitutes competency. The catch was that physicians would consider patients incompetent if they refused treatment. This, however, has been changing. In 1966, in a case in Washington, the court put forth a competency test: Can the patient understand the situation, the risks, and the alternatives? It does not matter whether the patient's choice is rational or not, as long as the patient is able to make a decision (Montange, 1974). A case in Massachusetts in 1979 came to the same conclusion. An elderly woman refused to have a gangrenous leg amputated despite the fact that refusing the amputation would lead to death. The court ruled that it was irrelevant that the patient's decision was irrational. What was relevant was that the patient was making a choice based on her own wishes and values ("Convincing the System, . . . " 1980).

CHILDREN AND REFUSAL OF TREATMENT

When a patient is a minor, the parents must authorize the treatment. If the physician (or others) disagrees with the parents' decision, the decision becomes subject to review. Veatch (1976, pp. 125–128) discusses situations in which the courts have been clear about upholding or not upholding the parents' choice. Where the child is not in danger of dying, the courts have made decisions based on the reasonableness of the parents' decision. Generally, if the omission of treatment would lead to the child being damaged, the court will override the parents' decision. There are, however, three acceptable reasons for refusing treatment: where the treatment carries substantial risk; where there is no clear need for treatment; and where the treatment can be delayed until the child can be consulted.

If a child is dying and can be restored to health through medical treatment, the courts will intervene. For example, blood transfusions have been ordered for children of Jehovah's Witnesses. Courts have decided that there is "no parental right to make martyrs of one's children" (Veatch, 1976, p. 125).

The Case of Chad Green

The case of Chad Green is one in which a court overturned parents' decision to withhold treatment. His story was presented by Marion Steinman (1978). In August 1977, Chad Green, a 20-month old boy, contracted acute lymphocytic leukemia, the most common form of childhood leukemia and the most curable. Chad Green was given intensive chemotherapy in Nebraska, where the family was living at the time, for a four-week period. The therapy was effective and Chad went into remission. However, the next stage of treatment involves injecting drugs into the spinal fluid and/or irradiating the brain. This protects against leukemic meningitis, since leukemic cells will invade the central nervous system, where drugs cannot reach them. The Greens decided to go to Massachusetts since Chad's grandparents lived there and because Massachusetts General Hospital did not do cranial radiation. In October 1977, Chad had his first injection into the spinal fluid. The Greens also put Chad on a nutritional program. They believed that the chemicals Chad was taking were poisoning his body, and that the nutritional program would counteract the chemicals. After the third injection, Chad needed another drug, which was to be given 10 times daily in injections for two consecutive weeks. The greens refused to give Chad this treatment. At the same time, Diana Green, without telling the physicians, stopped giving Chad the pills he had been taking. Therefore, all Chad was getting was the spinal injections. By December, Chad was totally off chemotherapy.

In February 1978, Chad again began showing symptoms of a relapse. The Greens, however, refused a bone marrow test and told the physicians that Chad was no longer on chemotherapy. On February 22, 1978, Dr. Truman, the physician in the case, petitioned Plymouth County Probate Court for the appointment of a temporary guardian who could consent to chemotherapy for Chad. The court allowed the petition, and two court-appointed guardians took Chad back for treatment. The same process began again: Chad had the bone marrow test, which showed acute lymphocytic leukemia. He went through the four-week intensive therapy; he went into remission; the spinal injections began. The Greens, however, were still against the chemotherapy, and on March 29th, the District Court in Higham ruled in favor of the Greens. This decision was overruled by the Superior Court, with whom the Massachusetts Supreme Court ultimately agreed. Meanwhile, in January 1979, the Greens went into exile in Tijuana, Mexico, after a warrant was issued for their arrest on a civil contempt charge. They treated Chad with laetrile and their nutritional program. On October 3, 1979, Chad Green, a 3-year-old leukemia victim, died in Mexico.

The Issue of Defective Infants

The law is not clear on the parent's right to refuse treatment for those infants who are born with defects, such as a spina bifida child or a child with Down's syndrome. Spina bifida is a congenital defect in which the two sides of the spinal column are not joined. It leads to nerve damage, paralysis, and possibly hydrocephalus, since there may be a blockage of the cerebrospinal fluid. Without treatment, the child may still die or may grow up severely retarded and suffer from paralysis from the waist down (Grisez & Boyle, 1979, p. 283). Children born with Down's syndrome often have other complications such as intestinal blockage, which must be treated for the child to survive.

There has been some argument that physicians and parents may be criminally liable if treatment is withheld from defective infants (Cantor, 1975; Robertson & Fost, 1976). In two cases, the courts ordered treatment. In one, a Maine judge ordered the implantation of a food tube in a baby's stomach, although the baby was severly deformed and would never regain full consciousness. In another case, a Long Island judge made an infant with Down's syndrome a temporary ward of the state so that an operation could be done to relieve an intestinal blockage (Cantor, 1975,p. 71).

However, "withholding treatment seems to have become a widespread, if not frequent event" (Robertson & Fost, 1976, p. 883). One survey of pediatricians in Massachusetts found that half would recommend withholding treatment for those children with Down's syndrome who have an intestinal blockage (Robertson, 1976). For children with spina bifida, physicians have selectively treated those children they felt would have the best chances of survival (Grisez & Boyle, 1979, pp. 153–154).

Anthony Shaw (1973), a pediatric surgeon, discusses a number of his cases where treatment was withheld. For example:

> Baby B was referred at the age of 36 hours with duodenal obstruction and signs of Down's syndrome. His young parents had a ten-year-old daughter and he was the son they had been trying to have for 10 years; yet, when they were approached with the operative consent, they hesitated. They wanted to know beyond any doubt whether the baby had Down's syndrome. If so, they wanted time to consider whether or not to permit the surgery to be done. Within 8 hours a geneticist was able to identify cells containing 47 chromosomes in a bone-marrow sample. Over the next 3 days the infant's gastrointestinal tract was decompressed with a nasogastric tube, and he was supported with intravenous fluids while the parents consulted with their ministers, with family physicians in their home community and with our geneticists. At the end of that time the B's decided not to permit surgery. The infant died 3 days later after withdrawal of supportive therapy. (p. 886)

The decision to withhold treatment from defective infants is generally made in terms of the "quality of life" the infant is likely to have. The problem is, as Grisez and Boyle (1979) point out: "The crux of the matter is that different people have different quality-of-life standards. No one is able to judge fairly what a day of life is worth to some other person. It would be arbitrary to accept quality-of-life standards as a basis for providing less protection for the lives of certain classes of individuals" (p. 259).

EUTHANASIA

"Euthanasia," which comes from Greek terms meaning "the good death," has come to encompass four different policies: (1) making the terminal stage as painless as possible, but not hastening death; (2) making the terminal stage as painless as possible, but condoning jeopardizing the patient's life in the process; (3) ceasing treatment; or (4) actively participating in ending the patient's life (Reiser, 1975, p. 31). Euthanasia may be applied to persons with painful, terminal diseases; to persons in irreversible comas; to infants who suffer from gross mental or physical defects; or to other defective persons such as the senile or the retarded.

The various connotations for the term *euthanasia* arise because of the various types of euthanasia. Major distinctions are between active and passive euthanasia; direct and indirect euthanasia; and voluntary and involuntary euthanasia.

Active and Passive Euthanasia

The major difference between active and passive euthanasia is that active euthanasia involves committing an act that would result in a person's death, whereas passive euthanasia involves omission of an act. Other terms for active and passive euthanasia are positive euthanasia and negative euthanasia, respectively. An example of active euthanasia occurred in 1973, when Lester Zygmaniak shot his brother George. George Zygmaniak had been in a motorcycle accident and was irreversibly paralyzed from the neck down. Lester Sygmaniak responded to George's pleas to be killed. An example of passive euthanasia occurs whenever a physician decides not to resuscitate a patient, or when a plug is pulled from a respirator.

Some ethicists see no difference between active and passive euthanasia. Rachels (1975) gives two cases that are exactly alike except that one involves killing and the other involves letting someone die:

> In the first, Smith stands to gain a large inheritance if anything should happen to his six-year-old cousin. One evening while the child is taking his bath, Smith sneaks into the bathroom and drowns the child, and then arranges things so that it will look like an accident.

> In the second, Jones also stands to gain if anything should happen to his six-year-old cousin. Like Smith, Jones sneaks in planning to drown the child in his bath. However, just as he enters the bathroom Jones sees the

child slip and hit his head, and fall face down in the water. Jones is delighted; he stands by, ready to push the child's head back under if it is necessary, but it is not necessary. With only a little thrashing about, the child drowns all by himself, "accidentally," as Jones watches and does nothing. (p. 79)

Obviously, in the preceding cases, omission and commission are both wrong. However, as Veatch (1967, p. 92) points out, these cases do not show that commission and omission are the same. They do show, however, that omission may be just as wrong as commission in some cases.

Joseph Fletcher (as discussed in Macguire, 1975) also sees the distinction between omission and commission as being very hazy: "What, morally, is the difference between doing nothing to keep the patient alive and giving a fatal dose of a painkilling or other lethal drug? The intention is the same, either way. A decision not to keep a patient alive is as morally deliberate as a decision to end a life" (p. 116).

Despite the fact that the outcomes and the motives for active and passive euthanasia may be the same, Maguire (1975) and Veatch (1976) discuss the differences:

1. They may differ in their psychological effects. Commission may lead to a great deal of guilt for the bereaved. However, omission may be just as hurtful to the bereaved if the memories of the dead person are of a long and painful illness.

2. Commission must be deliberate, whereas omission may result from not being able to make a decision.

3. In omission, the agency is diffuse. There is no one person who is responsible for the death. No one person is responsible for not administering the treatment.

4. The cause of death is different. As Ramsey (1970) points out: "In omission, no human agent causes the patient's death, directly or indirectly. He dies his own death from causes that it is no longer merciful or reasonable to fight by means of possible medical interventions" (p. 151).

5. The long-range effects on society may be different. There is a possibility that if we allow active killing of the dying, we may consequently allow active killing of others. This is know as the *wedge argument*. This argument has been applied to what occurred in Naxi Germany. Naxi Germany used the principle of euthanasia to kill the mentally ill and the "useless eaters" (Wilson, 1975, p. 35). In 1939, all state institutions had to submit reports on patients who had been unable to work the previous five years. Patients were then selected for eu-

thanasia. Children were handled by the Realms Committee for Scientific Approach to Severe Illness Due to Heredity and Constitution (Reiser, 1975, p. 43). Eventually, "euthanasia" was used to kill those races deemed inferior: the Jews, Poles, Russians, and Gypsies.

Hospital authorities make decisions concerning passive euthanasia regularly. This was highlighted when Massachusetts General Hospital specified formal policy about letting people die. All critically ill patients are classified as follows ("Helping the Dying Die," 1976):

- Class A: "Maximal therapeutic effort without reservation."
- Class B: Same as A but "with daily evaluation because probability of survival is questionable."
- Class C: "Selective limitation of therapeutic measures." In these cases, there might be orders not to resuscitate, a decision not to give antibiotics to cure pneumonia, and so on.
- Class D: "All therapy can be discontinued."
- Class D is generally only for patients with brain death or those who have no chance of regaining "cognitive and sapient life" (p. 1105).

Patients may be moved into different classes as their situations change.

The law makes distinctions between active and passive euthanasia. Legally, active euthanasia is absolutely prohibited since motive is no defense for killing. Table 6.2 presents the courts' decision in "mercy killings." Dr. Sander and Dr. Montemarano, claimed that their patients were already dead before they were injected with potassium chloride, in Dr. Montemarano's case, and with the air bubbles in the case of Dr. Sander. Both doctors, and the majority of the laymen, were acquitted, the laymen on the basis of temporary insanity.

Physicians also distinguish between active and passive euthanasia. The American Medical Association (AMA) House of Delegates adopted the following statement to serve as a guideline for physicians (1973):

The intentional termination of the life of one human being by another— mercy killing—is contrary to the policy of the American Medical Association.

The cessation of the employment of extraordinary means to prolong the life of the body when there is irrefutable evidence that biological death is imminent is the decision of the patient and/or his immediate family. The advice and judgment of the physician should be freely available to the patient and/or his immediate family.

Table 6.2. U.S. Court Decisions in Some Widely Publicized "Mercy-Killings"

First Degree Murder	Lesser Homicide	Acquitted	Acquitted on Grounds of Temporary Insanity	Refused to Indict
Roberts Michigan 1920 fixed poison for wife life imprisonment	*Repouille* New York 1939 chloroformed 13-year-old mongoloid son susp. 5–10 yr. sentence	*Greenfield* New York 1939 Chloroformed 17-year-old imbecile son	*Braunsdorf* Michigan 1950 shot 29-year-old invalid daughter *Kirby* New York 1832 drowned 2 children	*Johnson* New York 1938 accused of suffocating cancer-stricken wife
Noxon Massachusetts 1943 electrocuted 6-month-old mongoloid son life imprisonment then life sentence then life parole	*Mohr* Pennsylvania 1950 killed blind & cancer-stricken brother 3–6 year sentence & $500 fine	*Haug* Pennsylvania 1947 indicted for drugging invalid mother	*Nagel* Arizona 1953 shot 28-year-old invalid daughter *Reichert* New York 1942 shot 26-year-old mental patient brother	*Reinecke* Illinois 1967 accused of strangling 74-year-old cancer-stricken wife

Dr. Sander
New Hampshire 1950 indicted for injecting air in vein of dying cancer patient

Werner
Illinois 1958 indicated for suffocating bedridden wife

Zygmaniak
New Jersey 1973 indicted for shooting paralyzed brother

Dr. Montemarano
New York 1973 accused of drugging dying cancer patient

Paight
Connecticut 1949 shot cancer-stricken father

Waskin
Illinois 1969 shot cancer-stricken mother

Reprinted with permission from *Freedom to Die* by O. Ruth Russell. Copyright © 1975 by Human Services Press, New York.

189

Direct and Indirect Euthanasia

Direct and indirect forms of euthanasia are similar to passive and active forms. The distinction between direct and indirect killing lies in whether or not death is the primary intention of the act. The major indirect form of euthanasia is the use of painkilling drugs. In order to lessen the suffering of the patient, greater and greater dosages of a painkiller may be administered. In doing so, however, death may be hastened. Since the primary intention in giving the medication was to lessen pain, the death would be indirect.

In a study of specialists in internal medicine, Deana Crane (1975) found that 43 percent of the physicians and 29 percent of the residents were willing to take the risk of inducing respiratory arrest in a terminal cancer patient by increasing the narcotics dosage.

Voluntary and Involuntary Euthanasia

Voluntary euthanasia refers to euthanasia with patient consent, while involuntary euthanasia does not involve the patient's consent. The arguments against voluntary euthanasia are that the patient may not be making a decision based on personal wishes, but may be consenting to relieve another's suffering; that people may be under a temporary depression when deciding; and that medication may induce confusion so that the person is unable to make a decision. The problem with voluntary euthanasia is that it is irrevocable (Kamisar, 1958). Once the decision is made and the treatment stopped, one cannot change one's mind.

However, proponents of voluntary euthanasia believe that a person has the right to decide whether or not to live, and that safeguards, such as requiring a period of time between the request for euthanasia and the act itself, should be included. As pointed out previously, most competent adults do have the right to refuse treatment.

What occurs when a patient is not in a position to refuse treatment, that is, when a patient is in a comatose state? The Living Will is a document that allows a person to specify what treatment, if any, he or she would want given certain conditions. The following is the Living Will distributed by Concern for Dying:

> To My Family, My Physician, My Lawyer, and All Others Whom It May Concern
>
> Death is as much a reality as birth, maturity and old age—it is the one certainty of life. If the time comes when I can no longer take part in de-

cisions for my own future, let this statement stand as an expression of my
wishes and directions, while I am still of sound mind.

If at such a time the situation should arise in which there is no reasonable
expectation of my recovery from extreme physical or mental disability, I
direct that I be allowed to die and not be kept alive by medications, artificial means or "heroic measures." I do, however, ask that medication be
mercifully administered to me to alleviate suffering even though this may
shorten my remaining life.

This statement is made after careful consideration and is in accordance
with my strong convictions and beliefs. I want the wishes and directions
here expressed carried out to the extent permitted by law. Insofar as they
are not legally enforceable, I hope that those to whom this Will is ad-
dressed will regard themselves as morally bound by these provisions.

"The Living Will" reprinted with permission from Concern for Dying, 250 West 57th Street,
New York, N.Y. 10107

Although not a legal document, the Living Will or a similar document has been passed by a number of state legislatures (see Table 6.3).
   Involuntary euthanasia involves those patients who are comatose but
who have written no living will. It may also pertain to those who are
not competent to make decisions. Two recent cases have aroused a
great deal of interest.

Karen Ann Quinlan. On April 15, 1975, Karen Ann Quinlan, a 21-
year-old woman, went into a coma. She was admitted to St. Clare's
Hospital in Denville, New Jersey, and was placed on a respirator. In
July, her father, Joseph Quinlan, signed a release to permit the physicians to turn off the respirator, which the physicians refused to do.
They felt that to turn off the respirator would be an act of homicide.
Joseph Quinlan then went to court to be appointed Karen Ann's
guardian "with the express power of authorizing discontinuance of all
extraordinary means of sustaining vital processes." Karen's parents argued that she would have wanted to be removed from the machine;
they reported that Karen Ann had discussed the fact that she would
not want to be kept alive at all costs. The judge of the Superior Court,
Judge Muir, decided in favor of the hospital. The judge argued that
Karen Ann Quinlan was still alive; she did not meet the Harvard criteria for brain death, and "there is a duty to continue the life assisting
apparatus, if within the treating physician's opinion it should be
done. . . . There is no constitutional right to die that can be asserted by
a parent for his incompetent adult child." He considered that to turn

Table 6.3. "Living Will" Legislation, also known as "Natural Death" or "Right-to-Die" Ac

State	Became Law	Time After Which Directive Must Be Reexecuted	Form Provided	Hospital and Physician Legally Protected Unless Negligent	Binding on Physician	Can Be Executed by Adult in Good Health	In Order to Be Binding, Must Be Reexecuted After Patient Becomes Terminal
Arkansas (Act 879)	July 1977	None	No	Yes	Same as New Mexico	Yes	No
California (A.B. 3060)	Jan. 1977	5 years	Yes	Yes	Yes, if directive signed 14 days after patient becomes terminal	Yes, but not binding unless patient is terminal	Yes
Idaho (S.B. 1164)	July 1977	5 years	Yes	Yes	Same as New Mexico (if patient is terminal and cannot communicate)	Same as California	Yes
Kansas (S 99)	April 1979	None	Suggested form	Yes	Yes	Yes	No
Nevada (A.B. 8)	July 1977	None	Yes	Yes	No	Yes	No (but directive is not binding at any time)
New Mexico (S.B. 16)	June 1977	None	No	Yes, but physician must show "reasonable care and judgment"	Yes, but no penalty if physician does not comply	Yes	No
North Carolina (S.B. 504)	July 1977	None	Yes	Physicians are protected; hospitals not specifically protected	No	Yes	Same as Nevada
Oregon (S.B. 438)	June 1977	5 years	Yes	Yes	Same as California	Same as California	Yes
Texas (S.B. 148)	Aug. 1977	5 years	Yes	Yes	Same as California	Same as California	Yes
Washington (H 264)	March 1979	None	Suggested form	Yes	No	Yes	No

Reprinted with permission from Concern for Dying, 250 West 57th St., New York, New York 10107.

Void While Patient Is Pregnant	Provides for an Agent to Act on Behalf of a Minor	Provides for "Ombudsman" for a Patient in a Skilled Nursing Facility	Provision for Revocation	Penalties for Hiding, Destroying, or Falsifying Directive or Revocation	Other Provisions
No	Yes	No	No	No	Physician need not determine validity. Physician need not certify illness as terminal except for minors and incompetent patients. Proxy may act for incompetent patient. Signer may request life-sustaining procedures.
Yes	No	Yes	Yes	Yes	Physician must determine validity of directive and witnesses. Concealing evidence of revocation constitutes murder. Directive must be placed in patient's medical record.
No	No	No	Yes	No	Physician need not determine validity. Only operative if patient is comatose or unable to communicate with physician. Specifically does not cover persons not signing directives.
Yes	No	No	Yes	Yes	Physician need not determine validity. Patient has responsibility of notifying physician of existence of document.
Yes	No	No	Yes	Yes	Physician need not determine validity. Directive must be placed in patient's medical record. Similar documents executed before law went into effect "have same effect" as directives executed under the law.
No	Yes	No	Yes	Yes	Physician need not determine validity. Court must certify agent's decision when minor is involved. Minor may counter agent's decision. Directive must be placed in patient's medical record or physician's case file.
No	No	No	Yes	No	Physician need not determine validity. Hospitals not specifically protected but can cite law as a defense. Clerk of court must validate directive. No age provisions. Brain death defined.
No	No	Yes	Yes	Yes	Physician need not determine validity. Directive must be placed in patient's medical record.
Yes	No	No	Yes	Yes	Basically the same as the California law except (1) physician need not determine validity and (2) no provision for ombudsman for patients in skilled nursing facilities.
Yes	No	No	Yes	Yes	Physician need not determine validity. Patient has responsibility of notifying physician of existence of document.

off the respirator would be an act of homicide. The Quinlans then appealed to the New Jersey Supreme Court, which overturned Judge Muir's ruling. One of the major concerns was the violation of Karen's right to privacy:

> We think that the State's interest contra weakens and the individual's right to privacy grows as the degree of bodily invasion increases and the prognosis dims. . . . It is for this reason that we determine that Karen's right of privacy may be asserted in her behalf, in this respect, by her guardian and family under the particular circumstances presented by this record. (Matter of Quinlan, 1976)

Judge Hughes of the Supreme Court decided that if there were no reasonable possibility of Karen ever becoming conscious, the life-support systems could be removed without any civil or criminal liability. Karen Ann Quinlan was then weaned from the respirator. At the writing of this book, she was still alive.

Joseph Saikewicz.   Joseph Saikewicz (as discussed by Grisez & Boyle, 1979, pp. 275–277) developed acute myeloblastic monocetic leukemia, which is considered incurable. However, chemotherapy is generally administered with the hope that the therapy will be successful and that the patient will go into remission. The treatment is painful, has serious side effects, and requires the patient's cooperation. Without the treatment, the patient will definitely die in a short time but will die painlessly. The difficulty with this case was that Mr. Saikewicz was a severely retarded, institutionalized 67-year-old. A guardian was appointed for Mr. Saikewicz. After investigating the situation, the guardian recommended that Mr. Saikewicz not be given chemotherapy. The recommendation was accepted by the probate court, but the judge also referred the case for review. The Supreme Court of Massachusetts approved the lower courts' decision on July 9, 1976. A full opinion was issued on November 28, 1977. Meanwhile, Mr. Saikewicz died on September 4, 1976. The decision to withhold treatment was not based on Mr. Saikewicz's incompetency. Rather, the court reaffirmed "that the noncompetent person has the same rights with respect to care as the competent person" (p. 275). The reason that treatment was withheld was that it would have led to a great deal of pain and disorientation for Mr. Saikewicz.

The decisions made in these two cases show that competency is not an issue in terms of euthanasia. It is the interests of the patient that are important. If competency were to become an issue in involuntary euthanasia, the wedge argument could then apply.

RELIGION AND EUTHANASIA

Catholicism, orthodox Judiasm, and orthodox Protestantism are opposed to any form of active euthanasia but allow forms of passive euthanasia.

Catholicism

The Catholic view of euthanasia was recently reaffirmed by Pope John Paul II. It was first stated by Pope Pius XII in 1957 in his *allocutio* to Italian anesthesists. Direct euthanasia is strictly forbidden. If self-administered, it is suicide, and if death is administered by another, it is homicide. Passive euthanasia is limited by the distinction between ordinary and extraordinaary procedures. Ordinary measures are always required to be applied to a patient; otherwise, it is morally the same as killing the patient. However, the exclusion of extraordinary treatments where there is no reasonable hope of recovery is acceptable. The difficulty with the distinction between ordinary treatment and extraordinary treatment is that these are relative terms. For example, mouth-to-mouth resuscitation was once considered an extraordinary procedure (Hendin, 1974, p. 18).

There are differences attached to the meanings of "extraordinary" and "ordinary." Paul Ramsey (1970) discusses three differences between the ways in which doctors and moralists would use these terms:

1. The physician is likely to make the distinction between customary versus unusual procedures without taking into account the medical history of the patient, as the moralist would.
2. To the moralist, the decision to stop extraordinary means is basically the same as starting them. For the physician, it is more difficult to stop a procedure, once it is begun.
3. Moralists would view the patient as a person and take that into account, while the physician would take a more narrow view.

Gerald Kelly (1958), a Catholic theologian, sees the differences between physicians' and moralists' definitions of "extraordinary" and "ordinary" in the following manner: Physicians would define "ordinary" measures as "standard, recognized, orthodox, or established medicines or procedures of that period, at that level of medical practice, and within the limits of availability. Extraordinary measures are fanciful, bizarre, experimental, incompletely established, unorthodox, or not recognized." Moralists define ordinary measures as "all medicines, treatments and operations which offer a reasonable hope of benefit without excessive pain, or other inconveniences, and extraordinary means offer no reasonable hope of benefit and are excessively expensive, painful and inconvenient" (p. 129).

The differences that Ramsey and Kelly discussed were evident in the case of Brother Joseph Charles Fox, a member of the Order of the Society of Mary. At the age of 83, Brother Fox suffered a heart attack during surgery for a hernia. He went into a coma and was placed on a respirator. His friend, Father Philip Eichner, asked the hospital authorities to take Brother Fox off the respirator, but they refused. Father Eichner took the hospital to court and used, as the basis of his testimony, the fact that when he and Brother Fox had discussed Pope Pius XII's *allocutio*, Brother Fox had stated that he did not want "extraordinary" means used. Father Eichner was defining the word as Kelly and Ramsey said the moralists would. The hospital authorities, however, did not see these measures as extraordinary; furthermore, they did not wish to stop a procedure once it had been started. (The Court granted the petition of Father Eichner on December 6, 1979; the District Attorney immediately appealed but lost his appeal on March 27, 1980; meanwhile, Brother Fox had died in January [Annas, 1980].)

Judaism

Judaism, too, does not sanction positive euthanasia. The biblical basis for this is found in the words of King David. A young survivor of a battle against the Philistines saw King Saul, who was in terrible pain from a wound. The King begged to be killed, and the survivor obeyed him. When David heard of this, he had the man executed, saying, "You have been convicted by the testimony of your own lips of having taken the life of God's anointed" (Silver, 1974, p. 121). However, during the Middle Ages, two types of euthanasia were practiced: it was believed that you could enable a dying person to die more quickly if you removed the pillow or if you placed the synagogue keys under the dying person's pillow. The former was prohibited by law in the fourteenth century; the latter was condemned as being magical (Wilson, 1975, p. 25).

In terms of passive euthanasia, the degree of acceptance is related to the orthodoxy of the theologian. The Orthodox tradition is best reflected by Rabbi Immanuel Jakobovits (1961) writing in the *Hebrew Medical Journal*: "Jewish law sanctions the withdrawal of any factor—whether extraneous to the patient himself or not—which may artificially delay his demise in the final phase" (p. 251). The final phase, however, refers to an individual being expected to live only three days or less. Conservative and Reform Jews would define passive euthanasia with fewer limitations on the prognosis of the dying individual (Hendin, 1974, p. 81).

Protestantism

Protestant theologians provide very different views on euthanasia. Karl Barth (as discussed in Wilson, 1975) believes that human life belongs solely to God, and that we cannot be certain that we are helping a patient when we allow him or her to die. Allowing a patient to die is as wrong as killing the patient. At the other end of the debate on euthanasia is Joseph Fletcher. Fletcher (1968) defines euthanasia as merciful release from incurable suffering. He feels that the decision for or against euthanasia must depend on the situation. It is not a question of passive versus active euthanasia, nor of using ordinary versus extraordinary measures. For Fletcher, the situation in which the dying person exists is the determining factor. Basically, he sees three positions that can be taken:

1. The absolutist view, which sees life as the highest good and death as the worst evil, and so would be against any form of euthanasia.
2. Stoic-indifference, which sees life as meaningless and assigns no value to life.
3. Pragmatic-situation ethic, in which life and death may both be considered good depending upon the specific circumstances. "In this view life, no more than any other thing or value, is good in itself but only by reason of the situation; and death, no more than any other evil, is evil in itself, but only by reason of the situation" (p. 365).

Hence, euthanasia is not inherently good or bad.

The Council for Christian Social Action of the United Church of Christ (1973) adopted a statement that falls between Barth and Fletcher. They believe that it is ethically and theologically proper to avoid artificial and/or painful prolongation of death, and for a person to executive a living will. If a person has not made his or her wishes known and death is certain, then artificial means should no longer be used to keep the patient alive. "We believe there comes a time in the course of an irreversible terminal illness when, in the interest of love, mercy and compassion, those who are caring for the patient should say 'enough'."

Arguments Opposing Euthanasia

Arguments against euthanasia generally involve the roles of God and humanity; the role of medicine; and the danger of abuse (Russell, 1975). The religious arguments are: (1) God, and only God, should decide when life should end; (2) the Sixth Commandment says "Thou shalt not kill"; and (3) suffering must be accepted as part of God's plan.

Fletcher (1979) disputes all three arguments: (1) If only God should decide when life ends, then it is also interference to prolong life through modern technology. (2) The translation of the Sixth Commandment is incorrect; it should be "Thou shall do no murder," which means that one should not unlawfully kill. Besides, those who justify war and capital punishment cannot condemn euthanasia on this basis. (3) We make decisions regarding when people should suffer. No one would use this argument to refrain from using anesthesia in a surgical procedure. "It is much more realistic to take as our regulative principle the rule that 'Blessed are the merciful, for they shall see mercy' " (p. 197).

The arguments involving the role of medicine include the following: (1) the Hippocratic Oath prohibits doctors from practicing euthanasia; (2) there is always the possibility of a mistaken diagnosis, or that a cure may be discovered; and (3) euthanasia would destroy the relationship between physician and patient (Russell, 1975, pp. 209–210).

Again, these arguments may be disputed. The Hippocratic Oath states the following:

> I will follow that method of treatment which, according to my ability and judgment I consider for the benefit of my patients, and abstain from whatever is deleterious and mischievous. I will give no deadly medicine to anyone if asked, nor suggest any such counsel.

The promise is to benefit the patients, not to prolong life. O. Ruth Russell (1975) points out that the clause concerning deadly medicine was put in to prohibit physicians from conspiring with politicians to kill their opponents (p. 209).

The chance of a mistaken diagnosis or a future cure is highly unlikely. In order to safeguard against the former, more than one medical opinion should be received. With regard to the latter, it is not likely that a cure could undo the damage that has taken place. Although the refutation of the argument seems to make sense, there have been cases, such as the following, that allow this argument against euthanasia to stand (*Newsweek*, 1975):

> Dr. Robert Glaser, president of the Kaiser Family Foundation in Palo Alto, California recalls a 70-year-old man with multiple myeloma, an incurable malignancy of the bone marrow, who seemed to be going progressively downhill. Physicians at a large medical center decided to administer only painkillers, and to keep the patient comfortable during his last days. They also referred him to a hospital nearer his home. But there a new doctor took over and decided to try another course of chemotherapy to treat the myeloma. As a result, the patient went into partial remission and has enjoyed another four years of a relatively active life. (p. 68)

If euthanasia were legalized with safeguards, patients might have more confidence in the doctor–patient relationship, since they would know that the physician would carry out their wishes.

Perhaps, though, the most difficult argument against euthanasia is that abuses might follow. Although proponents of euthanasia say that the wedge argument, discussed previously, is not pertinent to American society, that "as long as we have a free society in which policies are openly discussed and legislation arrived at by democratic processes, there is no need to have such fears" (Russell, 1975, p. 214), the wedge argument cannot be totally dismissed. In a study of 570 college students, conducted by Helge Mansson (1972), 326 approved a project to kill the "unfit" as a solution to the problems of overpopulation and personal misery.

The major argument for euthanasia is that everyone has a basic right to die with dignity, that to force people to suffer is both degrading and cruel (Flew, 1969). Yet as Ramsey (1970) points out, can there be death with dignity?

SUMMARY

This chapter has looked at three ethical issues surrounding death: the definition of death, the right to refuse treatment, and euthanasia. Brain death as determined by the Harvard criteria is beginning to be the standard definition. One must be sure that the criteria for determining death stems from one's concept of death.

With regard to refusing treatment, most competent adults have a legal right to do so. The right of parents to refuse treatment for children has been decided on the basis of the reasonableness of the decision.

In order to study euthanasia, one must define the type of euthanasia that is meant: active or passive euthanasia, direct or indirect, voluntary or involuntary. Legislation, medicine, and religion make a large distinction between active and passive euthanasia. Further distinction is made between the use of ordinary and extraordinary measures. There are very clear cut arguments for or against euthanasia. As with most complex moral issues, both the pros and cons are significant.

LEARNING EXERCISES

1. Write your own living will.
2. If you were terminally ill with acute myeloblastic monocetic leukemia, the same disease that Joseph Sackewicz had, would you undergo chemotherapy? Discuss your decision.
3. Speak to your physician about the ethical issues discussed here. Do you and your physician agree on these issues? How do you feel this discussion will affect your relationship?
4. Design a model statute for a definition of death.

AUDIOVISUAL MATERIAL

The Right to Die. 56 min/color/1974. McMillan Films.
   A television news documentary that explores extraordinary treatment in terminal cases, the right of the terminally ill to commit suicide, and mercy killing.

Whose Life Is It Anyway? 53 min/color/1975. Eccentric Circle Cinema Workshop, University of California Extension Media Center, Concern for Dying.
   A young sculptor, paralyzed in an accident, wishes to refuse treatment, although this will result in his death. The film depicts various professionals' attitudes toward the sculptor's wishes.

Who Should Survive? 26 min/color/1972. University of California Extension Media Center.
   The film deals with the birth of a child with Down's syndrome and what happens when the parents refuse life-saving surgery. It raises issues of passive versus active euthanasia, the right to refuse treatment for minors, and staff reactions to the experience.

The Right to Live: Who Decides? 15 min/color/1972. University of Arizona Bureau of AV Services.
Our values concerning who should live and who should die are dramatically portrayed in these excerpts from the film *Abandon Ship* with Tyrone Power.

REFERENCES

Alexander, M. The rigid embrace of the Narrow House: Premature burial and the signs of death. *Hastings Center Report*, June 1980, *10*, 25–31.

American Medical Association. *The physician and the dying patient.* Report of the Judicial Council, 1973.

Annas, G. Quinlan, Saikewicz and Brother Fox. *Hastings Center Report*, June 1980, *10*, 20–21.

Black, P. McL. Definitions of brain death. In T. Beauchamp & S. Perlin (Eds.), *Ethical issues in death and dying*. Englewood Cliffs, N.J.: Prentice-Hall, 1978.

Brierley, J. B., Adams, J. H., Graham, D. L., & Simpson, M. Neocortical death after cardiac arrest. *Lancet*, September 11, 1971, 560–565.

Cantor, N. L. A patient's decision to decline life-saving medical treatment: Bodily integrity vs. the preservation of life. *Rutgers Law Review*, Winter 1972, *26*, 228–264.

Cantor, N. L. Law and the termination of an incompetent patient's life-preserving care. In J. Behake & S. Bok (Eds.), *The dilemmas of euthanasia*. Garden City, N.Y.: Anchor Press, 1975.

Capron, A., & Kass, L. A statutory definition of the standards for determining human death: An appraisal and a proposal. *University of Pennsylvania Law Review*, November 1972, *121*, 87–118.

Convincing the system to leave you alone. *Concern for Dying*, Winter 1980, *6*, 2–6.

Council for Christian Social Action, United Church of Christ. *The right to die*. Washington, D.C., February 17, 1973.

Crane, D. Physicians' attitudes toward the treatment of critically ill patients. In J. Behake & S. Bok (Eds.), *The dilemmas of euthanasia*. Garden City, N.Y.: Anchor Press, 1975.

Fletcher, J. Elective death. In E. F. Torey (Ed.), *Ethical issues in medicine*. Boston: Little, Brown, 1968.

Fletcher, J. *Morals and medicine*. Princeton, N.J.: Princeton University Press, 1979.

Flew, A. The principle of euthanasia. In A. G. Downing (Ed.), *Euthanasia and the right to die*. London: Peter Owen, 1969.

Glaser, R. Innovations and heroic acts in prolonging life. In O. Brim, H. Freeman, S. Levine, & N. Scotch (Eds.), *The dying patient*. New York: Russell Sage Foundation, 1970.

Grisez, G., & Boyle, J. *Life and death with liberty and justice*. Notre Dame, Ind.: University of Notre Dame Press, 1979.

Harvard Medical School, Ad Hoc Committee of the Harvard Medical School to Examine the Definition of Brain Death. A definition of irreversible coma. *Journal of the American Medical Association*, August 5, 1968, *205*, 337–340.

Helping the dying die: Two Harvard hospitals go public with policies. *Science*, September 17, 1976, *193*, 1105–1106.

Hendin, D. *Death as a fact of life*. New York: Warner Paperback, 1974.

Jakobovits, I. The dying and the treatment under Jewish law. *Hebrew Medical Jurnal*, 1961, *2*, 126–152.

Kamisar, Y. Some non-religious views against proposed mercy-killing legislation. *Minnesota Law Review*, May 1958, *42*, 969–1042.

Kass, L. Death as an event: A commentary on Robert Morrison. *Science*, August 20, 1971, *173*, 698–702.

Kelly, G. *Medico-moral problems*. St. Louis, Mo.: Catholic Hospital Association, 1958.

Kennedy, I. The Kansas statute on death—an appraisal. *New England Journal of Medicine*, 1971, *285*, 946–950.

Maguire, D. *Death by choice*. New York: Schocken Books, 1975.

Mansson, H. Justifying the final solution. *Omega*, 1972, *3*, 79–87.

Matter of Quinlan, 70 N.J. 10, 355 A 2nd 647 (1976).

Montange, C. Informed consent and the dying patient. *Yale Law Journal*, July 1974, *83*, 1632–1664.

Morison, R. Death—Process or event? *Science*, August 20, 1971, *173*, 694–698.

Newsweek, November 3, 1975, *86*, 68.

Rachels, J. Active and passive euthanasia. *New England Journal of Medicine*, January 9, 1975, *292*, 78–80.

Ramsey, P. *The patient as a person*. New Haven, Conn.: Yale University Press, 1970.

Reiser, S. The dilemma of euthanasia in modern medical history: The English and American experience. In J. Behake & S. Bok (Eds.), *The dilemmas of euthanasia*. Garden City, N.Y.: Anchor Press, 1975.

Robertson, J. Discretionary non-treatment of defective newborns. In A. Melunsky & G. Annas (Eds.), *Genetics and the law*. New York: Plenum Press, 1976.

Robertson, J., & Fost, N. Passive euthanasia of defective newborn infants: Legal and moral considerations. *Journal of Pediatrics*, 1976, *88*, 883–889.

Russell, O. R. *Freedom to die*. New York: Human Sciences Press, 1975.

Shaw, A. Dilemmas of informed consent in children. *New England Journal of Medicine*, October 25, 1973, *289*, 885–890.

Silver, D. The right to die? In J. Reimer (Ed.), *Jewish reflections on death*. New York: Schocken Books, 1974.

Steinman, M. A child's fight for life: Parents vs. doctor. *New York Times Magazine,* December 10, 1978, *160*.

Veatch, R. *Death, dying and the biological revolution*. New Haven, Conn.: Yale University Press, 1976.

Wilson, J. *Death by decision*. Philadelphia: Westminster Press, 1975.

7

Suicide

The phenomenon of suicide has existed throughout civilization. Attitudes toward this type of behavior have fluctuated, but the notion that any individual would voluntarily choose self-destruction has never been totally accepted by society. Death by suicide remains an enigma and a paradox.

In this chapter we discuss demographic data related to suicide, the different theories of suicide, the current emphasis on suicide prevention, the impact of suicide on surviving families and friends, and the health care professional's response to suicide.

DEMOGRAPHIC DATA

The suicide rate in the United States is 12.6 per 100,000; it currently ranks as one of the 10 leading causes of death. The variables associated with suicide include age, sex, race, marital status, and socioeconomic level. Suicide rates gradually rise during adolescence, increase sharply in early adulthood, and parallel advancing age up to the age bracket 75 to 84, when it reaches a rate of 27.9 suicides per 100,000 (Kastenbaum & Aisenberg, 1976, p. 211). Male suicides outnumber female suicides at a ratio of three to one. More whites than nonwhites commit suicide. Suicide is more prevalent among the single, widowed, separated, and divorced. It is generally presumed that suicide rates are highest at both extremes of the socioeconomic ladder.

These statistics, however, can be misleading. The suicide rate in young people has risen sharply since the 1950s. In 1954 the suicide rate for the age group 15 to 24 was 4.2 per 100,000; in 1974 it rose to

10.9 (Klagsbrun, 1976, p. 17). The reasons for this are multiple and complex. Adolescence marks the transition into adulthood; it is tumultuous. Researchers suggest that the fragmentation of family life, the shifts in cultural mores, the pressures of parents with high expectations, and the myth of happiness contribute significantly. Klagsbrun (1976) refers to this rapid increase as the "hidden epidemic" in our society. Amongst this age group, college students were reported to have suicide rates of from 15 to 20 per 100,000 students each year. In a new survey, Schwartz and Reifler (1980) challenge these figures and indicate that their findings suggest a rate of only 7 per 100,000 per year.

The suicide rate for nonwhites has also increased significantly. Woodford (1965) suggests that since 1946 the suicide rate of blacks has doubled. He attributes this increase to the Black Movement and its concomitant increased opportunity for mobility, role shifts, and social stress. Professor Robert Davis's research at the Institute for Research on Poverty at the University of Wisconsin–Madison also supports Woodford's findings.Davis (1979) reports that (1) the suicide rate for 15 to 19-year-old nonwhite females exceeds that of white females; (2) for blacks males, ages 20 to 24, it equals or surpasses that of white males; (3) for nonwhite males and females, ages 15 to 34, the suicide rate is higher than it has been in more than 50 years; (4) for blacks between the ages of 15 and 24, it is higher than for the total black population; and (5) suicide among blacks peaks between ages 25 and 34 (p. 3). He expresses concern that "suicide and other forms of life-threatening behavior have become an acceptable behavior form for young blacks; that in fact, a role model that was not acceptable in the past is now so; that maybe young black people are accepting self-destruction as an acceptable form of coping" (p. 3).

Although the overall suicide rate for American Indians parallels the national average, at some reservations it ranges from five to ten times the national average (Resnik & Dizmong, 1977, p. 217). Most American Indian suicides occur from adolesence through early adulthood. The young American Indian is thwarted in the search for identity, autonomy, and independence by a society that produces conflicting values between reservation life and mainstream America. Resnik and Dizmong (1977) conclude that the American Indian adolescent copes "frequently with suicide; with alcoholism; with violence, even homicide; with reckless driving; with victim-precipitated homicides. We do not believe this is necessarily specifically Indian; we believe it can apply to other minority group children" (p. 224).

Webb and Willard (1975) challenge the reported high suicide rates of American Indians. They suggest that Indian suicide has not been investigated from an ethnocentric perspective. They also question the validity of the research since it has been designed to demonstrate the need for a suicide program or to evaluate an existing program; findings could be distorted to satisfy research objectives.

It is difficult to evaluate the suicide rate among Spanish-speaking people in the United States. Suicide statistics classify people as "white," "black," or "other." Frederick and Lague (1972) report that in 1971 there were over 9 million Spanish-surnamed individuals in the United States of Mexican, Puerto Rican, and Latin American origin. They assume that since this population is faced with the same economic and identity problems as blacks and American Indians, their suicide rate is also increasing.

Dublin (1963) notes that Orientals have suicide rates that are comparable to, or higher than, those of white Americans (p. 35). Kastenbaum and Aisenberg (1976) attribute this finding to the Oriental Americans' relative ease in being assimilated into the American culture, an intact family structure, a higher socioeconomic class than other minority groups, and a traditional acceptance of suicide.

It is particularly interesting to note that among professionals, physicians have the highest suicide rate and teachers, the lowest (Dublin, 1963, p. 63). "The current annual suicide rate among American physicians removes from society a number equal to that of an average medical school graduating class" (Ross, 1973, p. 145). Ross (1973) reports that the physician suicide rate between 1965 and 1967 was 33 per 100,000, double that for white American males. The suicide rate for female physicians is even higher, at a rate of 40.5 per 100,000 and nearly four times that of the general female population over age 25. The medical subspecialty that has the highest rate of suicide is psychiatry. Blachly et al. (1968) made a comparison of the suicide rate of 16 medical specialties and found that pediatricians had the lowest rate, 10 per 100,000, and that psychiatrists had the highest rate, 61 per 100,000.

Medical students also have a higher incidence of suicide when compared to a reference population matched for age, sex, race, and residence. Wekstein (1979) struggles to explain this high incidence and notes:

> A hypothesis suggests itself that many aspirants for medical careers seek and attempt to achieve omniscience, omnipotence and virility by identifying themselves with the esteemed and exalted role of the physician. The attempt to achieve such goals is incompatible with reality and is doomed to failure. . . . The motivation to practice medicine in order to obtain magical powers that do not exist and are not inherent in any profession can lead to death-oriented behavior when the narcissistic bubble bursts. (p. 49)

Suicidologists, those people interested in the study of suicide, suicide prevention, and the phenomena of self-destruction, frequently object to the compilation of statistics. Klagsbrun (1976) believes that suicide, not death, is the last taboo topic in our society. This stigma leads to underreporting and "covering up" suicidal behavior. Carse and Dallery (1977) discuss the difficulty inherent in labeling a death a suicide. "No death will be declared a suicide unless it has been so determined by a coroner" (p. 191). Coroners frequently rely on information provided by police, physicians, and relatives. They also suggest that even when facts are not in question, there may be conflicting explanations. Wekstein (1979) notes "statistics on suicide are synthetic; that is, they are concocted products and their inaccuracy and unreliability are an open secret" (p. 58). Kastenbaum and Aisenberg (1976) also question the value of compiling demographic data: "If all of the interacting variables discussed are basic to suicide, then why do not all of those in the high risk group kill themselves? And what explains the occasional suicide of the young, married, middle-class Irish or Italian born Catholic girl?" (p. 231). These statistics provide some basic information about "who" but provide little insight into "why."

THEORIES OF SUICIDE

The motivation for suicide is perplexing and not yet resolved. Attempts to examine and explain the etiology of suicide fall into four general categories: (1) philosophical, (2) sociological, (3) psychoanalytic, and (4) preventionist.

Philosophical

Philosophers have not provided a specific theory of suicide. Their major contribution to the study of suicide has been their willingness to struggle with the issue of self-destructive behavior and the meaning of life and death. Choron (1972) believes that "philosophers seem to have been instrumental in bringing about the permissive and tolerant view of suicide that generally prevails today" (p. 107).

The current philosophical approach, existential suicide, is closely linked to the writings of Camus. He believed that suicide was the only serious philosophical question. For Camus (1955) life is absurd and meaningless. Paradoxically, this also means that death is absurd, and Camus opposes the temptation of suicide. The existential dilemma for the individual is to live in this "absurd state" where one is in constant confrontation with the world. "It is this revolt that gives life its value and confers majesty on it; it is essential to 'die unreconciled and not of one's free will' and to preserve to the bitter end one's integrity and pride" (Choron, 1972, p. 138). Many suicidologists disagree with Camus's premise and believe that lack of meaning in this life is a strong motivation for suicide.

Choron (1972) provides an excellent discussion of "Philosophers on Suicide," which is summarized in Table 7.1. It is particularly interesting to note Spinoza's rejection of a natural impulse to self-destruction, since this is diametrically opposed to Freud's assumption that it is a basic trait of the human psyche. Voltaire used a "sociological approach" and concluded that suicides occurred more frequently in urban areas because city dwellers were more prone to melancholia, because suicidal tendencies were inherited, and because some were

Table 7.1. Philosopher's Position on Suicide

Philosopher	Position on Suicide	Rationale
Pythagoras: 582 B.C.	Antisuicide	Belief that the individual must wait for God to release the soul.
Plato: 427–347 B.C.	Antisuicide	Suicide contradicts God's will—believed in the immortality of his true self.
Aristotle: 384–322 B.C.	Antisuicide	Suicide is a cowardly act; contrary to the "right rule of life."
Epicurus: 341–270 B.C.	Antisuicide	"Wise man neither seeks to escape life nor fears the cessation for neither does life offend him nor does the absence of life seem to be evil."
Greek Stoic: 200 B.C.	Neutral	Rational decision on which is preferable in any given situation.
Seneca: 3 B.C.–65 A.D.	Prosuicide	If you like life, live; if you don't, go back where you came from.
Epictetus: A.D. 60–132	Neutral	One can choose to "play or not play,"
Montaigne: 1533–1592	Prosuicide	Objected to Church's position; challenged the belief that only despair led to suicide.
Descartes: 1596–1650	Antisuicide	Belief that good in life always outweighs the bad; wanting to die is an error in judgment.

Table 7.1. *(Continued)*

Philosopher	Position on Suicide	Rationale
Spinoza: 1632–1677	Neutral	Denied human impulse for self-destruction; suicide is possible only from external pressures.
Voltaire: 1694–1778	Prosuicide	Cited psychological and sociological reasons.
Montesquieu: 1689–1755	Prosuicide	Individual right to choose suicide.
Rousseau: 1712–1778	Prosuicide	Suicide is humanity's natural right; God endowed us with reason and so suicide is "acceptable to God."
Hume: 1711–1776	Prosuicide	Suicide is neutral crime against God or humanity or society. "No one throws away his life as long as it is worth living."
Kant: 1724–1804	Antisuicide	Human duty is to self-preservation; therefore suicide is a vice.
Schopenhauer: 1788–1860	Ambivalent	Suicide is vain, foolish act but defends the right of the individual to suicide.
Nietzsche: 1844–1900	Prosuicide	To deprive people of the right to die is cruel; suicide is another way to reach "eternal return of the soma."
Hartmann: 1842–1906	Antisuicide	While life is undesirable, it is humanity's duty, through the intellect, to move toward "cosmic redemption," where mankind will decree its own distinction.

motivated by a desire for revenge. Choron (1972) observes: "These conclusions were widely accepted by subsequent students of suicide, and although the first three have been disregarded in recent times, the motive of revenge has been recognized and stressed" (p. 125).

Sociological

Emile Durkheim's study of suicide in 1897 attempted to understand suicidal behavior by examining social forces. He claimed that the high suicide rate at the close of the nineteenth century in Europe was related to particular factors in the environment. A major component of his thesis was the capacity of the individual to be adequately integrated into the prevailing social structures. He categorized (1951) four types of suicide: egoistic, where the individual feels alienated, has no specific ties, and is poorly integrated into society; altruistic, where the individual feels it is necessary and expected, and is overly integrated; anomic, where the individual experiences sudden shifts and a breakdown of social institutions, and where society is unable to provide adequate regulation; and fatalistic, where the individual experiences excessive regulation. Carter (1976) notes that a fifth category, egocentric suicide, has been suggested by George De Vos. Egocentric suicide places a greater emphasis on frustration and aggression in contrast to the loss and despair of egoistic suicide (Carter, 1976, p. 329).

Psychoanalytic

Suicide was the subject of the Vienna Psychoanalytic Society meeting in 1910. At that time Freud cautioned, "I have an impression that in spite of all the valuable material that has been brought before us, we have not reached a decision on the problem that interests us" (Wekstein, 1979, p. 5). Freud continued to question self-destructive behavior. "Mourning and Melancholia," published in 1917, dealt with the dynamics of depression and, in reconstructing the process, explained:

> An object-choice, an attachment of the libido to a particular person had at one time existed; then owing to a real slight or disappointment coming from this loved person, the object-relationship was shattered. The result was not the normal one of a withdrawal of libido from this object and a displacement of a new one . . . it was withdrawn into the ego. . . . Thus the shadow of the object fell upon the ego and the latter could henceforth be judged by a special agency, as though it were an object, the forsaken object. (p. 249)

He formulated the view that suicide was a form of aggression against an internalized love object. Since the person both loves and hates at the same time, this aggression is markedly ambivalent.

Karl Menninger elaborated on Freud's theory of aggression turned inward. He (1938) felt that any suicide is driven by three conscious or unconscious wishes: the wish to kill, the wish to be killed, and the wish to die. Psychoanalytically, suicide can be seen as murder in the 180th degree (Shneidman & Mandelkorn, 1967, p. 3). Menninger also discusses specific human behavior he labels chronic, focal, and organic suicides. These individuals continue to live in spite of a self-destructive lifestyle.

Hendin's (1965) study of suicide stresses that the psychodynamics of depression are insufficient to explain suicide. "The patient's attitudes and fantasies with regard to death and dying are extremely important in the motivation of suicide, whether or not depression is present" (Hendin, 1965, p. 185). These fantasies frequently view death as a gratification or a form of atonement. Feelings of dependency, loneliness, hopelessness, and alienation also contribute to the act of suicide. The psychoanalytic approach assumes that vicissitudes of instinctual drives and unconscious motivation give rise to suicidal behavior.

Preventionist

Shneidman, Farberow, and Litman are generally associated with analyzing suicide from a prevention perspective. The Suicide Prevention Center in Los Angeles was established in 1958 to "save lives, to integrate with other agencies within the community and to obtain systematically organized data that can be employed in research designs" (Farberow & Shneidman, 1965, p. 7). They concluded from research there that the majority of suicides have a recognizable presuicidal phase. In reconstructing events preceding a death by means of a "psychological autopsy" to help answer "why," "how," and "what," they have concluded that suicidal behavior is a form of communication. They coined the phrase, "a cry for help," to underscore "the messages of suffering and anguish and the pleas for response that are expressed by and contained within suicidal behaviors" (Farberow & Shneidman, 1965, p. xi).

Shneidman (1973) also believes that any suicide is colored with ambivalence—"to cut one's throat and cry for help in the same breath" (p. 82). His taxonomy of death-related behavior includes intentioned, unintentioned, and subintentioned death:

1. In intentioned death, the individual takes a direct active role in bringing about death. Intended suicide is subdivided into four categories. First, the "death-seeker" commits suicide "in such a manner that rescue is realistically unlikely or impossible" (Shneidman, 1973, p. 82). Second, the "death-initiator" believes death will occur soon and precipitates the event. Shneidman (1973) uses the example of "older hospitalized persons in the terminal stage of fatal illness . . . with remarkable and totally unexpected energy" who succeeded in killing themselves. Third, the "death-ignorer" believes that life will continue

in some other fashion. The final category is the "death-darer," the person who tempts fate by engaging in risky methods such as Russian roulette.

2. Unintentioned death occurs when the individual plays no significant role in precipitating death. Although one might assume that in this category, everyone would prefer not to die, Shneidman suggests that there are different attitudes. The "death-welcomer" is glad that death will occur; the "death-acceptor" is resigned to his or her fate; the "death-postponer" endeavors to forestall death; the "death-disdainer" does not believe death will occur; and the "death-fearer" is fearful and fights the notion of death.

3. "The subintentional death is one in which the person plays some partial, covert, subliminal or unconscious role in hastening his own demise" (Shneidman, 1973, p. 87). This category is the most provocative, for Shneidman contends that the individual allows suicide to occur and that this behavior is "unconscious." He (1976) identifies several types of behavior on a "continuum of expectation and possibility of death" (p. 89). The "death-darer" and the death-chancer play a game to court death with odds calculated in their favor. The "death-hastener" unconsciously brings about or exacerbates a physiological imbalance. The individual who has a destructive lifestyle, such as alcohol, drug, or dietary abuses, or who refuses to follow medical orders for a specific condition, is considered to be a death-hastener. A "death-facilitator" will passively make death easy. Shneidman cites unexpected deaths in hospitals and refers to the work of Weisman and Hackett (1961, 1962; Weisman, 1972) to support this category. The "death-capitulator" plays a psychological role, usually through fear, in terminating life. Voodoo deaths fall into this category. Finally, the "death-experimenter" lives on the brink of death, "usually by excessive use of alcohol or drugs— seemingly wishing a chronically altered, usually befogged state of consciousness" (Shneidman, 1973, p. 9). Wolfgang (1959) describes a form of suicide by murder. The individual purposively chooses a superior adversary and thus brings about his or her own death. Shneidman includes this "victim-precipitated" homicide as another form of subintentional death.

The issues regarding subintentional deaths for health care professionals and society at large are multiple. Do we accept these deaths as suicides? Are they preventable? What modality of intervention would be most effective?

Charmaz (1980) criticizes the preceding approaches because they tend to separate suicidal individuals from the context of their experience. "Ordinarily, suicide is taken to say something basic about only the individuals who commit it and perhaps their immediate social relationships, but not something basic about the society in which it takes place" (Charmaz, 1980, p. 235). She believes that the psychoanalytic view eliminates the individual's capacity to understand; that Durkheim's theory is only a preliminary set of ideas; and that the preventionist approach is a form of social control (pp. 241–249). She does not specifically find fault with Shneidman's approach, but expresses concern that "other suicide preventionists may apply their perspective more concretely and without the sensitivity of their progenitors" (p. 249). For her, the suicidal crisis is a crisis of self within a specific social structure. It is crucial to understand how the multiple variables are "subjectively experienced, acted upon and become a source of interaction with others" (p. 262). Suicidal individuals experience increasing social isolation as they experience hopelessness, helplessness, and failure.

Charmaz labels this the closed world of suicide and draws the analogy of Plath's (1975) metaphor of the bell jar. Charmaz's (1980) analysis is based on her conviction that our current values are still "built on the residue of the Protestant ethic with its underlying emphasis on individualism" (p. 254). She acknowledges being influenced by the Marxist critique of capitalist society, and points to a need for basic structural changes. Her discussion is thought-provoking and does define gaps and discrepancies in the current approach to suicide prevention. Systemic change is a slow process. In the meantime, the suicidal crisis requires immediate action. The health care practitioner feels compelled to act in the here and now. The life that is saved today is the life that matters.

SUICIDE PREVENTION

"Once every minute or even more often, someone in the United States kills himself or tries to kill himself with conscious intent. Sixty or seventy times every day these attempts succeed. In many instances they could have been prevented by some of the rest of us" (Menninger, 1957, p. vii). The zeitgeist of suicide today is prevention. Death by suicide often is perceived as "useless," "meaningless," and a "waste of a life." Intervention/prevention allows us to exercise some control over what ultimately will be an inevitable event. Although both Szasz (1971) and Hillman (1964) question the ethics involved in suicide prevention, there are sufficient data available to support the hypothesis that many suicidal individuals are glad to be "rescued." How can we assess whether a person is "suicidal"? Shneidman et al. (1965) prepared a fact and myth sheet to dispel the folklore or mythology of suicide:

Myth: People who talk about suicide won't commit suicide.

Fact: Suicide threats must be taken seriously. Seventy-five percent of people who commit suicide have given warnings of their intentions.

Myth: Suicide happens without warning.

Fact: Suicidal people give clues, warnings and indication of intent. Alertness to these clues is essential.

Myth: Improvement after a suicidal crisis means that the risk is over.

Fact: Most suicides occur within 90 days of the emotional crisis when the person appears to recover. Improvement is equated with increased energy. Physicians, relatives and others should be especially cautious and watchful.

Myth: Suicide and depression are synonymous.

Fact: There are other reasons for suicide. Depression does remain the best indication of potential suicide.

Myth: All suicidal persons are insane.

Fact: The majority of suicides are unhappy, temporarily overwhelmed. It is circular reasoning to say that suicide is an insane act, and therefore suicidal persons are insane.

Myth: Suicide is a single disease.

Fact: Suicide is expressed in various forms and shapes. An accurate taxonomy or classification has not yet been developed.

Myth: Suicide is immoral.

Fact: Behavior and customs are neither external nor universal.

Myth: Suicide can be controlled by legislation.

Fact: Legislation may have opposite effects: the person will be sure he'll be successful to escape punishment and after unsuccessful attempts will be fearful to seek help.

Myth: Suicide is inherited.

Fact: Suicide does not run in families.

Myth: Suicide is the "curse of the poor" or a "disease of the rich."

Fact: Suicide cuts across all strata—it is "democratic."

Myth: Suicidal people are fully committed to dying.

Fact: Most suicidal people are ambivalent. Intervention by proper assessment of distress signals can prevent suicide. (pp. 13–14)

What are the prodromal clues—the distress signals, the cues, the "cries for help"? Litman (1966) discusses the following:

1. Verbal communications—Statements may be direct: "I wish I were dead" or indirect: "How do you leave your body to medical school?"
2. Suicide attempts—In over one-third of suicide deaths there is a history of a previous attempt.
3. Symptomatic actions—People communicate by actions such as giving away important personal possessions, taking dare-devil chances, increasing alcohol and drug intake, and irregular work attendance.
4. Depression—Symptoms are psychological, physiological, and social such as loss of energy, loss of interest in usual pleasures, sleeplessness, loss of appetite, withdrawal from social life.
5. Treatment failures—Disabling illness, unresponse to treatment, diseases that impair respiration are more often associated with suicide.
6. Excessive reactions—Excessive emotional preoccupation with a specific condition such as pregnancy, obesity, or cancer.
7. Panic reactions—Sudden blind panic, such as after an automobile accident while rescuers attended his badly injured wife, her husband hanged himself. (pp. 169–170)

Shneidman (1965) suggests another approach to recognize prodromal clues:

1. Verbal.   Similar to Litman's.
2. Behavioral.   Suicide attempt or "dry run," putting one's affairs in order, giving away possessions (Litman's symptomatic actions).
3. Situational.   Anxiety prior to surgery, particularly mutilative surgery; family discord; financial worry.
4. Syndromatic.   These are specifically related to a medical or surgical hospital setting and include depression; disorientation; defiance (refuses treatment, is demanding, insists upon privileges, has a low frustration tolerance); dependence; and dissatisfaction (is very demanding, insists nothing is being done, threatens to leave against medical advice)

If these prodromal clues are present, it is important to evaluate the individual's suicidal potentiality. Litman (1965) suggests a tactful information-gathering series of questions going from the more general to the more specific. The following should be included in the assessment:

1. Suicide plan. Include queries about method, time, and place. Obviously, someone indicating having bought a gun to shoot him- or herself tomorrow is a high risk, as are people who set specific deadlines.
2. Severity of symptoms. Severe agitation, helplessness, combined with frantic need to do something; hopelessness that worsens when offered help.
3. Basic personality. Stable versus unstable; what type lifestyle?
4. Precipitating stress. Should be evaluated from the patient's viewpoint and can include loss of a spouse, employment, or health. Is it a special anniversary date? Although this may be taken lightly by someone evaluating stress, do not overlook the loss of a patient who may represent the person's only love object.
5. Resources. Physical, financial, and interpersonal assets.
6. Reaction of significant others. Are they supportive?

Intervention can be primary, secondary, and tertiary. In the primary stage, the assessment is made and appropriate action should be taken. If lethality is low, support from family, friends, and the like may be sufficient. High lethality requires referral to a mental health practitioner, mental health center, or crisis center. During this stage it is particularly important that the potential suicidal person is "heard." Statistics suggest that 75 percent of completed suicides have visited a physician within six months of the suicide. Since the individual rarely reveals spontaneously that he or she is contemplating suicide, physicians should be aware of the prodromal clues of suicide and feel comfortable enough to question the patient. This obviously applies to nurses, social workers, clergy—the world at large. Frederick (1973) terms this first step of intervention "psychological first aid." After evaluation has been made, the caretaker should continue to be available to supply direct support, and to assist the suicidal individual in following through on appropriate recommendations.

In caring for the dying patient, statements such as "I can't go on" or "I wish this were over," or actions such as writing a will are more commonplace. They should not be ignored, however. Time should be taken to explore the intent of the communication. It frequently represents a "cry for help," a plea not to be abandoned and forgotten because of the terminal status.

Secondary intervention may include a variety of modalities, including individual or group therapy, electroconvulsive therapy, and hospitalization. A traditional practice in the hospital is to place a suicidal individual on 24-hour observation and to remove all potentially harmful objects. Carter (1976) questions the efficacy of this behavior, as "the ego of the depressed patient may be lowered further" (p. 340). She underscores the philosophy of suicide prevention centers—that "one must convey to the suicidal person that someone cares deeply" (p. 341).

Tertiary prevention or postvention takes place if a suicide has been completed; its intent is to enable the survivor-victims to cope.

IMPACT ON SURVIVORS

Shneidman (1973) believes that the largest public health problem is the "alleviation of the effects of stress in the survivor-victims of suicidal death" (p. 33). By extrapolation, Wekstein (1979) estimates that the total number of survivors is in excess of a quarter of a million (p. 41). Death by suicide is more traumatic and stigmatizing for survivors. They must deal with feelings of guilt, shame, anger, and ambiguity. The recent emphasis on suicides being "preventable" casts an additional burden, as survivors question "why" they were not able to prevent the act, or whether they "drove" the individual to suicide. Survivors also have to deal with the initial inquiry around the circumstances of the death, sometimes being "suspected of murder."

Charmaz (1980) analyzes the social responses to suicide that "set in motion a chain of destructive events" (p. 272). Stigma fosters the development of shame; survivors question their capability to have prevented the event; lack of social support heightens guilt and inhibits grief, which culminates in mourning being distorted and aborted. Children are particularly traumatized by the suicide of a parent. They feel rejected, abandoned, and responsible for the suicide. Families often respond to the stigma of suicide by creating a story for the children to explain the death. This family myth does not protect the child and contributes to further distortion.

For Cain (1977) the legacy of suicide includes reality distortion, tortued object-relations, guilt, disturbed self-concept, impotent rage, identification with the suicide, depression, and self-destructive search for meaning and incomplete mourning.He (1977) remarks that society "affords virtually no institutions or mechanisms for relieving the unique burdens bequeathed the suicide's bereaved" (p. 232). The newsletter *Thanatology Today* has received numerous requests for this type of resource but reports a "dearth of clinical materials." The September 1979 issue describes a program in Chicago sponsored by Catholic Charities. The program, entitled Living Outreach to Survivors (LOSS), uses a group approach for participants to help one another. LOSS is not limited to Catholics; "the whole social service approach of Catholic Charities is to serve everyone" (Rubey, 1979, p. 2).

Sharon Valente, RN, MN, and Corine Hatton, RN, MN, are working with families of suicides in the Los Angeles area at the Center for Health Sciences. They report that their program "has no funding" and they had not developed a free system based on ability to pay; "often various members are seeing other therapists and they are financially strapped at the time they need our group" (Valente, 1980, p. 2).

Shneidman (1973) describes the postvention work of Alfred Herzog in Philadelphia with parents of adolescent suicides. His work delineates three psychological stages of postvention care: (1) resuscitation—working with the family in the first 24 hours; (2) rehabilitation—consultation with the family for the first six months; and (3) renewal—tapering off of sessions and the mourning process from six months on (Shneidman, 1973, p. 34).

THE HEALTH CARE PROFESSIONAL'S RESPONSE TO SUICIDE

If suicide has such a devastating effect on family and friends, how is the health care team affected? Do they respond in a similar fashion? If so, are support systems available?

Research indicates that staff reaction to a patient's suicide is similar to that of family and friends. Litman (1965) interviewed over 200 therapists and concluded: "The reaction of therapists emphasized fears concerning blame, responsibility and inadequacy" (p. 574). Kayton and Freed (1967) believe that the initial response of staff "suggested a similarity to a traumatic neurosis" (p. 187).

Light (1972) did an analysis of psychiatrists' response to suicide based on his observed reactions to five suicides over a two-year period, a sample of 366 suicide cases, and the attitudinal studies of 80 to 100 therapists not directly involved in a suicide. He concluded that the psychiatrist experiences guilt, heightened love, loss, and anger. "Particularly evident may be a sense of betrayal grounded in the organization of the therapeutic work" (Light, 1972, p. 824). He incorporates his findings with those of Kayton and Freed (1967) and suggests three stages of response: (1) numbness and disbelief; (2) anger and grief mixed together; and (3) denial or sadness and dissipation of feelings over time.

Staff members all experience a sense of failure. Light (1972) believes that these feelings of failure are dissipated by "diagnostic talk" (going over notes to find clues and psychodynamic forces leading to the final act); "Professional talk" (determination of whether, when, and who made a mistake, and how improvements can be made); and the "suicide review" conducted several months after a patient has committed suicide. "The reviewer squarely placed the fault, but then excused it very kindly and said everyone is fallible" (Light, 1972, p. 834). The review serves as a mode to reaffirm the staff's sense of worth. Nurses and social workers also experience anxiety, increased sense of responsibility, and fear of participating in a catastrophe (Carter, 1976; Frederick, 1973; Heilig & Klugman, 1965).

Staff responds very differently to a suicide attempt or failed suicide. Weber (1973) reports a shift from concern to annoyance, anger, and disdain. Responses varied among nurses and physicians. Nurses responded positively to 50 percent of the suicide attemptors and hostilely or punitively to 5 percent. Physicians responded positively to 10 percent and hostilely or punitively to 30 percent. This study only represents a small sample of health care practitioners, but it is wise to bear in mind how our attitudes and values color our response to suicidal behavior.

SUMMARY

The preceding delineates in some small measure the complexity of suicide as a psycho-socio-dyadic, existential phenomenon and stresses the dimension of suicide as a public health problem. The etiology of suicidal behavior continues to elude us. Throughout history, societies have responded to suicide in cruel ways. Bodies of suicides have been dragged through the streets, impaled on stakes, left at public cross-roads, and refused burial. Suicides' property was confiscated. Although attitudes have changed considerably, there are contradictory data about the predominant attitude of society toward suicide today.

More research is needed to refine and define statistics related to suicidal behavior. The current emphasis on suicide prevention has not resulted in a decline in the suicide rate. In spite of the more than 200 prevention centers throughout the United States, rates continue at an all-time high. More education is required to sensitize everyone to "cries for help." This multidimensional issue requires an interdisciplinary approach that also includes significant others.

Health care practitioners should be alert to the needs of the survivor-victims. Survivors need the opportunity to express feelings in a nonjudgmental environment. Since the stigma of suicide often dominates responses to the survivor, special efforts should be made to identify and encourage environmental support. Caregivers must also be aware of their own attitudes and emotional responses to suicidal patients and to death by suicide.

Suicide prevention represents the last frontier where we can demonstrate to ourselves that death is preventable. We should always keep in mind that death is humanity's universal lot.

LEARNING EXERCISES

1. Is suicide ever justifiable? If so, under what conditions?
2. Role play with other members of the class what you might say to a friend who is indicating suicidal thoughts.
3. Read Sylvia Plath's *The Bell Jar*. If you had been a health professional consulted by Plath, how might you have intervened?
4 Find out what is available in your community for suicide prevention.

AUDIOVISUAL MATERIAL

Suicide Prevention in the Hospital. 30 min/black and white/1968. National Audio-Visual Center.

In the film, Dr. Norman Farberow discusses how to recognize and deal with suicidal patients in the hospital.

Suicide Prevention and Crisis Intervention: A Series of Case Histories. 25 to 35 min each/12 black and white/1972. Charles Press, Michigan State University.
A comprehensive series of films that include six interviews dramatizing several suicidal individuals. Emphasis is placed on practical issues and the response of health care workers, social workers, police, clergy, and teachers.

Ronny's Tune. 18 min/color/1978. Wombat Productions.
The complex responses by family members to a teenage son's suicide are dramatically portrayed.

Suicide: But Jack Was a Good Driver. 15 min/color/1974. CRM/McGraw-Hill Films.
By using the example of two teenagers dealing with their friend's possible suicide, the film provides a discussion of adolescents' attitudes toward suicide, identifies warning signals, and provides suggestions about relating to, and dealing with, individuals who are suicidal.

REFERENCES

Blachly, P. H., Deshar, W., & Roduner, G. Suicide by physicians. *Bulletin of Suicide*, December 1968, *1*(1).

Cain, A. Survivors of suicide. In S. Wilcox & M. Sutton (Eds.) *Understanding death and dying: An interdisciplinary approach.* Port Washington, N.Y.: Alfred Publishing, 1977.

Camus, A. *The myth of Sisyphus and other essays.* New York: Random House, 1955.

Carse, J., & Dallery, A. (Eds.). *Death and society: A book of readings and resources.* New York: Harcourt Brace Jovanovich, 1977.

Carter, F. M. *Psycho-social nursing* (2nd ed.). New York: Macmillan, 1976.

Charmaz, K. *The social reality of death.* Reading, Mass.: Addison-Wesley, 1980.

Choron, J. *Suicide.* New York: Scribner's, 1972.

Cresswell, P. Suicide: The stable rates argument. *Journal of Biosocial Science*, 1974, *6*, 151–161.

Davis, R. Sociologist views black suicides in the seventies. *Thanatology Today*, September 1979, *1*(6), 2–3.

Dublin, L. L. *Suicide: A sociological and statistical study.* New York: Ronald Press, 1963.

Durkheim, E. *Suicide.* New York: Free Press, 1951.

Farberow, N., & Shneidman, E. (Eds.). *The cry for help.* New York: McGraw-Hill, 1965.

Frederick, C. J. The role of the nurse in crisis intervention and suicide prevention. *Journal of Psychiatric Nursing,* January–February 1973, *11*, 24–31.

Frederick, C., & Lague, L. *Dealing with the crisis of suicide* (Public Affairs Pamphlet No. 406A). New York: Public Affairs Committee, October 1972.

Freud, S. Mourning and melancholia. In J. Strachey (Ed. and translator) *Standard edition of the complete psychological works of Freud* (Vol. 14). London: Hogarth Press, 1957.

Heilig, S., & Klugman, D. The social worker in a suicide prevention center. In H. Parad (Ed.), *Crisis intervention: Selected readings.* New York: Family Service Association of America, 1965.

Hendin, H. Suicide: Psychoanalytic point of view. In N. Farberow & S. Shneidman (Eds.), *The cry for help.* New York: McGraw-Hill, 1965.

Hillman, J. *Suicide and the soul.* New York: Harper & Row, 1964.

Kastenbaum, R., & Aisenberg, R. *The psychology of death.* New York: Springer, 1976.

Kayton, L., & Freed, H. Effects of suicide in a psychiatric hospital. *Archives of General Psychiatry,* August 1967, *17,* 184–194.

Klagsbrun, F. *Too young to die: Youth and suicide.* Boston: Houghton Mifflin, 1976.

Light, D. Psychiatry and suicide: The management of a mistake. *American Journal of Sociology,* 1972, *77*(5), 821–838.

Litman, R. When patients commit suicide. *American Journal of Psychotherapy,* 1965, *19*, 570–576.

Litman, R. E. Acutely suicidal patients: Management in general practice. *California Medicine,* March 1966, *104*, 168–174.

Menninger, K. *Man against himself.* New York: Harcourt Brace, 1938.

Menninger, K. Foreward. In E. S. Shneidman & N. Farberow (Eds.), *Clues to suicide.* New York: McGraw-Hill, 1957.

Plath, S. *The bell jar.* New York: Bantam Books, 1975.

Resnik, H. L. P., & Dizmong, L. H. Suicidal behavior among American Indians. In J. Carse & A. Dallery (Eds.), *Death and society.* New York: Harcourt Brace Jovanovich, 1977.

Ross, M., M.D. Suicide among physicians. *Diseases of the Nervous System,* March 1973, *34,* 145–150.

Rubey, Rev. C. Chicago Archdiocese aids survivors of young suicides. *Thanatology Today,* September 1979, *1*(6), 2.

Schwartz, A., & Reifler, C. College suicides overstated by half. *Thanatology Today,* August 1980, *2*(5), 4–5.

Shneidman, E. Preventing suicide. *American Journal of Nursing,* May 1965, *65*(5), 111–117.

Shneidman, E. *Deaths of man.* New York: Quadrangle, 1973.

Shneidman, E. S., & Farberow, N. (Eds.). *Clues to suicide.* New York: McGraw-Hill, 1957.

Shneidman, E., Farberow, N., & Litman, R. The suicide prevention center. In N. Farberow & E. Shneidman (Eds.), *The cry for help.* New York: McGraw-Hill, 1965.

Shneidman, E., & Mandelkorn, P. *Suicide—It doesn't have to happen* (American Association of Suicidology pamphlet). Los Angeles: Neuro-Psychiatry Institute, University of California, 1967.

Szasz, T. The ethics of suicide. *Antioch Review,* 1971, *31,* 7–17.

Valente, S. Suicides' families: Structures more normal than believed. *Thanatology Today,* March 1980, *1*(12), 2.

Webb, J., & Willard, W. Six American Indian patterns of suicide. In N. Farberow (Ed.), *Suicide in different cultures.* Baltimore, Md.: University Park Press, 1975.

Weber, T. Psychological reactions of emergency room staff to suicide attempters. *Omega,* 1973, *3,* 103–109.

Weisman, A. *On dying and denying.* New York: Behavioral Publications, 1972.

Weisman, A., & Hackett, T. Predilection to death. *Psychosomatic Medicine,* 1961, *23,* 232–256.

Weisman, A., & Hackett, T. The dying patient. *Forest Hospital Publications,* 1962, *1,* 16–21.

Wekstein, L. *Handbook of suicidology: Principles, problems and practice.* New York: Brunner/Mazel, 1979.

Wolfgang, M. E. Suicide by means of victim-precipitated homicide. *Journal of Clinical and Experimental Psychopathology*, 1959, *20*, 345–349.

Woodford, J. R. Why Negro suicides are increasing. *Pageant*, October 1965, 13–16.

8

Funerals

Funerals have existed since the beginning of mankind. Sixty thousand years ago, Neanderthals buried their dead with a ceremony (Fulton, 1976, p. 23). They have existed in some form in all societies. The funeral has been universally important for both the society and the individual. It is a rite of integration as well as separation (Fulton, 1979, pp. 249–253). The funeral serves to reinforce the integration of the community, the family, the religious group, and the ethnic group while helping the bereaved begin their separation from the deceased.

In the past 20 years, the funeral in American society has been under attack as a meaningless ritual involving extravagant expense. Major criticism has been aimed at the funeral industry. This chapter looks at the funeral in American society. Has it become meaningless? How has the funeral industry influenced the American funeral? What is the role of religion?

THE FUNCTIONS OF THE FUNERAL

Paul Irion (1966) asks whether the funeral today has value or is only a vestige of our history. Besides the overt or manifest function of disposing of the body, the funeral performs other more covert or latent functions both for the bereaved and for the society. For the individual, the funeral performs the following functions:

1. It increases the reality of death. One feeling at the beginning of grief is denial; that the person you love could not have died. As the final rite the funeral brings home the reality that death has occurred.

227

2. The funeral provides "consensual validation" for the mourner (Irion, 1976), since the mourner is joined by others who are also feeling the loss. Sanction is given to the expression of feelings, since the people gathered at the funeral share the same emotions to some degree. Furthermore, the tributes paid to the deceased, which emphasize the worth of the person, show the bereaved that the deceased is worthy of the pain that is being felt (Cassem, 1976).

3. In a common sense function, the funeral provides the bereaved with something to do (Cassem, 1976). It provides specific role behaviors so that the bereaved does not have to think about how he or she should act. The bereaved must meet with the funeral director, set up the funeral, and follow the appropriate ritual.

4. The funeral also provides the bereaved with support during the beginnings of grief by providing a network of relationships to which they may turn.

5. The funeral helps people gain a greater perspective on life and death. It is "a necessary series of interactions which help realize death, a social reality, and the promise that we, too, shall die" (Weissman, 1976, p. xv).

The funeral is important for the society because it performs the following functions:

1. The funeral reaffirms the cohesiveness of the family. The joke that people in a family only see each other at funerals stresses this function. It is a time when family members come together in a unit to partake in a ritual. By doing so, they demonstrate visibly the importance of family networks in the society while showing the bereaved that they are not alone.

2. The funeral acts as a mirror of the values and expectations we have of each other (Weissman, 1976). For example, in our society we value self-control, discipline, and self-reliance. At funerals, we admire those people who behave in this manner. Although it is appropriate to feel grief, it is inappropriate to become hysterical or to act without self-control, thus reaffirming certain values in the society.

3. A funeral may reinforce the social order. When well-known persons in positions of power or prestige die, the funeral may become a public event where the people in the society pay homage not only to the deceased but to the position he or she once held. When John F. Kennedy died, the American people participated in his funeral through television. This not only allowed us to mourn the man but also made us aware of the importance of the presidency. Funerals may fur-

ther reinforce the social order by varying with the class and or age of the deceased.

4. Funerals also reaffirm religious and ethnic identity. The majority of funerals are religious ceremonies; even those people who do not attend a church or synagogue often choose a religious ceremony for their death. Ethnic group identity is also important. For example, although the majority of Irish and Italian people are Roman Catholics, their funerals reflect ethnic differences. To an outside observer, an Italian wake and funeral seems a much more mournful event than an Irish wake and funeral, where there may be a great deal of drinking, eating, and talking.

5. Funerals serve as rites of passage. They are ceremonies marking the transition from one status to another status (Van Gennep, 1960). There are three phases: separation from the previous status, transition to the new status, and incorporation into the new status. It is a rite of passage both for the deceased and the bereaved. Separation between the deceased and the living is seen at the committal rites, where the deceased is buried. The transition stage occurs during the funeral; it is a way of maintaining a relationship with the deceased. After the funeral, there are rites to incorporate the newly deceased with the dead. This can occur in prayers said for the soul of the deceased. The funeral also serves to incorporate a bereaved spouse into the family and community, although he or she is assuming a new status as widower or widow.

A critique of funerals today is that they no longer have value. Yet as we look at the functions of the funeral, both societally and individually, we see how valid the funeral still is. Although the community may no longer totally participate in the funeral, family and friendship networks do. Funerals provide the bereaved with a sense of community while reestablishing the importance of primary networks to the larger community. Those who say that the funerals of yesterday were worth more because they were simpler and less extravagant are probably idealizing history.

THE HISTORY OF THE AMERICAN FUNERAL

Extravagance in funerals always existed in our country, except for a short time after the Pilgrims settled here. When the Puritans arrived in New England, the dead were buried with an absence of ceremony and a lack of emotion (Stannard, 1977, p. 103). Since the soul was already at its predestined fate, the body was thought of as meaningless. Funeral sermons were no different than other sermons, and were not delivered upon burial. No religious prayers were said for the deceased, for fear that praying for the deceased would lead people to believe the Catholic doctrine of purgatory, rather than the Puritan belief of pre-destination (Harmer, 1963, p. 70). However, according to Stannard (1977), this lack of ritual lasted for only about two decades. In 1649 the Boston Artillery officers requested

> one barrell and a halfe of the countryes store of powder to acknowledge Boston's great worthy dew love & respects to the late honoured Govner [John Winthrop], which they manifested in solemnizing his funerall. (Shurtleff; in Stannard, 1977, p. 110)

These cannons may have symbolized the beginning of extravagant funerals in New England.

For the Puritans in the latter half of the seventeenth century, funerals became very elaborate. The body of the deceased was washed and dressed, and the body was laid out in the home or in the church. Gloves were sent to those people who were invited to the funeral. (According to Harmer [1963, p. 70] one Boston minister collected 2,940 pairs of gloves in 30 years, which he then sold for a substantial sum.) The church bell was rung on the day of the funeral and the procession went to the burial ground, either with members of the procession carrying the coffin or having it carried on a hearse. It was important for the coffin to be properly lined and made of good wood. After the burial, a feast was held at the home or the church, at which time people were given gold funeral rings to mark their attendance. The funerals were obviously very costly; "even in the cases of the wealthiest individuals, it was not uncommon for funeral expenses to consume 20 percent of the deceased's estate" (Stannard, 1977, p. 113).

In order to control the giving of gloves and rings, which was becoming a financial burden, government regulations came into effect. In 1721, Massachusetts passed a "law which forbade the giving of scarves, gloves (except six pairs to the bearers and one pair to the minister), wine, rum and rings" (Harmer, 1963, p. 70).

In other colonies, such as New York and Virginia, funerals were just as extravagant if not more so:

> It is said that the obsequies of the first wife of Hon. Stephen Van Rensselaer (of Albany) cost twenty thousand dollars. Two thousand linen scarfs were given, and all the tenants were entertained for several days. (Earle, 1977, p. 34)

The poor also had elaborate funerals. The following is a list of expenses for the funeral of one Ryseck Swarb, which was taken care of by the church (Earle, 1977, p. 35):

	Guilders
3 dry boards for a coffin	7
3/4 lb. nails	1
Making coffin	24
Cartage	10
Half a vat & an anker of good beer	27
1 gallon rum	21
6 gallons madeira for women and men	84
Sugar and cruyery	5
150 sugar cakes	15
Tobacco and pipes	5
Grave digger	30
Use of pall	10
Wife Jan Lockermans	36
	275

After the American Revolution, funerals continued to be elaborate in the cities, although there were laws limiting the amount that could be spent. However, in the Western territories and in rural areas, funerals became more simple out of necessity. The family was a participant in the funeral ritual. The deceased was washed by the family and viewed in the home. The family wagon served as a hearse. This is the "ideal" funeral envisioned by those who tend to wish for the way things were. However, this occurred for only a proportion of the population and only lasted until the Civil War. The Civil War saw the development of the funeral industry as a business (Harmer, 1963, pp. 73–75).

During the Civil War, families of dead soldiers wanted them brought home for burial. This was an opportunity for embalmers to descend on the battle areas to preserve the remains of the deceased: "The war gave the opportunity for further experimentation, a measure of perfection in the process, and a foothold for a full-time vocation" (Bowman, 1959, p. 117). With embalming came an emphasis on the body for the funeral ritual.

At the same time, casket manufacturers began to create more sophisticated products. In 1848 Almond Fisk came up with a casket that would prevent putrefaction—a metallic burial case. The demand for this type of coffin led to its mass production. By 1889, there were 194 coffin factories. Gone was the small coffin shop and the demand on local cabinetmakers to make coffins (Harmer, 1963, pp. 91–92).

With increasing urbanization, it was no longer suitable to have the funeral in the home, since homes were getting smaller. Also, there was no place to embalm and "beautify" the body. Hence, the funeral home became the place to prepare the body, have the viewing, and even hold the funeral.

There was an attempt to beautify death. Flowers came into fashion at funerals, though they were strongly opposed. Flowers were viewed as pagan and wasteful. As Haberstein and Lamers (1955) point out, the opposition was to the extensive use of flowers.

Mouring cards became popular. These were cards given to friends at the funeral that expressed hopeful views of death such as the following:

"There is no death." What seems so is transition;
   This life of mortal breath
Is but the suburb of the life elysian,
   Whose portal we call death.

The Mourning Card of James Pelling; quoted in Haberstein and Lamers, 1955, p. 401

Today, it seems that we are combining the extravagance of the Colonial funeral and the beautification of the nineteenth-century funeral. The funeral generally costs a considerable amount, and it is considered important for the deceased to be presented as beautifully as possible. One major difference, however, in today's funerals is that the mourners are no longer active participants in the rites; instead, we are passive observers (making, perhaps, the rite of separation more difficult). All the details of the funeral are left up to the funeral directors, who are both overseers of the funeral and businessmen.

THE FUNERAL INDUSTRY

The funeral industry has generally been criticized for taking advantage of the bereaved. Jessica Mitford in 1963, in *The American Way of Death*, gives example after example of unethical funeral practices, where the bereaved are pressured into spending more than they can afford. In 1978, *The New York Times* found similar practices. They report the following case: In arranging his brother's funeral, a man wanted a plain pine box. The funeral director said that the box was not large enough, and the brother's legs would have to be cut off to make him fit into the box. The bereaved brother ended up purchasing a more expensive coffin (April 24, 1978, p. B9). This is an extreme example, but undertakers also do such things as saying that embalming is legally required (it is not) and charge amounts greater than those originally quoted. Spokesmen for the funeral industry agree that some unethical practices go on, but say that they occur in only a minority of cases, and that the number of complaints is small when compared with the more than 2 million funerals conducted every year.

The funeral industry is a $4 billion business (*New York Times*, 1978). There are 22,500 funeral homes ranging from small, family-owned homes to those owned by large conglomerates. An average funeral is expensive; costing $2,350 in an urban area of the Northeast (the cost is slightly lower in other parts of the country) (Consumers Union, 1977, p. 27).

Included in the funeral prices are removal of the body; use of the funeral home; embalming and restoration; the coffin; the use of a hearse and other limousines; arranging for the burial permit, death benefits, newspaper death notices, and religious services; arranging and caring for the flowers; and providing a guest register and acknowledgment cards. There are additional costs for the burial and vault (Consumers Union, 1977, p. 32).

How do funeral directors justify the expense? With 22,500 funeral homes and about 2 million deaths per year, each funeral home should do about 88 services per year. However, funerals are not equally distributed. Half of all funeral homes have less than 60 funerals per year (Consumers Union, 1977, p. 21). With the majority of funeral homes having such a small volume, the price of the funeral must be adequate to meet costs and show a profit. The two major expenses for funeral homes are overhead and personnel costs. In 1975, a funeral home and equipment cost $120,000 for a firm doing fewer than 100 funerals a year; they cost more than $600,000 for a home doing more than 300 funerals a year (Consumers Union, 1977, p. 18). It is considered important for a business to have an elegant, comfortable funeral home. One director told the authors how proud he was of his new funeral home, which had fireplaces in each of the viewing rooms and comfortable Colonial-style furniture. He also pointed out that his business tripled when he moved into the new funeral home. People apparently wanted to have funerals in an attractive setting.

Personnel, the major operating expense, may consist of any number of undertakers, receptionists, and managers, who must be on call 24 hours a day. The costs of an average funeral also must help pay for services provided for the indigent and for the credit extended to those who cannot pay immediately. The funeral director feels that he or she is performing a service for the community that very few want to do, preparing and taking care of the deceased's body.

According to the funeral directors' trade associations, there is very little profit in funerals. The National Funeral Directors Association (NFDA), representing 14,000 members, claims that the average profit per funeral in 1975 was only $53. The Federated Funeral Directors of America, having a membership of 1100, claim that the profit was $168 per funeral. The National Selected Morticians, a trade association with 860 members, sees the profit as only $44 per funeral (Consumers Union, 1977, pp. 18–19). It is interesting that the three major trade associations cannot agree on the amount of profit. Despite this low margin of profit, Service Corporation International, part of an international chain of 171 funeral homes, had a net income of over $4 million on gross revenues of less than $8 million (*New York Times*, April 23, 1978, p. 51).

Since the funeral industry is privately owned, why shouldn't funeral directors be allowed to maximize their profits, as in any other business? The funeral business is dealing with very vulnerable people. Funerals are often paid for by the elderly and by bereaved spouses, people least likely to be able to afford the expenses involved. Unlike other purchases, there is a lack of time for comparison shopping, and it seems that undertakers are unlikely to quote prices on the telephone (*New York Times*, April 28, 1973, p. 51). To comparison shop, one would have to go from funeral home to funeral home, a very difficult task when one is bereaved.

Yet, despite the imperfections of the funeral industry, clients are generally happy with the funeral director. The 68 widows and widowers studied by Glick, Weiss, and Parkes (1974) generally felt that the funeral director was supportive. Phyllis Silverman, who has worked extensively with widows, reported that widows found the funeral director to be more helpful than the physician or the clergyman (Dempsey, 1975, p. 173). In a study directed at finding out specifically how the bereaved felt about the funeral and the funeral director, Khlief (1975) consistently found that the bereaved thought highly of the funeral director, were satisfied with the funeral costs, and were happy with the presentation of the body.

Fulton's study (1965) of the attitudes of the American public had similar findings: most had positive attitudes toward the funeral director. Many of those with negative attitudes had little direct information about funerals. Fulton concludes that some of the anger we may feel toward the funeral director is anger toward death:

> The guilt generated by desire on the part of the bereaved to rid themselves quickly of the body and by the death itself, the possible confusion and anxiety in the selection of the "right" casket, and the attitude of the funeral director as the constant reminder and associate of death, prompt the public to lash out at him. (p. 101)

Funeral Costs

Funeral costs consist of six major parts: professional fees, the coffin, embalming, extras, the vault, and the cemetery (Consumers Union, 1977).

Professional Services.   This is an arbitrary fee generally in the range of $450 for the services of the funeral director. It includes arrangements and supervision of the funeral. Another service now being offered is grief therapy. There is disagreement as to whether the funeral director is trained to do this. *The New York Times* (April 25, 1978, p. 20) reviewed the catalogues of five schools of mortuary science: three schools required two psychology courses; one school required one such course; and one required only one course. Pine's study (1975) of 8,227 funeral directors found that 34 percent had a high school education or less; only 21 percent had completed college (p. 187). Funeral directors, however, "say they have a special insight into the trappings of death, a part of which comes from the ancient stigma to which they have been subjected as caretakers of the dead" (*New York Times*, April 25, 1978, p. 20). It must be noted that the funeral director is the one person to whom the bereaved may talk about the death. The physician and nurse do not have a responsibility to the bereaved, since their patient has died; and seeing a psychiatrist or a psychologist may carry with it a stigma for many bereaved. The funeral director becomes the only professional to whom the bereaved may turn.

The Coffin or Casket.   The price of the coffin will play a large part in determining the price of the funeral and the profits of the funeral director. Generally, the greater the price of the coffin, the higher the profit for the funeral director. There are many instances of funeral directors pressuring their customers into buying more expensive caskets than they intended:

> We'll take the $650 casket.
>
> Yes, but she *was* your mother. Surely something in a better casket would be more befitting her memory. Now this $800 casket. . . . (Consumers Union, 1977, p. 80)

But this salesmanship may be unnecessary since coffins may be arranged in the selection room so that the consumer will not purchase the cheapest one. Wilber Krieger developed the approach in his book *Successful Funeral Management* (as discussed in Consumers Union, 1977, pp. 72–75; and Mitfod, 1963, pp. 24–26). It is a method of arranging coffins so that the consumer will generally spend slightly above the average; the coffins are divided by price into four quartiles. In the "avenue of approach" are those caskets that sell for more than the median, in the third quartile; to the left is an aisle called "Resistance Lane," which has the cheapest caskets on the left and most expensive ones on the right. The contrast between the two sets is so great that the buyer usually ends up purchasing a casket for slightly above the average price. The "carefully planned strategy of the display room allows as much freedom of choice as a loaded gun" (Consumers Union, 1977, p. 74).

Embalming. Embalming involves replacing the blood of the deceased with formaldehyde in order to preserve the body. This allows the body to be displayed in an open coffin. Funeral directors claim that embalming is important since it protects against infectious diseases such as tuberculosis. However, this explanation is questioned by medical experts. Dr. Michael Baden, a medical examiner, stated the following:

> The unembalmed body is not a danger to living persons. There would be a danger of contracting tuberculosis from a dead body only if the funeral director cut into the body. If the body is not cut, there is no danger. It's much the same with hepatitis. There would have to be contact with open sores in order for there to be danger of infection. (*New York Times*, April 23, 1978, p. 51)

Another rationale for embalming and restoration is that it allows viewing of the body. Here, again, there is much debate as to whether this is psychologically helpful. Some thanatologists believe that viewing the body gives people a chance to say good-bye to the deceased. It is claimed that it also facilitates realization of the death, since the bereaved are seeing the deceased laid out in the coffin. Others believe that viewing the body places too much emphasis on a "lifeless shell" and not on who the person actually was. Since the goal of restoration is to make the deceased as lifelike as possible, viewing may actually postpone the reality of death. The findings of Parkes (1972, pp. 152–153) illustrate the debate. Eight widows viewed the corpses of their husbands. Three had unpleasant memories of it, while four were pleased. (One expressed no reaction.) They referred to how peaceful the corpse looked. Similar findings appeared in the study of Boston widows and widowers (Glick, Weiss, & Parkes, 1974). Half the widows and a quarter of the widowers were upset by viewing the corpse; the others were not.

Embalming is not mandated by state law except under certain circumstances—if the body is to be transported on a common carrier; and, in some states, if death occurs from a communicable disease or if burial does not take place within a certain time limit. Many states consider refrigeration an alternative to embalming.

One undisputed fact is that embalming is important for the funeral industry. It is not important in and of itself; embalming is not a major funeral cost. It is important because it permits viewing of the body, and all the extra expenses associated with it. One might also question whether people would buy cheaper coffins if there were no viewing.

Extras.   Extras include burial clothes, flowers, limousines, out-of-town transportation of the body—that is, anything that is not part of the casket, the embalming, or the cemetery. These items can add hundreds of dollars to the total.

Vaults.   Vaults are containers that enclose the coffin in the ground. They are not required by law, although they may be required by cemeteries since they keep the ground from collapsing when the coffin disintegrates. Vaults may be purchased either through the cemetery or the funeral director, though they are generally less expensive when purchased through the cemetery.

Cemetery Costs.   Cemetery expenses of about $1,000 include the plot itself, the grave marker, and opening and closing the burial plot. In 1977, Consumers Union found a modest earth burial cost $900—$250 for the plot, $250 for opening and closing the grave, and $400 for the monument. One alternative is to have the body placed in a crypt in a mausoleum. This may cost up to $2,000. Here, too, there are costs for opening and closing the crypt and for perpetual care.

The following is an actual bill for a funeral in 1973 in Westchester County, New York (Consumers Union, 1977, pp. 120–121):

Mahogany casket	$804
Enclosure, pine	85
Removal of body	25
Embalming	125
Preparation room use	20
Use of funeral home—two days	250
Arrangements, supervision	175
Use of hearse	53
Use of limousine	47

Mass of the Resurrection	60
Memorial prayer cards	14
Register book	5
Acknowledgement cards	13
Four pallbearers at $15	60
Death notice in newspaper	17
Twelve transcripts of death certificate at $2	24
Gratuities	8
Headstone	300
Two-plot grave	200
Opening grave	60
Blanket of roses	50
	$2395

The preceding was considered a modest funeral for the community.

Why do we spend so much on funerals? According to Pine and Phillips (1971), "monetary expenditures have taken on added importance as a means for allowing the bereaved to express (both to themselves and others) their sentiments for the deceased" (p. 138). Extravagance at funerals may be a way of assuaging guilt. As a widower quoted in Taylor (1979) remarked: "Her death left unfinished business between us and it comforted me to spend more than I could afford on the funeral" (p. 379). An expensive funeral is a way to communicate love; it may be an attempt to gain social status; or it may be another indication of our standard of living (Irion, 1966, pp. 55–56). As noted previously, one function of the funeral is to reinforce our values, and one of our values is consumption. How different is going into debt for a funeral from going into debt for a vacation or a car? It is the American way (Jackson, 1963, p. 85).

For those who wish to lower the costs of funerals, memorial societies help to provide an alternative. Memorial societies are nonprofit organizations formed by consumers that assist people in "achieving simplicity, dignity and economy" in their funerals. They do not conduct funerals but help people in arranging for them. Anyone may join a memorial society for a fee of about $15. Today there are 150 memorial societies serving over 750,000 members (*New York Times*, April 23, 1978, p. 51). According to Consumers Union (1977, pp. 214–219), there are three different types of memorial societies. A contract society has a contract with at least one undertaker to provide society members with funerals at less than regular costs; the undertaker makes a profit by having a higher volume. A cooperating society has an understanding between the undertaker and the society to provide lower-cost funerals, but there is no formal agreement. An advisory society acts as an information center.

Although making economic common sense of funerals has been the goal of memorial societies, they have not been accepted with total enthusiasm. There has been pressure from the funeral industry, calling memorial societies insensitive and unnecessary to the needs of the bereaved. Memorial societies have had difficulty reaching the poor, the group who could benefit most from using them. The societies are viewed as being for the upper- and middle-class professional. The major reason for the lack of enthusiasm is our avoidance of death. Joining a memorial society forces us to think about our own death and the deaths of those we love, and to plan for those deaths.

THE RELIGIOUS FUNERAL

Even though religion may not be as important in people's lives as it once was, it is still important in death. The nonreligious funeral is still in the minority. Each religion has its own structure and beliefs concerning death.

Catholicism

Although there are ethnic differences, the Roman Catholic funeral generally follows a specific ritual. The first part of the ritual, the wake, is the vigil before the funeral. Generally lasting two days, it is the time when the community, the bereaved's friends, and colleagues come to pay their respects. Flowers are sent and cards are left, announcing that prayers are being said for the deceased. The casket may be open or closed. In the evening, a priest will hold a wake service that will include prayers and readings from the Bible. The rosary may also be said.

The funeral is incorporated in the Mass. A procession by the family will bring the casket to the church from the funeral home. "The casket is covered with a white pall, symbolic of the white robe of baptism. The priest himself wears white vestments, emphasizing the joy of faith that overcomes the sadness of death" (Butler, 1974, p, 106). The paschal candle, representing the new life of Christ, is lighted and placed at the casket. The service consists of prayers, Bible readings, a homily that may include references to the deceased, the Eucharist prayer (which includes a celebration of Christ's death and resurrection, and an offering of the sacrifice), and Communion. A euology is not given. The rite of commendation ends the Mass, the last farewell before the body is buried.

The funeral procession proceeds to the cemetery, where a public committal rite is held. The family then returns home. A month after the death, a month's Mass is celebrated. Anniversary Masses are celebrated every year on the anniversary of the death.

For the dying, there is the ritual of anointing. Prior to the Second Vatican Council in 1973, extreme unction, or the last rites, were administered to those who were very near death. Today, the ritual of anointing is performed on anyone considered seriously ill. This allows both the dying person and the family to participate in the ritual. At death, the Viaticum (a special type of Communion) is given. If sudden death occurs, the priest leads the family in prayers.

Catholics believe in life after death. However, before entering the kingdom of heaven, the soul must be purified, and the mystery of love perfected in purgatory. The living offer prayers that the period in purgatory will not last too long, that the soul will not suffer greatly, and that God will take the soul to heaven. The funeral rites celebrate the passage from death to life and the deceased's entering "the fellowship of saints." (For further discussion, see Butler, 1974; and Nowell, 1972.)

Judaism

The Jewish system of mourning is based upon the halakah, a detailed system of law that specifies behavior after someone's death. When death occurs, immediate plans are made for burial. There is a tearing of the mourner's clothes, terrah, to symbolize the grief. Years ago, every Jewish community had its holy society, the Chevra Kadisha, whose charge it was to care for the body of the deceased and to prepare it for the funeral. Today, funeral directors have generally taken over these arrangements. The body is ritually cleansed so that it may enter God's presence in purity. Then, whether rich or poor, since in death all are equal before God, the body is dressed in a white linen shroud.

The presence of a casket at the funeral is required to emphasize the rite of separation. However, viewing is considered disrespectful. The funeral service generally takes place at the funeral home and is officiated by a rabbi. Appropriate psalms are said to give comfort to the bereaved and to glorify the dead. The prayer "El Molay Rachamim" is said, which asks God to have compassion on the soul of the deceased. "The euology of the dead (Hesped) is usually included in the service to recognize not only that a death has occurred but that a life has been lived" (Grollman, 1974, p. 126).

There is a procession to the cemetery where the burial service is ended. Kaddish, a prayer praising God and praying for the establishment of God's kingdom on earth, is said. The prayer of condolence is also recited: "May the Lord comfort you among all the other mourners of Zion and Jerusalem."

When the mourners arrive home, it is customary for them to wash their hands to ritually cleanse themselves. Neighbors and friends bring food, including hard-boiled eggs, which symbolize the continuation of life. The Shiva period begins; it lasts for seven days. As signs of mourning, the bereaved do not wear leather; they sit on low stools and cover all mirrors, so that they may not be concerned with vanity. A seven-day candle is lighted representing the soul of the deceased.

After Shiva, the bereaved may return to normal activity, but must avoid places of entertainment for 30 days. This ends the mourning period except when a parent has died. Then mourning proceeds through the following 11 months, during which Kaddish is said at daily services. Commemoration of the cemetery plaque is called the unveiling. It occurs after the 30 days of mourning but before the first anniversary of the death. Every year the anniversary of the death is commemorated by lighting a candle and reciting Kaddish. Memorial prayers are also said at synagogue four times per year: Yom Kippur, Shemini Atzeres, the eighth day of Passover, and the second day of Shavons.

Judaism does have a specific belief in the afterlife. Grollman (1974) discusses some concepts Jewish people have regarding death.

1. Death is inevitable.
2. The human spirit does not die: "Man is immortal; in body, through his children; in thought, through the survival of his memory; in influence, by virtue of the continuance of his personality as a force among those who come after him; and ideally, through the identification with the timeless things of spirit" (p. 131).
3. There is some belief that the soul will be rewarded or punished depending upon the life that was led.
4. The dead will be resurrected with the coming of the Messiah.
5. The soul may enter a new body and begin a new life.

Jewish people vary in their beliefs about the last three concepts:

> There are many thoughts, yet none is declared authoritative and final. The tradition teaches, but at the same time seems to say there is much we do not know and still more we have to learn. And even then, only God can completely discern the mysteries of life and death. (Grollman, 1974 p. 135)

(For further discussion, see Grollman, 1974; and Riemer, 1974.)

Protestantism

There are many differences among Protestants regarding funerals because of all the various denominations. In order to get a picture of the Protestant funeral, Irion (1966) sent a questionnaire to 160 ministers representing 10 major denominations. The following pattern emerged: After the body is prepared by the undertaker, it is first viewed by the family. Then there is public visitation, which may be a few hours or all afternoon and evening. The funeral is usually held on the afternoon of the third day after the death, in the chapel of the funeral home. One-third of the 2,000 funerals conducted by the ministers questioned by Irion took place in church. Scriptures are read and prayers are said. Generally the scripture passages reflected four themes: "the Christian hope for resurrection, the sustaining power of God, the Christian understanding of death, and the Christian understanding of life" (p. 16). Prayers involved intercession for the bereaved and thanksgiving to God. A funeral sermon is said that might include references to the deceased.

After the funeral service, there is a procession to the cemetery where a brief committal service is held to signify the breaking of ties with the dead. Then the bereaved return home. In some communities, a supper may be served by friends and neighbors. One alternative to the traditional service is the memorial service where the casket is not present.

Jordan (1974) presents a good discussion of the Protestant theology of death. As does the funeral ritual, Protestant theology varies from denomination to denomination, from a belief in no afterlife to a belief in reincarnation. However, most beliefs in an afterlife focus on resurrection and immortality. In resurrection, the being enters a new dimension of eternal life; in immortality, the soul continues its existence after death. There are also different views of heaven and hell. Hell is defined by some as a realm of everlasting torment; others do not believe in the existence of hell at all. Heaven is seen as involving communion with God, saints, and other persons in heaven. For some, heaven allows for spiritual development, while for others it is a place of passive rest.

Despite the variations, Jordan points out commonalities with which most Protestants agree:

- Death is a mystery, and we cannot fully comprehend the meanings surrounding death.
- Death is a corporate event in the fellowship of believers.
- The impact of death is realized and experienced in the community of

faith, and it calls forth the caring resources of the congregation to the bereaved.

- The religious resources and rituals of the faith group are significant to the bereaved in dealing with the death event. (p. 83)

ALTERNATIVES TO THE TRADITIONAL FUNERAL

Besides the traditional funeral and burial, there are three alternatives for disposition of the body: cremation, donation of the body to medical science, and cryonics.

Cremation

Cremation occurs after the funeral ritual unless there is direct cremation—an immediate disposition of the body. In the United States few people have chosen this alternative. Although cremation has existed throughout history, cremation did not develop in the United States until 1876, when the first American crematory was set up by a Washington physician, primarily for sanitary reasons. But cremation never really became popular. In 1976 only slightly more than 7 percent of the dead in the United States were cremated (Consumers Union, 1977, p. 157).

The body is cremated in the container in which it was brought to the crematory. This container may be a regular wooden casket, or it may be pressed wood or cardboard. Generally, the crematory requires a container made from an inflexible material. Once the body has been incinerated, the ashes of the bones are left. These cremated remains are placed in an urn or a special container, with special care taken that the ashes are properly labeled. Urns may be deposited in a columbarium, a structure attached to a crematory that has recesses in the walls for keeping the cremated remains; or the urns may be buried or kept on one's mantle.

Most religions in the United States do not oppose cremation, including most Protestant denominations. Although Roman Catholicism still favors burial, in 1963 Canon laws prohibiting cremation were rescinded. Cremation is allowed under the following conditions: if cremation is customary in a country; if there is danger of disease; if a grave site cannot be obtained that is suitable because of cost or distance; or if the law requires cremation, as it does in Japan (Consumers Union, 1977, p. 166). To be cremated one must obtain permission from the chancery office of the diocese.

244 • DEATH AND DYING

Orthodox Judaism prohibits cremation because of the belief in resurrection of the body with the coming of the Messiah. Conservative Judaism is also opposed to cremation, but permits the burial of cremated remains in a Jewish cemetery. Reform Judaism allows cremation.

Two advantages of cremation are that the remains take up less space, and that it can be cheaper than burial: a vault is not needed; a coffin is unnecessary, and there are no grave-opening and -closing fees. (However, the funeral service may still be expensive.) The disadvantages are that it is not as familiar a method of disposal, and it does not provide a site to go to in remembering the dead.

As Irion (1966) points out, though the values of cremation and burial may be the same:

> The rapid dissolution of the body indicates with considerable clarity that death has occurred, that relationships have been ended, that things can never again be as they have been in the past. (Pp. 207–208)

Donation of the Body to Science

Another choice is to leave one's body to medical science. The Uniform Anatomical Gift Act, approved in 1968 by the National Conference of Commissioners on Uniform State Laws, serves as the basis for legislation in all states for allowing people to leave their bodies, or any part thereof, to medical or dental schools without requiring permission of next of kin. The following is typical of the form that must be completed by a potential donor:

1. _____ , in the hope that I
    (Print or Type Your Name Here)

may help others, hereby make this anatomical gift, if medically acceptable, to take effect upon my death. I give my entire body for the purposes of transplantation, therapy, medical research or education. Signed by the donor and the following two witnesses in the presence of each other.

| _____ | _____ |
| Signature of Donor | Date of Birth of Donor |

1. _____ 2. _____
    Signature of Witness   Signature of Witness

| _____ | _____ |
| Address (Street and Number) | Address (Street and Number) |

| _____ | _____ |
| City, State and Zip Code | City, State and Zip Code |

There is no guarantee that the medical school will accept the body. Also, once the medical school is finished with the body, the final disposition must still be arranged, although the medical school will assume responsibility.

Except for Orthodox and Conservative Judaism, religions approve of donating one's body to a medical school.

CRYONICS

Cryonics or cryogenics is based on cryobiology, the science of life at low temperatures. Those who believe in cryonics are frozen once they are legally declared dead. The hope is that both a cure for the terminal illness and technology for thawing will be developed so that the deceased may come back to life and get well. The cryonics movement was inspired by Robert C. Ettinger, who published *Prospect of Immortality* in 1964. The idea is to "freeze–wait–reanimate."

Dempsey (1975) describes the process:

> Blood is drained from the veins; arteries and lungs are perfused with a glycerol fluid to retard cellular damage; and the patient is then wrapped in aluminum foil and stored, like frozen food, at a temperature of $-79°$ C. . . . A sealed capsule becomes what is hoped the temporary home of the "deceased." Temperature is further reduced to $-196°$ C through the use of liquid nitrogen; this ensures that no further cellular deterioration takes place. And here, in cryonic suspension, the patient awaits ultimate resurrection. (p. 189)

In 1975, 15 persons were in cryonic suspension. There are two reasons why it has not become popular. It is very expensive: to be frozen and cared for costs about $20,000 (Hendin, 1973, p. 171). Furthermore, few believe that cryonics will really work. What cryonics does symbolize is the ultimate denial of death.

SUMMARY

The value of the funeral ritual has been criticized, yet it still performs a number of valuable functions both for the individual and for society. The funeral has been criticized because it has become an extravagant affair. However, throughout our history, funerals have generally been extravagant. Today funeral costs include the funeral director's professional fees, the coffin, embalming, extras, the vault, and the cemetery plot. The funeral industry has been attacked for unethical practices, yet the bereaved tend to find the funeral director helpful.

Religion is still very important in terms of determining funeral ritual. Catholicism and Judaism both have very specific rituals, whereas Protestantism differs by denomination.

In addition to the standard funeral and burial, people may choose to dispose of their bodies through cremation, donation to medical science, or cryonics. However, relatively few people in the United States have chosen these alternatives.

One can summarize the chapter by saying that the funeral is not only a vestige of history but is also of contemporary value.

LEARNING EXERCISES

1. Speak to a clergyman about the funeral rites in his or her religion.
2. Call three funeral homes and ask about their prices. Were they willing to give you the information? How did the prices compare?
3. Debate whether the funeral is a vestige of the past or has present-day value.
4. Describe the type of funeral you would plan for yourself. Could you discuss this with members of your family? Why or why not?

AUDIOVISUAL MATERIAL

Religious Viewpoints on Death. Filmstrip with audiocassette/19. Educational Perspectives Associates. Program Number 3 of Dimensions of Death series.
The ritual in theology surrounding death is presented for three major religions—Catholicism, Judaism, Protestantism.
Since "The American Way of Death". 59 min/color videocassette. The Public Television Library Video Program Service.
The funeral industry is examined: how funeral directors are trained, the difficulties in getting a low-cost funeral, and the high cost of cremation.
Freeze: Wait: Re-Animate. 58 min/audiocassette. Pacifica Tape Library.
The cryonics movement is described, with a commentary by Isaac Asimov.
The Great American Funeral. 55 min/color videotape/1965. Mass Media Associates.

A critical analysis of the funeral industry that includes interviews with ministers, morticians, cemetery owners, people in ancillary industries, and Jessica Mitford.

REFERENCES

Bowman, L. *The American funeral*. Westport, Conn.: Greenwood Press, 1959.

Butler, R. The Roman Catholic way in death and mourning. In E. Grollman (Ed.), *Concerning death: A practical guide for the living*. Boston: Beacon Press, 1974.

Cassem, N. The first three steps beyond the grave. In V. Pine, A. Kutscher, D. Peretz, R. Slater, R. DeBellis, R. Volk, & D. Cherico (Eds.), *Acute grief and the funeral*. Springfield, Ill.: Charles C Thomas, 1976.

Consumers Union. *Funerals: Consumers' last rights*. New York: Norton, 1977.

Dempsey, D. *The way we die*. New York: McGraw-Hill, 1975.

Earle, A. M. Death ritual in colonial New York. In C. Jackson (Ed.), *Passing, the vision of death in America*. Westport, Conn.: Greenwood Press, 1977.

Ettinger, C. W. The prospect of immortality. New York: Doubleday, 1964.

Fulton, R. The sacred and the secular. In R. Fulton (Ed.), *Death and identity*. New York: John Wiley, 1965.

Fulton, R. The traditional funeral and contemporary society. In V. Pine, A. Kutscher, D. Peretz, R. Slater, R. DeBellis, R. Volk, & D. Chenico (Eds.), *Acute grief and the funeral*. Springfield, Ill.: Charles C Thomas, 1976.

Fulton, R. Death and the funeral in contemporary society. In H. Wass (Ed.), *Dying, facing the facts*. Washington, D.C.: Hemisphere, 1979.

Glick, I., Weiss, R., & Parkes, C. M. *The first year of bereavement*. New York: John Wiley, 1974.

Grollman, E. The Jewish way in death and mourning. In E. Grollman (Ed.), *Concerning death: A practical guide for the living*. Boston: Beacon Press, 1974.

Haberstein, R., & Lamers, W. *The history of American funeral directing.* Milwaukee, Wis.: Bulfin Printers, 1960.

Harmer, R. M. *The high cost of dying.* New York: Collier Books, 1963.

Hendin, D. *Death as a fact of life.* New York: Warner Books, 1973.

Irion, P. *The funeral: Vestige or value?* Nashville, Tenn.: Abingdon, 1966.

Irion, P. The funeral and the bereaved. In V. Pine, A. Kutscher, D. Peretz, R. Slater, R. DeBellis, R. Volk, & D. Cherico (Eds.), *Acute grief and the funeral.* Springfield, Ill.: Charles C Thomas, 1976.

Jackson, E. *For the living.* Des Moines, Iowa: Channel Press, 1963.

Jordan, M. The Protestant way in death and mourning. In E. Grollman (Ed.), *Concerning death: A practical guide to the living.* Boston: Beacon Press, 1974.

Khlief, B. Attitudes to the funeral, funeral director and funeral arrangements. In O. Margolis, H. Raether, & A. Kutscher (Eds.), *Grief and the meaning of the funeral.* New York: MSS Information, 1975.

Mitford, J. *The American way of death.* New York: Simon & Schuster, 1963.

New York Times, April 23, 1978, *1*, 51.

New York Times, April 24, 1978, *1*, B9.

New York Times, April 25, 1978, 20.

Nowell, R. *What a modern Catholic believes about death.* Chicago: Thomas More Press, 1972.

Parkes, C. M. *Bereavement.* New York: International Universities Press, 1972.

Pine, V. *Caretaker of the dead.* New York: Irvington Publishers, 1975.

Pine, V., & Phillips, D. The cost of dying: A sociological analysis of funeral expenditures. In F. Scott & R. Brewer (Eds.), *Confrontations of death.* Corvallis: Oregon State University, 1971.

Riemer, J. (Ed.). *Jewish reflections on death.* New York: Schocken Books, 1974.

Stannard, D. *The puritan way of death.* Oxford: Oxford University Press, 1977.

Taylor, C. The funeral industry. In H. Wass (Ed.), *Dying, facing the facts.* Washington, D.C.: Hemisphere, 1979.

Van Gennep, A. [*The rites of passage*]. M. Vegedom & G. Caffee, trans.). Chicago: University of Chicago Press, 1960.

Weissman, A. Why is a funeral. In V. Pine, A. Kutscher, D. Peretz, R. Slater, R. DeBellis, R. Volk, & D. Cherico (Eds.), *Acute grief and the funeral*. Springfield, Ill.: Charles C Thomas, 1976.

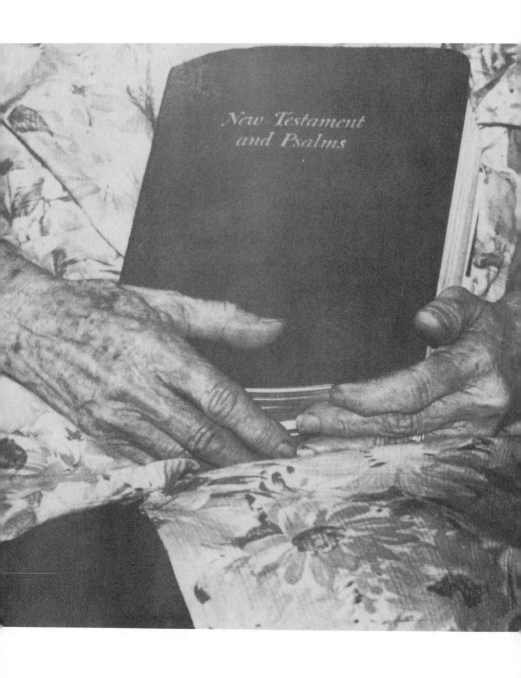

9

Grief and Bereavement

When we get married, most of us believe that we will live together with the one we love for the rest of our lives. When we die, we will die together. However, most of us will not die together; one of the couple, usually the wife, will experience grief and bereavement. Most women can expect to become widows and remain widows for about nine years. In 1975, 12.1 percent of the women living in the United States were widows; only 2.4 percent of the men were widowers. There were 10,104,000 widows and 1,817,000 widowers (Lopata, 1979, p. 34). As women get older, they are more likely to be widowed. Between the ages of 45 and 54, only 7.2 percent of the women are widowed. This figure increases to over 25 percent for ages 60 to 64, and to over 50 percent for women between 70 and 74 (Lopata, 1979, p. 36). Despite the likelihood that about half our population will experience the loss of a spouse, we are ill prepared for the grief we will feel.

This chapter focuses on the process of grief and bereavement, and then examines the problems associated with the role of widow and widower. It deals primarily with the loss of a spouse, since the loss of a child is discussed in Chapter 5.

First, grief and bereavement must be distinguished. Bereavement is the actual state of the deprivation caused by the loss. It is an objective state. Grief is a psychological state characterized by mental anguish. It is the response of emotional pain to the loss.

GRIEF

Grief is a process through which the bereaved must go if they are to become whole persons again. It is a time of great ambivalence:

The bereaved may be desperately lonely, yet shun company; they may try to escape from reminders of their loss, yet cultivate memories of the dead; they complain if people avoid them, embarrassed how to express their sympathy, yet rebuff that sympathy irritably when it is offered. (Marris, 1974, p. 28)

The ambivalence comes from a desire to return to the past, yet to reach out to the future. During a period of grief, the present may be meaningless.

There are two very different theories of why we grieve. For Freud (as discussed by Glick, Weiss, & Parkes, 1974; and Goldsmith, 1972), the grieving process allows us to break our ties with the lost object. The libido, or our mental energies, must be withdrawn from the deceased, but this is very painful. The person focuses on the deceased and tries to bring back memories. In bringing these memories to consciousness and in looking at them, the survivor severs the attachment to the deceased.

For Bowlby (1961), grieving is an attempt to reestablish ties and is not a process of withdrawing them. In grief, we are continuously trying to find the lost object. Obviously, though, this is extremely frustrating. Eventually, this frustrated search for the deceased lessens. However, as Bowlby points out, it is necessary to go through this yearning in order eventually to recover.

Although the two theories posit different dynamics underlying the grief, the behavioral results may be similar: there is intense pain and an intense focus on the deceased.

Grief consists of a number of stages: shock and numbness, intense grief (which consists of yearning, anger and guilt, and disorganization), and finally reorganization (Bowlby, 1961; Parkes, 1970). (Other theorists have posited more stages; however, their stages may be subsumed in the three already mentioned. For example, Kavanaugh, 1972, sees the bereaved as going through seven stages: shock, disorganization, volatile emotions, loss, loneliness, relief, and reestablishment.)

Shock and Numbness

The most immediate reaction to a death is generally a feeling of numbness. The bereaved cannot believe that the death has occurred. It is a time when feelings are not yet admitted to consciousness. This stage works as emotional anesthesia, for to allow the feelings of grief at this point would be totally overwhelming. This is why the bereaved may appear to be doing so well at funerals. They may not break down; they may greet everyone with a handshake and say: "I'm so glad you could come. Doesn't he look lovely?" Yet on examination, the bereaved is saying exactly the same thing to everyone. He or she is acting as an automaton. When John F. Kennedy was shot, we all admired the behavior of his widow, and how she acted during the funeral. Perhaps at this time she was exhibiting the first stage of grief, which allowed her to act with such dignity.

The numbness of the bereaved may fool others into believing that they are doing well. After a few hours to a few days, however, the numbness should wear off, and the bereaved will enter the next stage.

Intense Grief

The intensity of the grief is not necessarily related to the degree of love felt for the individual who has died; rather, it is related to the degree of feelings, both negative and positive, one had toward the dead person.

C. S. Lewis (1961), chronicling his grief over the death of his wife, expresses the feelings that occur in this stage:

No one every told me that grief felt so like fear. I am not afraid, but the sensation is like being afraid. The same fluttering in the stomach, the same restlessness, the yawning. I keep on swallowing.

At other times it feels like being mildly drunk, or concussed. There is a sort of invisible blanket between the world and me. I find it hard to take in what anyone says. Or perhaps, hard to want to take it in. It is so uninteresting. Yet I want the others to be about me. I dread the moments when the house is empty. If only they would talk to one another and not to me. . . .

And no one every told me about the laziness of grief. Except at my job—where the machine seems to run on much as usual—I loath the slightest effort. Not only writing but even reading a letter is too much. Even shaving. What does it matter now whether my cheek is rough or smooth? They say an unhappy man wants distractions—something to take him out of himself. Only as a dog-tired man wants an extra blanket on a cold night; he'd rather lie there shivering than get up and find one. It's easy to see why the lonely become untidy; finally, dirty and disgusting. (p 1–2)

In the first phase of intense grief, there is continued pining and searching for the deceased. The thoughts and behavior of the bereaved are focused on the lost person. There is a perceptual set for the lost person; the bereaved believes in the person's presence. The bereaved's thoughts are constantly concerned with the deceased, and attention is directed toward objects associated with the lost person.

Hallucinations are not uncommon. For example, in one study, 46.7 percent of 293 bereaved people had postbereavement hallucinations (Rees, 1975), including both visual and auditory hallucinations; 11.6 percent of those studied stated that they spoke with the deceased. The majority of the bereaved found the hallucinations helpful, although some of them questioned their own sanity. Rees reported some of the reactions:

> I think she got me my present house. I find hearing her breathing disturbing, but I like the feeling she is in the house.
>
> I feel him guiding me.

There is also anger and guilt. Anger will be reflected by irritability and bitterness. It may be directed at all those nearby, the doctors who took care of the deceased, at God, and at the deceased. The bereaved are angry at the deceased for causing such pain. Young survivors are angry because they are left alone to raise the children. Older bereaved ask what happened to the retirement plans they made together.

The bereaved may be angry at God: If God were a just God, how could He have taken my spouse? He (or she) was such a good person, while there are so many bad persons still alive.

Anger is also directed at oneself in terms of guilt. The bereaved go through many "if only I hads." An example of this comes from author Robert Anderson (1974) over the death of his wife:

> I made the discovery of the very small lump in my wife's breast. I had no idea what it was. I said nothing until a solicitation from the Cancer Society listed the warning signals of cancer. For years after, I cursed my own ignorance and the negligence of all the doctors who had never taught my wife breast self-examination. For years, with hot flashes of anger and guilt, I went over and over those weeks of delay. Why didn't I mention even in passing the small lump in her breast? My brother is a doctor; why didn't I check with him? A simple phone call. For years I rewrote compulsively that scene in my head, playing it differently—I mention the lump to my wife; we go to the doctor; we are in time, and my wife is alive. (p. 10)

During intense grief the bereaved will lapse into despair. They are disorganized. Apathy and aimlessness are two predominant feelings. There is a sense of futility and emptiness, and a loss of patterns of interaction. These feelings of despair may come and go as the bereaved start to reorganize their lives. As they take each step, such as finding a new friend, or a job, the depression begins to lift until the final stage reintegration occurs.

Reintegration

Reintegration, or recovery, has occurred when the bereaved are functioning normally again. A sense of continuity in life must be reestablished. As Marris (1974) points out, this is done, "not by ceasing to care for the dead, but by abstracting what was fundamentally important in the relationship and rehabilitating it" (p. 34). It is giving up the deceased without giving up what the deceased meant to the bereaved.

A Cleveland surgeon, Dr. George Crile (1969), depicts the final stage of grieving, a little more than a year after his wife had died:

> I still live in the same house. Many of the same birds, the wood ducks and the swan, are still in our back yard. Many of the relics that Jane and I collected in our travels are about our house. But there are no ghosts. Memories that were for a time inexpressibly sad have once again become a source of deep pleasure and satisfaction.
>
> Since we know nothing of death except that it comes to all, it is not unreasonable to be sad for the person who has died. The sorrow that I once felt for myself, in my loss, now has been transformed to a rich memory of a woman I loved and the ways we traveled through the world together. (p. xxiii)

One never totally gets over the grief. On special occasions, such as birthdays or anniversaries, the depression may reoccur. The memories continue to exist, but they may become good memories.

PATHOLOGICAL GRIEF REACTIONS

Sometimes the bereaved does not reach the stage of recovery. There are three reactions that are distortions of normal grief:

1. *Delayed Grief:* Here, the bereaved feels little sorrow and continues on with life. The bereaved will act very busy and will be very calm. This may last a few weeks or even longer. Suddenly, the grief may be triggered by the loss of some object, such as a wristwatch; or it may occur when the circumstances surrounding the death are recalled. A person with a very severe reaction to a recent death may be grieving for a death that occurred years ago. For example, Lindemann (1944)

discusses a woman who grieved intensely for her mother, but who actually was engrossed in fantasies concerning her brother, who had died twenty years before.

2. *Inhibited Grief:* The bereaved never feels the grief. Instead they may develop various physical conditions, such as ulcerative colitis, asthma, or rheumatoid arthritis.

3. *Chronic Grief:* The grieving continues; the person can never get beyond the intense yearning for the person, the anger, the guilt, and the despair.

According to Marris (1974), these patterns exaggerate the normal aspects of grief—"the impulse to escape from everything connected with bereavement, the worsening of physical health, the despair or refusal to surrender the dead. And in each, counterbalancing impulses have been suppressed. The process of normal grief seems to be a working out of conflicting impulses: while in abortive grief patterns, the conflict is never resolved" (p. 28). The depression, panic, guilt, and ill health that are felt in these distorted forms of grief do not differ in kind, but rather in duration and intensity, from normal grief reactions (Parkes, 1972, p. 117).

Who is most likely to have a poor outcome? Bornstein et al. (1973); Maddison (1968); and Maddison and Walker (1967) have attempted to answer this question. Bornstein et al., studying the elderly bereaved, found that only 13 percent of the poor-outcome group lived with their families, compared with 46 percent of the nondepressed group. The major predictor for Maddison, studying widows whose husbands were aged 45 to 60, was the perception of the supportiveness of the environment; the widow with a bad outcome felt that the people in her environment had not permitted her to express her feelings, that they wanted her to control herself. The widow perceived that the people she interacted with did not allow her to talk about the past. As Maddison stresses, these are the widow's perceptions and not necessarily the reality. Hence, social support and perceived social support are important in defining those bereaved who are at high risk.

The Symptomatology of Grief and Bereavement

Throughout the process of grieving, the bereaved may suffer from various physical symptoms. Normal grief is normal only in a statistical sense, since grief is such a different state from what we consider healthy (Engel, 1961).

Much of what we know about the symptomatology of grief stems from the work of Erich Lindemann (1944). In 1942, a nightclub, the Cocoanut Grove, caught fire: 499 people died; 200 survived. Many of the survivors, although physically well, kept complaining of physical symptoms such as shortness of breath, insomnia, and loss of appetite. One of the psychiatrists treating the survivors was Lindemann. He proceeded to study 101 bereaved persons, including the survivors of the fire, and recorded his observations. He found that "acute grief is a definite syndrome with psychological and somatic symptomatology" (p. 141). Within grief, there was (1) somatic distress, especially respiratory disturbances; (2) preoccupation with the image of the deceased while feeling emotionally distant from others; (3) guilt; (4) hostile reactions; and (5) loss of patterns of conduct.

Further studies have confirmed Lindemann's findings. Clayton et al. (1972) found that three symptoms occurred in over half the bereaved patients they studied: sadness, difficulty in sleeping, and crying. Other symptoms included loss of appetite and weight, loss of interest in television, friends, and current events, and difficulty in concentration.

Physical health has been shown to deteriorate during bereavement. Parkes' study (1964) of the case records of 44 widows showed that each patient saw her GP on the average of 2.2 times every six months during the 18 months before her husband's death. It rose to 3.6 times during the first six months following bereavement. Wiener et al. (1975) found similar results in their study of the elderly bereaved. They further found that the bereaved were much more likely to be taking medication five to eight months after the death than a control group of nonbereaved elderly.

Besides being related to ill health, is grief related to death? Do people die of broken hearts? (Parkes, 1972). Although grief is not listed as a cause of death on a death certificate, epidemiological studies have shown that widows and widowers have a higher mortality rate than married people of the same sex and age. The difference in the mortality rate is highest for white males aged 25 to 34; it is 4.31 times greater for these widowers than for married men (Rees, 1972).

In a study of 4,486 widowers aged 55 and over, Young, Benjamin, and Wallis (1963) found an increase in the death rate of 40 percent during the first six months of bereavement. Seventy-five percent of these deaths were attributed to heart disease, particularly coronary thromboses and arteriosclerotic heart disease.

A statistical relationship, however, between bereavement and death does not answer Parkes' question. In order to do this, we must look at the hypotheses explaining the statistical relationship. Epstein et al. (1975) and Rees (1972) discuss the various hypotheses:

1. *The selection hypothesis*: The healthy among the widowed tend to remarry and select themselves out, leaving the widowed population with higher death rates. However, since the death rate is highest for those most recently bereaved, those who remarry would have to do so quickly. This is generally not the case.

2. *The homogamy or mutual choice of poor riskmates hypothesis*: Here, it is presumed that the unfit marry the unfit. Although individuals with similar physical disabilities may marry each other, it is unlikely that this hypothesis is true since the large increase in mortality occurs so rapidly after the death of a spouse.

3. *The joint unfavorable environment hypothesis*: The survivor and spouse shared an unfavorable environment so that what led to the death of the deceased will lead to the death of the other. However, except for a study by Ciocco done in 1940, which showed a tendency for married couples to die of tuberculosis, no other study has been able to document a relationship between causes of death in spouses.

4. *The non-grief-related behavior-change hypothesis*: Because the deceased spouse is no longer there, the survivor may be more likely to skip meals, to skip medicine, and generally not to take care of himself. This may be true for the elderly widower, who may have been cared for by his wife, but it is not generally true of widows.

5. *The desolation-effects hypothesis*: The effects of grief, including feelings of hopelessness, may result in physical vulnerability. The death of a spouse has been shown to cause the greatest amount of stress, which may then result in death.

This last hypothesis seems best to explain the statistical relationship between grief and death. People may indeed die from "broken hearts."

THERAPEUTIC INTERVENTION WITH THE BEREAVED

While we recognize the stages of grief, and although studies indicate that the bereaved represent a higher-risk population with regard to physical and/or emotional illness and even death, relatively few programs are available to provide support through this difficult period. Everyone assumes that the grieving individual will "get over it." Certainly this is true for the vast majority. The question is not so much whether the individual will "get over it" but rather how the health care team and the community can facilitate grief work and provide support to enhance his or her continued growth and development. Our sophisticated, technologically oriented culture promotes the development of elaborate schemes and programs; the obvious escapes our attention. The bereaved person often needs someone who will be able to sit and listen. This sounds simplistic, but we often feel pressured to give advice and counsel to escape our own feelings of helplessness. This "rush to help" often prevents us from hearing what the bereaved individual says is needed. Our cultural emphasis on competency, strength, and adequacy prevents the bereaved from experiencing the emotions necessary for appropriate resolution of grief.

Simos (1977) notes that repetition is necessary for the mastery of loss. The bereaved require repeated opportunities to verbalize their feelings in an attempt to make sense of their loss, to ask the unanswerable whys before acceptance of the loss can occur. One father (Hullinger, 1980), in discussing his response to his daughter's death, explained: "I needed the opportunity to talk over and over and over, to repeat and repeat and repeat. And to have somebody able to listen to that" (p. 2). This process begins as soon as the individual is told that death has occurred.

Currently the majority of deaths occure in institutional settings. The health care team, pressured by the demands of the setting and their own sense of failure, often allocates little time with family members after a patient has died. Even when death is expected, the family will respond with shock, numbness, and dismay. Physicians, nurses, and social workers often experience impatience with this response, and a common reaction is to withdraw while muttering, "But she knew he was dying." Some member of the health care team should remain available to assist family members as they incorporate the initial shock. Often this is perceived as a social work task, since the social worker is not responsible for ongoing, direct patient care. If possible, provision should also be made for some room where privacy is insured. Whether or not they were present at the exact moment of death, family members usually require reassurance that "everything was done."

Each family member has an individual response to death, and the health care practitioner must carefully observe and respond to these needs. A few common themes do emerge during this period: (1) ambivalence about seeing the person immediately following death; (2) how to tell other family members; and (3) beginning preparation for funeral arrangements. Family members will look to the health care practitioner as the "expert," and will require assistance in working through and arriving at decisions that are most meaningful for them. During the first few weeks following the death, family members usually have the support of their extended family and friends. While not essential, if members of the health care team have had an extended, intensive relationship with the deceased and family, attending the funeral or memorial service has salutary effects for everyone. The family welcomes the recognition of their needs and the respect for their dead, and the health care practitioner has an opportunity to "say good-bye."

After the initial phase the immediate family faces the difficult task of building a new life without the deceased. This period is particularly painful because they are frequently coerced by cultural mores into "forgetting about the dead." The expectation that "life goes on" makes no provision for how. One example of this is the minimum time off provided by places of employment. Most employers provide from three days to one week. If there is provision for an educational leave of absence, or a maternity leave, why not a bereavement leave?

Since there has been so little provision made by our existing institutions, a fast-growing phenomenon is the self-help movement. One example is the Widow-to-Widow program developed by Phyllis Silverman (1972, 1976b; Silverman et al., 1974). These programs are run by volunteers who are widowed and who are willing to use their experience to help others. "Those who participate in a Widow-to-Widow program are learning to deal with the transition as a means of preventing problems at a later date. They learn to cope, to find hope and to look forward to a future" (Silverman, 1977a, p. 270). A similar program, Compassionate Friends, has evolved to provide help for parents who have lost a child. For further information about self-help groups, the reader is referred to the references at the end of this chapter.

Childhood bereavement should not be overlooked. Furman's (1974) study of bereaved children suggests that a parent's death during childhood is a unique experience because the parent is an importantly loved person and is essential in the child's development. The parent who would normally assist the child in mourning is the very person being mourned. Furman (1977) suggests three social work tasks (which can be incorporated into the interdisciplinary team approach): (1) the bereaved family should be helped to maintain continuity of home and caregiving; (2) the surviving parent should be taught to help the child understand the reality of death and of the parent's death; and (3) the parent should be helped to understand the way a child mourns.

Anticipatory Grief

When people expect the death of someone close, they begin to experience their grief in advance. It is assumed that anticipatory grief offers the survivor time to work through a large portion of the trauma normally associated with loss. However, research findings do not bear this out. Rather, studies of the bereaved have found contradictory results when examining the adaptational value of anticipatory grief. Gerber et al. (1975) and Schwab et al. (1975) found that anticipatory grief could have negative consequences for the bereaved; Parkes (1973) found anticipatory grief to be helpful and adaptive; and Clayton et al. (1973) and Maddison (1968) did not find any relationship between bereavement and the grief reaction.

Clayton et al. (1973) compared the bereavement outcomes of 46 widows and widowers whose spouses had died within six months of being defined as having a terminal illness with 35 widows and widowers whose spouses died after being ill more than six months. There was basically no difference between the symptoms of the two groups at one month after the death.

When Clayton defined anticipatory grief, not in terms of time, but according to whether the bereaved had experienced the feelings associated with grief before the death, she also found no difference at the end of a year between those who had experienced the anticipatory grief and those who had not. (However, one month after the death, anticipatory grief tended to cause greater depression.)

Maddison (1968), in his study of 375 widows (132 in Boston and 243 in Sydney, Australia, whose husbands were aged 45 to 60), similarly found no relationship between bereavement outcome and expectedness of death. Sudden, unexpected death was not more likely to lead to a bad outcome.

Gerber (1975), who studied 81 widows and widowers, 16 of whom were survivors of an acute illness death (a death occurring without warning and prior knowledge of the condition; or a medical condition of less than two months' duration with the absence of multiple attacks and hospitalizations) and 65 with a chronic illness death (any condition of two or more months' duration), found no difference in the outcome of the two groups six months after the death. The two groups were not significantly different in terms of their number of physicians' office visits, in their use of psychoactive medication, or in the number of times the bereaved felt ill without consulting a physician. However, Gerber did find, when he looked at the bereaved whose spouses had died of a chronic illness, that there was a difference between those whose spouses had suffered from a chronic illness of longer than six months and those where the chronic illness was shorter. Those who witnessed the longer chronic illness did more poorly. This was especially significant for widowers.

Schwab et al. (1975) also found anticipatory grief to be dysfunctional; 68 percent of the 22 relatives whose decedents' illnesses were longer than one year had intense grief reactions at the time of the interview, compared to 30 percent of the 23 relatives whose decedents died within one year of an illness, or whose deaths were without warning. (The interval between the interview and the death ranged from one month to over one year.)

The preceding findings differ substantially from the findings of Parkes (1973). In his study of young Boston widows and widowers under 45, those whose spouses had a terminal incapacity of less than three days, with less than two weeks' warning, fared much worse than those whose spouses had a terminal incapacity of more than three days. Those unprepared for the death were more likely to feel disbelief and depression than those who were prepared. At the end of a year, they were still more depressed. Only 24 percent of the unprepared group was rated as having a good outcome compared with 59 percent of the prepared group. Differences still existed two to four years after the death.

Why are all these findings contradictory? The answer, in part, is that they are very different studies in terms of how they define anticipatory grief, what different age groups they studied, and the date at which they measured the outcome (see Table 9.1).

Another reason for the contradictions is that anticipatory grief is not inherently positive or negative, especially in terms of the ambivalence that is felt when a loved one is dying. As Aldrich (1974) points out: "A period of anticipation may provide a mourner with an opportunity to carry out grief work in advance of loss, but at the same time it complicates the working-through process by giving the hostile component of ambivalence a more realistically destructive potential" (p. 7). If the patient is not to be told that he or she is dying and a closed or mutual pretense awareness exists, it becomes difficult to work out the ambivalent feelings.

Furthermore, throughout anticipatory grief, the survivor must maintain hope; if not, the survivor is viewed as not having loved the person.

Table 9.1. Summaries of Anticipatory Grief

Study	Age of Bereaved	Definition of Anticipatory Grief	Date of Outcome	Relationship Between Outcome and Anticipatory Grief
Clayton et al.	Average age = 61	1. Illness shorter or longer than six months	One month after death	None
		2. Signs of anticipatory grief	One month after death	Anticipatory grief harmful
			One year after death	None
Maddison	Deceased between 45 and 60	Minimal warning	Fifteen months after death	None
Gerber et al.	Over 65	1. Acute illness/chronic illness	Six months after death	None
		2. Chronic illness shorter or longer than six months		Anticipatory grief harmful
Schwab et al.	All ages (16 of the 45 were over 65)	Illness shorter or longer than one year	One to 12 months after death	Anticipatory grief harmful
Parkes	45 and younger	Warning of more or less than three days	One year Two years Four years	Anticipatory grief harmful Anticipatory grief helpful

Anticipatory grief may lead survivors to feel that they gave up hope too early.

During the period of anticipatory grief, patients and all involved in their care, including the health care team, need as much support as possible. This period is particularly stressful for everyone. Both the patient and family are attempting to cope with uncertainties that lead to ambivalence, anger, and guilt. Family members can become preoccupied with their own grief and withdraw from the patient. Sometimes family members are at various levels of acceptance or have conflicting attitudes that isolate one family member from another. This is particularly difficult if the patient is a child, as the lack of understanding of one parent toward another can adversely affect their entire future. Premature mourning and the concomitant withdrawal of the family isolates the patient. This behavior frustrates the health care team if they cannot understand the underlying dynamics. At the same time, they are also struggling with their sense of impotence and having to shift from curing to caring. Their anger can just as easily be projected onto the family for "not caring" when they are actually unable to deal with their own feelings about "not curing."

The use of groups to help families discuss what must be faced and how to accomplish this is an extremely effective method of promoting better understanding during this period. It is particularly beneficial if members of the health care team can participate, or at least are informed of, the process. Lebow (1976) hypothesized that it is more desirable to encourage greater family involvement during the period of anticipatory grief. She postulated that while each family member was threatened by a sense of loss, each could be helped to enhance awareness and understanding of his or her relationship to others. She suggested six adaptational tasks: (1) remaining involved with the patient; (2) remaining separate; (3) adapting to role changes; (4) bearing the effects of grief; (5) coming to some terms with the reality of impending loss; and (6) saying good-bye. Obviously, tasks 1 and 2, which sound mutually exclusive, require understanding and creative therapeutic intervention. These techniques, however, need not be complex. For example, a family member can be encouraged to include the patient in all family decisions and communication. Often family members will convey to staff what they feel a patient needs, and must gently be reminded to ask the patient's preference. Similarly, family can be given "permission" by staff not to visit. At the Victoria General Hospice program, one day is set aside as "relatives' day off."

Instead of asking whether anticipatory grief is adaptive for all bereaved, studies should be addressing the questions: For whom is anticipatory grief adaptive? What is the optimal length of time for anticipatory grief? Under what conditions is anticipatory grief helpful? What was the nature of the relationship between the deceased and the bereaved?

ROLE CHANGES

Once the bereaved begin recovering from their grief, they are still faced with being widows or widowers. They are now single again, yet they are not single. The rules of behavior for a husband or a wife are clear in our society. What are the rules for the widow or widower? Widowhood is generally viewed as a temporary state, but a temporary state on the way to what? Where do you go from being a widow or widower? When do you stop being a widow or widower and become a single person? It is difficult to answer these questions since being a widow or widower, after the intense grief has passed, is an undefined role in our society.

Widows and widowers face specific problems in no longer being married, in being alone in a couples-oriented society. In Helen Lopata's (1979) study of widows, over 50 percent agreed with the statement: "One problem of being a widow is feeling like a fifth wheel." Younger widows may be perceived as a sexual threat by many of their friends; 37 percent of the women in Lopata's study agreed that other women are jealous of a widow when their husbands are around.

An attractive widow in her 40s, interviewed by one of the authors, reported how her relationship with her sister-in-law changed after her husband's death. While the widow's husband was alive, she always greeted her brother-in-law and sister-in-law with a hug and kiss. Now, when she went to kiss her brother-in-law, the sister-in-law gave her a dirty look.

Dating and sex become issues for the bereaved. Widows, especially, are not supposed to have any interest in sex. For example, a young widow interviewed by Kreis and Pattie (1969) reported: "My husband and I had a good sex life. Since he passed away, I've lived like a virgin. My minister was evasive when I mentioned my sense of frustration. He gave me that, 'Now, now, my dear,' but I got his message: 'Respectable women shouldn't have such desires, it isn't nice' " (p. 71).

When does it become all right for a woman to begin dating again? And when is it alright to have sex again? Although some would argue that the answers are best left to the individual, some societal guidelines would help alleviate the guilt the widow or widower may feel when beginning to date. As on widow asked, "When is it all right for me to take off my wedding band?"

Widows and widowers of different ages face specific problems. Lopata (1979, pp. 382–383) discusses the difficulties encountered by widows of various age groups:

Ages 30 to 54. With the death of the spouse, the income of the family will probably fall substantially. There are probably children who must be taken care of; yet there is a lack of inexpensive day-care.

Ages 55 to 65. Since the widow is not likely to have dependent children, she is not eligible for Social Security benefits, which may make her destitute. It is also harder for her to reenter the job market if she has not worked outside the home in a number of years. Although she may want to date, and eventually remarry, there is a paucity of eligible males.

Ages 65+. Here, the widow may be left relatively isolated. One effect of this may be that she is deprived of being touched. Although many studies have documented that touch deprivation in infants may have many negative effects, including death, there are no such studies of the elderly. What are the effects of touch deprivation in the elderly? We do not know. Yet it may be just as hurtful to the elderly as to infants.

Widowers, too, face a number of problems in dealing with their new role. The younger widower with children must find appropriate care for them that he can afford. He must now become more aware of his children's social and emotional needs, and become able to meet them. As Gerber (1975) points out: "His [the younger widower with children] awareness of how dependent he was on his spouse for maintaining the emotional level of the family is obvious only after the death" (p. 3).

The older widower may not be prepared to take care of himself. His wife was responsible for the housework, the cooking, and the cleaning, and the widower may not feel competent to do these jobs. Since the older widower may have retired, he in effect no longer has the two primary roles in our society: worker and spouse. As a result, he may begin to feel worthless.

The one major advantage a widower has over a widow is that it is easier for him to remarry, because there is a 5 to 1 ratio of widows to widowers (Gerber, 1975, p. 6). Many of the widowers are aware of this ratio. As one, aged 72, answered in response to a query concerning his plans: "I think I'll go down to Miami and look over the beaches for a future mate."

SUMMARY

Most of us are ill prepared for experiencing grief. Grief consists of three basic stages: shock and numbness, intense grief, and reorganization. In order to reach reorganization, it is necessary to feel the severe pain associated with grief; otherwise one may suffer pathological grief reactions. Associated with grief are various physical symptoms. The mortality rate of the bereaved is higher than the mortality rate of similar married men and women. Yet few programs exist for helping the bereaved to cope.

People may experience anticipatory grief. However, researchers have found contradictory results as to whether the effects of anticipatory grief are positive or negative.

The bereaved must face various other problems depending upon their age and sex.

LEARNING EXERCISES

1. Read Lynn Cain's book *Widow*. What are your reactions? Discuss her grieving process.
2. Make a survey of services in your community for the bereaved. What do your findings indicate about treatment of the bereaved?
3. Would you prefer to die before your spouse? Explain your response.
4. With regard to anticipatory grief—would you prefer for someone you love to die a sudden death or after a long-term illness?
5. Reexamine what your family's financial status would be if you or your spouse died. For example, do you have adequate life insurance?

AUDIOVISUAL MATERIAL

Conversation with a Widow. 30 min/videocassette/1977. University of Arizona.
   An interview with a recently bereaved widow depicting her grief. She discusses how hospital staff helped to facilitate her grieving process.

The Lost Phoebe. 30 min/color/1974. Perspective Films.
Based on Theodore Dreiser's short story about an elderly man who is unable to deal with the death of his wife, this film dramatizes the loneliness and sadness of bereavement.

The Long Valley. 59 min/color/1976. Time/Life Multi-Media.
A seminar on the stages of grief conducted by Colin Murray Parkes for persons who share their experiences of grieving. Medical personnel are included in this seminar.

Where is Dead? 20 min/color/1976. Encyclopedia Britannica Educational Corporation.
A 6-year-old's grieving process is presented, along with how her family enables her to understand the death of her brother.

REFERENCES

Aldrich, C. K. Some dynamics of anticipatory grief. In B. Schoenberg, A. C. Carr, A. Kutscher, D. Peretz, & I. Goldberg (Eds.), *Anticipatory grief.* New York: Columbia University Press, 1974.

Anderson, R. Notes of a survivor. In S. Troup & W. Green (Eds.), *The patient, death, and the family.* New York: Scribner's, 1974.

Bornstein, P. E., Clayton, P. J., Halikas, J. A., & Robins, E. The depression of widowhood after thirteen months. *British Journal of Psychiatry,* 1973, *122,* 561–566.

Bowlby, J. Process of mourning. *International Journal of Psychoanalysis,* 1961, *42,* 317–340.

Ciocco, A. On mortality in husbands and wives. *Human Biology,* 1940, *12,* 508.

Clayton, P. J., Halikas, J.A., & Maurice, W. L. The depression of widowhood. *British Journal of Psychiatry,* 1972, *120,* 71–78.

Clayton, P. J., Halikas, J. A., Maurice, W. L., & Robins, E. Anticipatory grief and widowhood. *British Journal of Psychiatry,* 1973, *122,* 47–51.

Crile, G. Memorial service, Kent Road, Cleveland Heights. In A. Kutscher (Ed.), *Death and bereavement.* Springfield, Ill.: Charles C Thomas, 1969.

Engel, G. Is grief a disease? *Psychosomatic Medicine,* 1961, *23,* 18–22.

Epstein, G., Weitz, L., Roback, H., & McKee, E. Research on bereavement: A selection and critical review. *Comprehensive Psychiatry*, 1975, *16*, 537–546.

Evans, G. *The* Family Circle *guide to self-help.* New York: Ballantine Books, 1979.

Furman, E. *A child's parent dies.* New Haven, Conn.: Yale University Press, 1974.

Furman, E. Bereavement in childhood. In E. Prichard, B. Orcutt, A. Kutscher, I. Seeland, & N. Lefkowitz (Eds.), *Social Work with the Dying Patient and Family.* New York: Columbia University Press, 1977.

Gerber, I., Cusalem, R., Hannon, N., Battin, D., & Arkin, A. Anticipatory grief and aged widows and widowers. *Journal of Gerontology*, 1975, *30*, 225–229.

Gerber, I. *The widower and the family.* Paper presented at the Second Annual Interdisciplinary Educational Conference on Bereavement and Grief, Yeshiva University, New York, 1975.

Glick, I., Weiss, R., & Parkes, C. M. *The first year of bereavement.* New York: John Wiley, 1974.

Goldsmith, C. *Anticipatory grief, a structural model.* Paper presented at Columbia-Presbyterian Medical Center, New York, April 14, 1972.

Hullinger, Rev. R. Parents of murdered children need special grief work. *Thanatology Today*, 1980, *2*(6), 3.

Kavanaugh, R. *Facing death.* Baltimore, Md.: Penguin Books, 1972.

Kreis, B., & Pattie, A. *Up from grief.* New York: Seabury Press, 1969.

Lebow, G. Facilitating adaptation in anticipatory mourning. *Social Casework*, 1976, *57*(7), 458–465.

Lewis, C. S. *A grief observed.* New York: Seabury Press, 1961.

Lieberman, M. *Self-help groups for coping with crisis: Origins, members process and impact.* San Francisco: Jossey-Bass, 1977.

Lindemann, E. Symptomatology and management of acute grief. *American Journal of Psychiatry*, 1944, *101*, 141–148.

Lopata, H. *Women as widows.* New York: Elsevier North-Holland, 1979.

Maddison, D. The relevance of conjugal bereavement for preventive psychiatry. *British Journal of Medical Psychology*, 1968, *41*, 223–233.

Maddison, D., & Walker, W. Factors affecting the outcome of conjugal bereavement. *British Journal of Psychiatry*, 1967, *113*, 1057–1067.

Marris, P. *Loss and change.* New York: Pantheon Books, 1974.

Parkes, C. M. The effects of bereavement on physical and mental health: A study of the case records of widows. *British Medical Journal*, 1964, *2*, 274–279.

Parkes, C. M. "Seeking" and "finding" a lost object: Evidence from recent studies of the reaction to bereavement. *Social Science and Medicine*, 1970, *4*, 187–201.

Parkes, C. M. *Bereavement: studies of grief in adult life.* New York: International Universities Press, 1972.

Parkes, C. M. Anticipatory grief and widowhood. *British Journal of Psychiatry*, 1973, *122*, 615.

Pasquale, F. Program Coordinator, Self-Help Institute, Center for Urban Affairs, Northwestern University, 2040 Sheridan Road, Evanston, Illinois.

Rees, W. D. Bereavement and illness. In B. Schoenberg, A. C. Carr, D. Peretz, & A. Kutscher (Eds.), *Psychosocial aspects of terminal care.* New York: Columbia University Press, 1972.

Rees, W. D. The bereaved and their hallucinations. In B. Schoenberg, I. Gerber, A. Wiener, A. Kutscher, D. Peretz, & A. Carr *Bereavement: Its psychosocial aspects.* New York: Columbia University Press, 1975.

Schwab, J. J., Chalmer, J. M., Conroy, S., Farris, D., & Markush, R. Studies in grief: A preliminary report. In B. Schoenberg, I. Gerber, A. Wiener, A. Kutscher, D. Peretz, & A. Carr (Eds.), *Bereavement: Its psychosocial aspects.* New York: Columbia University Press, 1975.

Silverman, P. Widowhood and preventive intervention. *The Family Coordinator*, 1972, *21*, 95–102.

Silverman, P. Bereavement as a normal life transition. In E. Prichard, J. Collard, B. Orcutt, A. Kutscher, I. Seeland, & N. Lefkowitz, (Eds.), *Social work with the dying patient and the family.* New York: Columbia University Press, 1977. (a)

Silverman, P. *If you will lift the load: A case book on mutual help for the widowed.* New York: Jewish Funeral Directors of America, 1977. (b)

Silverman, P., (Ed.). *Helping each other in widowhood.* New York: Health Sciences, 1974.

Simos, B. Grief therapy to facilitate healthy restitution. *Social Casework*, June 1977, *58*(6), 337–344.

Wiener, A., Gerber, I., Battin, D., & Arkin, A. The process and phenomenology of bereavement. In B. Schoenberg, I. Gerber, A. Wiener, A. Kutscher, D. Peretz, & A. Carr (Eds.), *Bereavement: Its psychosocial aspects*. New York: Columbia University Press, 1975.

Young, M., Benjamin, B., & Wallis, C. The mortality of widowers. *Lancet*, 1963, 2, 454–456.

10

Death from
A Cross-cultural Perspective

Serena Nanda

In some [Eskimo] tribes, an old man wants his oldest son or favorite daughter to be the one to put the string around his neck and hoist him to his death. This was always done at the height of a party where good things were being eaten, where everyone—including the one who was about to die—felt happy and gay, and which would end with . . . dancing to chase out the evil spirits. At the end of his performance, he would give a special rope . . . to the "executioner," who then placed it over the beam of the roof of the house and fastened it around the neck of the old man. Then the two rubbed noses, and the young man pulled the rope. Everybody in the house either helped or sat on the end of the rope so as to have the honor of bringing the old suffering one to the Happy Hunting Grounds where there would always be light and plenty of game of all kinds. (Freuchen, 1961, p.146)

Death is universally regarded as a significant event both for the individual and the social group. Every culture provides for its members a way of thinking about death, and of responding to it. Death everywhere is set off by ritual and supported by cultural beliefs and social institutions. It is surrounded by an atmosphere of the sacred and approached with intense emotions. This sacredness and intensity of feeling make it difficult to see the role culture plays in shaping not only beliefs and practices regarding death but also the feelings and emotions that accompany them.

273

In the United States, death is probably the most intensely felt of all life crises, yet also the least talked about. This chapter attempts to put American beliefs, emotions, and practices regarding death in a cross-cultural perspective, comparing the major dimensions of death, as it is experienced in our own culture, with those of other societies. It is hoped that this comparative approach will help us look at our own death responses more objectively, allowing us to think about alternative responses that might help individuals deal with death and dying in a more adequate way.

DEATH BELIEFS AND ATTITUDES

The opening quote in this chapter dramatically suggests that other cultures have attitudes toward death different from our own. These differences are partly reflected in beliefs about what happens after death. Undoubtedly, one of the most commonly held beliefs by non-Western peoples is that death is not the end of life, but rather a passage from the world of the living to another world, or spirit realm. Death is thus viewed not as immediate, but as a gradual transition from one status to another (van Gennep, 1960). In some cases the afterworlds are only vaguely described; in other cases detailed beliefs about the afterworld are an important part of a group's thinking about death. Frequently, life in the afterworld resembles or exactly duplicates life on earth. Among the Tikopia of Polynesia, for example, the soul makes courtesy visits to ancestral spirits guided by the same rules of etiquette that hold on earth. The souls of the dead keep their earthly status; and the system of clan dwellings, the special position of chiefs and ritual leaders, and the role of the married and the unmarried all broadly reflect Tikopian society. This reproduction of the social system functions to reinforce the belief that not only the individual but, more importantly, the society will continue even after its present members have died (Firth, 1967).

The knowledge of the continuance of society after one's own death is undoubtedly an important factor in the individual's acceptance of death. Where old people know that they are the last representatives of a once-vital culture, their individual deaths are made more poignant. Such is the case among many Native American tribes, whose cultural tradition and language are mainly carried by people in their 70s, 80s, and 90s. Another case of old people in this predicament has been movingly described by anthropologist Barbara Myerhoff in *Number Our Days* (1978), a case study of old Eastern European Jews in Venice, California. The knowledge that they are the last generation to know and love Yiddishkeit, the traditional Eastern European shetl (village) culture, is a source of great anxiety, and is a central focus in the concern these people have about their own death. These people, largely isolated from the society at large, as well as from their own children, fear the death of their culture as well as their own deaths. Furthermore, it appears that their fear of death is not as great as their fear of the debility, dependence, and invisibility that comes with advanced old age in a culture that values youth, action, and independence. This helps explain their sometimes querulous behavior, which Dr. Myerhoff sees as a bid for attention and interest among the only audience they have—themselves. Unlike members of many non-Western cultures, these Jews do not have a strong belief in an afterlife to sustain their hopes for the continuation of society. In this, they are similar to the larger society of the United States, where the individual soul of the deceased has no role to play in the society of the living.

A society in which conversations between the living and the dead are an important element in both religious and everyday life is the Gikuyu of East Africa. Jomo Kenyatta, in *Facing Mt. Kenya* (1965), points out that the term "communion with ancestors," rather than "ancestor worship," most accurately describes the relationship of the living and dead in this tribe. Because the Gikuyu believe that the spirits of the dead can be pleased or displeased by the behavior of the living, and can act accordingly, the ceremony of communing with the ancestral spirits is observed constantly in Gikuyu society.

In our own culture, the popular belief that the dead and the living are irrevocably separated from each other may be considered partly a consequence of our sense of time, in which sharp discontinuities are experienced between the past, present, and future. The American emphasis on forgetting the past, living for the present, and looking toward the future appears to correspond to our death beliefs, rituals, and attitudes. In this, we sharply contrast with other cultures in which past, present, and future are merged and the relationship between living and dead is continuous and ever-present. A dramatic example of this kind of belief is the Dreamtime of the aboriginal groups of Australia.

The Dreamtime is that long-ago time when the ancestors created all the animate and inanimate things of the cosmos, including the aboriginal people themselves. In all the important Australian tribal ceremonies, the Dreamtime is recreated through the telling of legends and the acting out of ritual. Traditionally, the aboriginals believed that each man's spirit came from a clan pool of spirits, entering his mother's womb at the time of conception and returning to the common pool after death. In order to pay this debt of creation to the ancestors, the Australians commemorate the events of the Dreamtime in their great initiation ceremonials. During these performances, the participants believe that they actually, in spirit, become the totemic ancestors. Thus, the Dreamtime contains within itself the past, present, and future; it is both temporal and eternal, forever connecting the living with their immediate and legendary ancestors (Elkin, 1964).

The continuity between the living and the dead is also elaborated in ideas of reincarnation, which are found in nonliterate, non-Western cultures, as well as in the major Eastern religions. Among the Central Eskimos, for example, the name of the last person to die in a settlement is given to the first child born thereafter, as the child is considered the reincarnation of the dead person (Boas; quoted in Mauss, 1979, p. 28). Hinduism and Buddhism both rest on complex philosophical ideas about how salvation (moksha) or a state of beatitude (nirvana) is attainable through a long series of reincarnations that are mystically related to the deeds (karma) of preceding lives. In both these religions, the ultimate outcome of the reincarnations is an undifferentiated and impersonal "oneness" with the universe. If one aspect of our fear of death is that it is basically a fear of separation and aloneness, as some psychoanalysts think, then the Hindu and Buddhist doctrines of union speak more directly and satisfyingly to that need than does the Western religious doctrine that views salvation as the continuity of the integrity of the personal self (Kakar, 1978, p. 36).

The social and psychological functions of such widespread beliefs are not difficult to understand. Societies regard themselves as ongoing systems, and the death of any member threatens the very existence of society. As Robert Hertz (1960, p. 78) so eloquently writes, "When a man dies, society loses in him much more than a unit; it is stricken in the very principle of its life, in the faith it has in itself." Death is perceived as antisocial, even unnatural. Society refuses to consider death irrevocable. Death is not seen as simply an end to life; it is also the beginning of a new existence. Thus, the idea of death is linked with that of resurrection—separation followed by a new integration.

Beliefs in an afterlife can be seen as meeting the threat that death makes to the social system. Such beliefs speak to the contradiction that exists between, on one hand, the continuity of the social system as a system of norms, groups, and beliefs and, on the other hand, the impermanence of its personnel—the conflict between the mortality of the human body and the immortality of the larger social body. From a comparative, cross-cultural perspective, Western beliefs of the meaning of death and the soul stand nearly by themselves. Others emphasize continuity—between past and present, living and dead, individual and community; we emphasize the discontinuities between past and present, the separation of the living and the dead, and the integrity of the individual soul and personality at the expense of the continuation of the community and the universe. These beliefs and values, as we shall see shortly, are manifest in the contrast between death rituals in our own and other societies; and they leave us badly prepared for death compared to other peoples.

PAIN, DYING, AND THE MILIEU OF DEATH

Very little has been written about the response to pain in other cultures, about the relationship of pain to dying, or about the milieu of the dying person, as opposed to the great body of work on death and beliefs about the afterlife. A small amount of experimental work done in the United States indicates that there does appear to be an important cultural dimension both in the experience of pain and in the emotional and behavioral responses to it (Wolff & Langley, 1977). Zborowski's work, as discussed in Chapter 4, indicates that the experience of, and response to, pain are tied up with attitudes toward sickness, health, the medical profession, and the commitment to emotional restraint as a cultural value.

A cultural dimension to pain experiences has also been noticed in the case of Alaskan Indians, who are reported to tolerate extreme pain very calmly for brief periods, provided it is accompanied by the hope of fast relief and recovery, but who are said to tolerate discomfort very poorly. Similarly, it has been reported that Alaskan Eskimos tolerate pain well if the prognosis is favorable, but poorly if the prognosis of the pain-causing disease or injury is unknown (Wolff & Langley, 1977, p. 319). Ruth and Stanley Freed (1979, p. 345), in their study of an Indian village, noted that while many aspects of Western medicine are not integrated into the Indian village health system, pain relievers are eagerly sought. Although there is now an important body of work on traditional healing systems in non-Western cultures and thus, by implication, a great deal of information on sickness and the sick role, information relating to the prolonged pain we associate with some terminal illnesses in our own society is lacking. In short, we have few good descriptions of how the dying person, as opposed to the dead person, is treated in non-Western cultures.

The few available descriptions are contradictory. An early historian

of medicine, Henry E. Sigerist, making reference to "primitive societies," distinguishes between the injuries and disabilities (such as skin
diseases) that nevertheless allow the affected individual to keep up
with normal life, and serious illness, accompanied by fever, that occasions complete isolation of the sick person from the group. Describing
the Kubu of Sumatra, he says: "The sufferer from such illness can no
longer take part in the life of the tribe. Sickness isolates him so completely that he is left helpless and in pain, even by his relatives. He is
shunned, as death is shunned . . . the sick man is dead to society even
before his physical death" (Sigerist, 1977, p. 380).

While it is true that in some societies bereavement begins before an
individual has died, we cannot take Sigerist's view as characteristic of
all "primitive" societies. Among the Cubeo of South America, for example, the dying do not appear to be shunned, although they are apparently not treated with any great concern, either. Goldman (1979,
p. 185) describes the dying of a headman who had been ill for several
weeks. The medicine men have given up on him, and his death was
therefore expected. Once this acceptance occurred, the dying man was
treated indifferently by his community. When at last the old man's
time seemed near, as indicated by the difficulty of his breathing, his
wife took up a death watch at his hammock. It was only after the man
died that the society mobilized itself by beginning the mortuary ritual.
Goldman reports that for neighboring tribes, those who are believed to
be fatally ill with no hope of recovery may even be buried alive. In
cases of voodoo death among the aboriginal tribes of Australia, it is
also reported that once those who believe themselves bewitched refuse
to take nourishment and show signs of decline, they are considered taboo and are isolated from the group out of fear.

On the other hand, Turnbull's (1961) description of an old woman's
death among the Pygmy foragers of the Ituri forest in Africa suggests
that among technologically simpler peoples, the dying person may be
a focus of concern and warmth. The Pygmies express various degrees
of illness by saying that someone is hot, with fever, ill, dead, completely
dead, absolutely dead, and, finally, dead forever. When someone is ill,
the women relatives will wail, but this is more of a ritual than spontaneous expression of grief. When someone "really dies," both kin and
friends of the deceased burst into uncontrollable expressions of grief.
Turnbull heard this wailing one evening when Balekimito, an old
woman who was the mother of the best hunter in the group, was carried into her son's camp. Turnbull (1961) writes:

"She had been ill for some time, but as she was an old woman nobody had
thought much of it. She had been ill before and not died completely, not

even just died. But now she had died completely and absolutely. . . and her son was running up and down, his face streaked with tears, beating himself on the head with his fists and crying that his mother was going to die forever. (p. 42)

The woman, in fact, was not yet dead; however, the room was filled with wailing men, women, and children. People waited both inside and outside her hut for the end, for her to die forever.

It is possible that the long dying process that is characteristic of some diseases in our own society is not frequent in these other cultures, which are nonurbanized and nonindustrial. Among the !Kung, who still live by hunting and gathering in the Kalahari Desert in southern Africa, such degenerative diseases as hypertension and coronary heart disease are unknown. People mainly die from accidents or respiratory ailments, and those who live into old age remain vigorous and alert—senility is unknown. The !Kung attitude in general is one of gratitude to the old for having worked to raise their children properly, and the old are generally treated very well, even when they are blind and totally dependent on the group. Researchers do point out, however, that this is more likely to be true for those old people with close relatives than otherwise, a point that parallels our own society with regard to hospital care (Fried & Fried, 1980, p. 155).

Among the LoDagaa of West Africa, whose mortuary ritual has been extensively described (Goody, 1962), the end of a person's life also takes place in the midst of the kin group. When a man is about to die, his brothers send young boys to tell others living in nearby villages. The dying man should be attended in his last hours by his sisters, his wives, and his sons. For the moment of his death, he should be sitting up, preferably in the arms of a close kinswoman. It is considered sinful for a man to die lying down, as if he were a slave with no one to take care of him. In such cases a payment must be made to the Earth priest, who then moves the corpse into the proper position. In this context, Goody quotes an informant, "If I suddenly got ill . . . my mother's sister would come to see me. If one of my matriclan doesn't come when I'm ill, to turn me over when I need it, who is there to help me? I'll die with my head on my mat." Because death is a matter of public concern, it is immediately marked by the wailing of women to inform the immediate neighbors, while the playing of xylophones spreads the news farther away. Messengers are sent out to inform kin in distant villages.

What seems apparent from these few examples of dying in other cultures is that whether the dying person is treated indifferently or with great care, he or she dies in the milieu of the community. At the moment of death, if not during the long illness that may precede it, the community responds to what is a matter of public, nor merely private, concern. Dying people in other cultures die in the midst of life going on around them. The surviving kin take an active part in death rituals, unlike the passive role to which kin are relegated in our own society, and must frequently be at the dying person's side to perform the proper rituals to facilitate the deceased's journey to the afterworld. Responses to the dying person may thus be viewed as responses both to a personal loss and to the loss experienced by the society at large. Grief reactions in other cultures appear to be directed effectively toward both consoling the bereaved persons closest to the deceased and toward reintegrating the society around the loss of the dead person.

GRIEF REACTIONS: COMMON CROSS-CULTURAL EXPERIENCES

Because people everywhere build long-term, interdependent relationships that produce feelings of attachment and caring, the end of these relationships produces emotional distress and disorganization in every culture. In spite of cultural differences, then, there are some universal, or at least very widespread, individual and social reactions to death. In all cultures, as in the United States, people react to death with expression of emotions—sadness, emptiness, fear, and anger.

Of all the expressions of grief associated with death, crying, or "wailing," is the most common (Rosenblatt, Walsh, & Jackson, 1976). The intensity of emotion expressed in some non-Western societies may seem shocking to Americans, where outward "bearing up" and emotional self-restraint are important values in funeral behavior. In the following scene among the Warramunga of Australia, a group of participants and spectators was leaving the area where a totemic ceremony had just been celebrated, when a piercing cry suddenly came from the camp where a man was dying:

> At once the whole company commenced to run as fast as they could while most of them commenced to howl. . . . Some of the men . . . sat down bending their heads forward . . . while they wept and moaned. . . . Some of the women . . . were lying prostrate on the body, while others were standing or kneeling around, digging the sharp ends of their yam sticks into the crown of their heads, from which the blood streamed down over their faces, while all the time keeping up a loud, continuous wail. Many of the men, rushing up to the spot, threw themselves upon the body. . . . To one side three men began wailing loudly . . . and in a minute or two another man of the same [totemic group] rushed on to the group yelling

and brandishing a stone knife. Reaching the camp, he suddenly gashed both thighs deeply, cutting right across the muscles, and unable to stand, fell down into the middle of the group. The (dying) man did not actually die until late in the evening. As soon as he had given up his last breath, the same scene was re-enacted, only this time the wailing was still louder, and men and women, seized by a veritable frenzy, were rushing about cutting themselves with knives and sharp-pointed sticks, the women battering one another's heads with fighting clubs. (Durkheim; quoted in Huntington & Metcalf, 1979, pp. 29–30)

This emotion, however sincerely felt, is nevertheless a ritual norm structured by kinship relations to the deceased. Durkheim demonstrated that the emotion generated by such rituals binds together individuals in society and reinforces the concept of society, as well as having more individual psychological functions. Such a structured, collective, yet powerful emotional expression is noticeable by its absence in grief behavior in the United States. The cross-cultural research of Rosenblatt et al. (1976) appears to show that the working through of grief and the resumption of a normal life takes less time when such intense emotional expression is collectively displayed as part of funeral celebrations. His finding that Americans experience grief longer and take longer to resume a normal pattern of life is not surprising in view of the relatively high inhibitions on grief display in our society.

Perhaps our own inhibitions about showing extreme emotion at death have led to the stereotype of the stoic Indian; although some Native American groups do value emotional self-control at death, the picture of the tight-lipped Indian, never expressing grief, contradicts the clinical and personal experiences of Native American nurses (Branch & Paxton, 1976, p. 96). It would appear that Indians will express grief if they are given a sympathetic environment in which to do so. It is perhaps the hostility or indifference they feel emanating from Anglo health personnel regarding their distinctive burial customs, their wish to use traditional healers, or the importance of family members surrounding and comforting the dying patient—all of which may interfere with hospital practices and procedures—that accounts for the repression of emotion in Native Americans, rather than any specific prohibition on grieving in their own cultures.

In considering the expression of grief in various cultures, it is relevant to consider the social position of the dying or dead person. Although most Americans would be quite reluctant to admit that the mourning of a person's death should, or does, correspond to their sex, age, or socioeconomic status, this does appear to be the case in all societies. In societies with high infant mortality, for example, a child's death does not occasion the extended ceremonies that take place for adults. In many societies a child is not considered a total social person until he or she has reached a certain age; dead children under that age are buried with hardly any ceremony. This seemingly casual attitude toward the death of children in some cultures is undoubtedly related to a high infant mortality rate. Where infant mortality is high, a relatively unemotional reaction to child deaths is probably adaptive. In India, for example, the infant mortality rate has always been high; even today, in a village very near the capital, New Delhi, Ruth and Stanley Freed report that death primarily strikes children under 4 years old (1980, p. 510). Popular Hinduism attributes the death of an infant to its bad actions in its last life. If a child dies, it is believed that its soul was overburdened by bad actions, and that it is better that such a child die so that it can be born again, shedding a bit of its bad actions in the process. These beliefs would appear to have some function in consoling the mother, particularly, who may find relief in the idea that the death was for the best. Among the Chinese, traditionally, the casualness with which the body of a dead child was disposed of—in a shallow grave—is explained by the Chinese belief that such children were not the genuine offspring of the stricken parents, but evil spirits, in the form of children, who sought to gain entrance into a household. Had they been received as proper children, they would bring disaster to the house, spreading disease and death to the other children.

Because a child is not considered a social person, its death often occasions less community response; the child has not yet taken on important social roles, and its loss to the community cannot be compared to that of an adult in the prime of life. Among the LoDagaa, whose customs are not atypical, no public grief is displayed for an unweaned child, and if a child dies within three or four months of its birth, even its parents may not mourn. Similarly, the death of a very old person does not occasion great public displays of grief, either. Such a person has usually ceased to maintain the affective relationships that would call forth the most important ritual expressions of grief, and has few surviving contemporaries to play the proper ritual roles. Even the political authority of such an old person as the head of the kinship group has often been taken over by another. Thus, like child, such a person is not involved in a meaningful social network, and this tempers the communal expression of grief (Goody, 1962, p. 139).

In addition to age, social status and relationship to the deceased account for intracultural variation in the expression of grief and in mourning behavior. In Chinese culture this is made explicit in the concept of mourning circles, the *wu fu*, or five degrees of mourning. The first of these was for one's parents and for a wife mourning her husband. In the second circle are grandparents and a husband mourning his wife. In the third circle are sisters and brothers; in the fourth circle, uncles and aunts; and in the fifth circle, remote relatives. For the death of a great-great-grandparent, however, joy, rather than grief, was expressed, because the person had lived to such a ripe old age (Fried & Fried, 1980, p. 174).

Although in our society, feelings of loss and sadness are considered the most appropriate ones to express at death. feelings of anger and aggression are frequently expressed in grief in other societies. Self-mutilation as described among the Warramunga of Australia is not uncommon; Rosenblatt et al. (1976) found that grief reactions involving aggression were described for 76 percent of a cross-cultural sample.

It is not difficult for professionals to understand why anger and aggression might accompany bereavement, perhaps even predominating over sorrow, when a very near and loved person has died. From a social point of view, the question is how to prevent the anger and aggression of the bereaved from damaging the social relations of the survivors and from inhibiting the reintegration of the group. Most societies try to channel the anger and aggression of grief along nondestructive paths. Here ritual activities and specialists play an important role by providing predictable and correct activities for the bereaved to engage in, minimizing the frustration that might come from not knowing what to do when death occurs. Ritual activities also keep the close survivors busy—often praying, singing, dancing, even engaging in sexual orgies that may divert aggressive energies into channels that do not result in harmful attacks on other persons. Ritual specialists are also useful in defining the often ambiguous feelings of bereaved persons as sorrow rather than anger; ritual itself may channel anger and aggression toward institutionalized targets—for example, out-groups—or—as we saw among the Warramunga—oneself.

In complex, socially stratified societies, where religious obligations in burial and mourning entail expense, anger toward one's poverty and toward established religious institutions may be a prominent emotion elicited by the death of a family member. In *A Death in the Sanchez Family*, Oscar Lewis (1970) exposes the wide range of emotions that come into play as a poor Mexican family tries to organize a decent burial for one of its members. As Lewis says in his introduction, "For the poor, death is almost as great a hardship as life itself." He goes on to describe that the difficulties the poor have in disposing of their dead are simply an extension of the difficulties they encounter in their powerless, impoverished lives: "Guadalupe died as she had lived, without medical care, in unrelieved pain, in hunger, worrying about how to pay the rent or raise money for the bus fare for a trip to the hospital" (p. x). Her survivors, being very poor themselves, had to spend a great deal of energy raising the money for her funeral; their anger at being exploited almost matches their grief at the death of their aunt. Consuelo, one of the nieces of the deceased. expresses her anger in these words:

> There are authors who have written that the Mexican cares nothing about life and knows how to face death. There are jokes and sayings and songs about it but I would like to see those famous writers in our place, undergoing the terrible, hideous sufferings we do, and then see if they are able to accept the death of any one of use with a smile on their lips, knowing that the person didn't have to die. . . . Maybe the older generation did have a philosophy of not attaching great importance to death, but I believe that was the result of the church . . . making them believe that they could achieve nothing here on earth, that they would get their reward in eternity. (Lewis, 1970, p. 35)

The anger and bitterness of the quote are disquieting, perhaps, as a response to death, but nevertheless are a reality for many poor people.

In some societies, however, anger and aggression are not inhibited nor suppressed, but rather culturally elicited as the appropriate, even honorable, expression of grief. Among the Kwakiutl tribes of the Northwest Coast of North America, the death of a close relative was experienced predominantly as an affront to one's dignity and status. The shame that was felt at a death had to be partly wiped out by holding a great feast (potlatch), at which great quantities of goods were distributed. Only by such feasts could the status lost by a death in the family be regained. A more aggressive way of handling a death was by head hunting, called "a killing to wipe one's eyes." This was a means of "getting even" by making another household mourn. When a chief's son died, the chief set out in his canoe to the village of a neighboring chief, who may have had nothing at all to do with the death. The bereaved chief would address his host, saying, "My prince has died today, and you go with him." Then he would kill the host chief. According to the Kwakiutl, this was a noble way to behave; a chief could not allow himself to suffer the humiliating degradation of status loss and struck back, not in revenge, but to wipe out the blemish on himself and his community. In death, as in life, the Kwakiutl were mainly concerned with their individual reputations and considerations of social status (Benedict, 1961, p. 216).

Another cultural context in which aggression is elaborated as a response to death is in those groups where either no deaths, or few deaths, are considered natural, and where the first question raised by the deceased's kin is "Who is to blame?" One of the societies where no death is blameless is that of Dobu, an island in the Western Pacific. The Dobuans live in perpetual distrust of everyone in their communities except for a very small group of trusted people. On Dobu every death is believed to be caused by "witchcraft, sorcery, poisoning, suicide or by actual assault." Every person on the island has knowledge of some spells for causing specific diseases or death. Therefore, after a death, the kin of the dead use various divination techniques to find out whose grudge killed their kinsman. They watch the corpse as the mourners walk by, and when the guilty person passes, the corpse is believed to twitch in one place or another. Since sorcery is most effectively practiced when two persons are friends or kin, the most suspicion often falls on those who have been closest to the deceased in the months before death (Fortune, 1932). Although most societies are not as ridden with suspicion as the Dobu, the projection of blame on others for a death appears to be a widespread, culturally institutionalized practice. Such institutions undoubtedly elicit aggression while channeling it onto institutionalized targets.

SUICIDE

As the chapter opening quote suggests, attitudes, frequencies, and methods of self-inflicted death are all influenced by culture. The few anthropological or culturally comparative studies of suicide in the literature (Bohannan, 1967; Devereux, 1961; Hendin, 1964) show very clearly that suicide is a socially meaningful action, and that the meanings are different in different societies. Certainly, the almost universally negative reaction to suicide in the United States, which is related to our "fear of death" syndrome, is not a reaction found in all cultures.

The Eskimo present a dramatic contrast to traditional American culture in their attitudes toward at least some kinds of self-inflicted death. The Eskimo traditionally are said not to fear death, and this appears to be true even today, where large-scale conversion to Christianity is typical. According to Freuchen (1961, p. 145), life is the central Eskimo concern, yet suicides are numerous; when "life is heavier than death," then no man hesitates to end his torment. This happens in old age, when a man can no longer hunt and may feel that he is a burden to his kin, in addition to feeling sadness at not being able to participate in the activities of the group.

Eskimo suicide contrasts with suicide in our own society, where every type of control is brought to bear on keeping the attempted suicide alive. Cultural meanings are invoked ("Suicide is a sin"); familial pressures are applied ("How could you abandon your spouse and children?"); psychological and even the legal forces of society are mobilized to prevent the individual from attempting suicide. An interesting point is that although active control and initiative are encouraged in every aspect of American life and culture, in death the individual is expected to remain passive.

It should not be assumed that suicide is a prevalent pattern in all non-Western, nonliterate societies; the meanings and practices vary enormously. Among the Zuni Indians of the Southwestern United States, for example, suicide is hardly known; to them, it is a rather exotic custom that occurs among white people (Benedict, 1961, p. 117). Among the Plains Indians, however, the theme of suicide was highly elaborated, notably in the custom of the "suicide pledge." A man undertaking this pledge tied himself to a stake by an eight-foot-long buckskin stole in the midst of one of the frequent battles involving the Plains Indians. He therefore could not retreat with his comrades if the battle was going against them. If he survived this death-courting experience, he was awarded the highest honors of the tribe. Plains Indians also understood suicide as a response to unrequited love; among the Mohave, for whom there were many categories of suicide, love suicide was associated with white people. The Mohave label many different types of death as suicide, most of which would not be recognized as such in our culture: stillbirths that are believed to be caused by the unwillingness of a future shaman to be born; the death of a suckling who has to be weaned because its mother is pregnant and who makes itself sick from spite; the death of twins at birth or before they get married; the pseudosuicide of a man who wishes to marry a kinswoman and permits a horse to be killed at his wedding in his place, thereby breaking the kinship bonds between himself and his bride; the victim of a witch who refuses to seek the help of a curer; an aging witch who incites his victim's relatives to kill him so that he can join the ghosts of his victims and thus retain his hold over them forever; a warrior who is tired of living and deliberately strays into enemy territory in order to be killed; the suicide attempts (which appear never to be successful) that occur as the closest kin of someone deceased attempts to jump on the Funeral pyre; and finally active suicides, which—judging from case histories—appear to involve people who kill themselves after they are disappointed or rejected in love, friendship, or affection by someone close to them (Devereux, 1961, p. 324).

Viewing suicide from a different perspective, it appears that there are similar motives in different cultures. Bohannan's (1967) conclusion about suicide in various African societies is that it springs from motives similar to those most frequently found in the United States—that is, domestic strife and the loss or fear of the loss of social status. In addition, the African societies studied by Bohannan and his colleagues have motives largely unknown here—for example, the fear of ghosts or other supernatural figures who are believed to have the power to cause one's death.

This motive brings us to a consideration of voodoo death, or death by sorcery or witchcraft In Cannon's (1942) classic article, he quotes a description of this phenomenon in Africa: "I have seen Kru-men and others die in spite of every effort that was made to save them, simply because they had made up their minds, not (as we thought at the time) to die, but that being in the clutch of malignant demons, they were *bound* to die" (p. 169). Although Cannon clearly accepts the view that this is therefore not suicide, Western observers might include this as subintentioned death—that is, a form of death in which the deceased plays an indirect, covert, partial, or unconscious role in his or her own demise.

The most vivid descriptions of this type of death come from Australian aboriginal societies in which the sorcerer is believed to work his magic by pointing a bone at the victim:

> The man who discovers that he is being boned . . . stands aghast, with his eyes staring at the treacherous pointer, and with his hands lifted as though to ward off the lethal medium, which he imagines is pouring into his body. His cheeks blanch and his eyes become glassy and the expression of his face becomes horribly distorted. . . . His body begins to tremble and the muscles twist involuntarily. He sways backwards and falls to the ground, and after a short time appears to be in a swoon; but soon after he writhes as if in mortal agony, and, covering his face with his hands, begins to moan. After a while he becomes very composed and crawls to his worley. From this time onwards he sickens and frets, refusing to eat

and keeping aloof from the daily affairs of the tribe. Unless help is forth-
coming in the shape of a countercharm . . . his death is only a matter of a
comparatively short time. (Basedow; quoted in Cannon, 1942, p. 172)

After a man has been boned, his social life collapses; he is in a taboo
state and is shunned by others out of fear. This state of social isolation
is itself suggestive of death, and is one of the many suggestions incorporated by the victim who is in a highly suggestible state and who co-
operates in withdrawing from life. Even before the victim dies, furthermore, the community holds a sacred ceremonial moving him from
the land of the living to the otherworld of the totemic ancestors. In
attempting to explain voodoo death, Cannon notes that a common element is that the victim, convinced that life is running out, refuses to
eat or drink and succumbs to weakness and death in a matter of days.
Cannon's view is that the extreme fear reaction causes a disastrous fall
of blood pressure, which in turn damages the organs necessary for adequate circulation. This, combined with the lack of food and water,
causes death. He thus sees voodoo death as similar to a true state of
shock in the medical sense, being induced by a prolonged and tense
emotion. Although later researchers (Lex, 1977) have suggested other
medical explanations, there is no contradiction of Cannon's basic point
that voodoo death is real, and that it is caused by repressed or obvious
terror. Since little intensive interviewing has been done and few life
histories taken for the few documented cases, it is difficult to know
whether listing them as suicide reflects our own categories, based on
our understandings of the workings of the unconscious, or native categories of victimology.

THE RITUALS OF DEATH: FUNERALS AND MOURNING

In all cultures death raises a series of problems pertaining to the obligations imposed on the survivors: the corpse must be looked after; the
deceased must be placed in a new status; the roles vacated by the deceased must be filled and their property disposed of; the solidarity of
the group must be reaffirmed; and the bereaved must be comforted
and reestablished in their relationships to others. In this section on the
rituals of death, funeral rites are dealt with first, followed by rituals of
mourning, with the focus on the mourning of spouses and especially
that of widows.

Mortuary or funeral rites have many functions: they give meaning and sanction to the separation of the dead person from the living; they help effect the transition of the soul to another, otherworldly realm; they assist in the incorporation of the spirit to its new existence. In most societies, the kin and the entire community are prominent in these rituals. Through performing mortuary rituals, as well as through observing mourning behavior, community members have a vital role in realizing a communal goal—the removal of the dead person's spirit so that it will not menace the living. This is most frequently accomplished by the practice of secondary treatment of the corpse.

Secondary treatment is the regular and socially sanctioned removal of some or all of the relics of the person from the place of temporary storage to a permanent resting place. It is one of the most frequent elements in death rituals in other cultures. Among the Berawan of Borneo, for example, there are two major ceremonies, separated by a period of anywhere from eight months to five years. The first ceremony begins immediately after the death. The corpse is displayed for a day or two, until it has been viewed by all the close kin. It is then put into a coffin or a large jar. At the end of a week, this is removed for temporary storage and is placed either in the longhouse or on a platform in the graveyard. At the second ceremony, people come from all over. The coffin or jar is brought to a small shed on the longhouse veranda. Every evening for about a week there is a party near where the jar of bones is kept. The bones are then transferred to their final resting place, either in a wooden mausoleum or in the niche of a massive, carved wooden post (Huntington & Metcalf, 1979).

In societies like that of the Berawan, where secondary treatment is practiced, death is not seen as immediate. Rather, there is a period during which the individual is believed to be neither alive nor fianlly dead. During this period, the process of decomposition of the corpse may be said to represent the liminality, or transition period, of the soul. As the body decays and is in an impermanent and miserable state of rotting, so the soul too, is in its impermanent and restless position, wandering around the living, perhaps seeking to pull others after it. It is at this time the corpse is most feared, and the fear of the corpse mirrors the fear of the spirit of the dead person. After the secondary treatment (burial or cremation of the bones), the soul of the deceased is considered to have reached and been integrated into the afterworld and is no longer feared. Secondary treatment rituals often are the official end to the mourning period and mark the point at which a surviving spouse may remarry.

The frequency of secondary treatment of the corpse corresponds to the widespread belief in the fear of ghosts. In fact, the United States stands almost alone of all the world's peoples in its cultural disapproval of perceptions and/or fear of ghosts (Rosenblatt et al. 1976). In other cultures, ghost fears may involve a fear of the dead coming back to extract revenge for past hurts or, more commonly, the fear that they may want to bring some of the living to join them. However these beliefs are phrased, they may be viewed as psychologically useful in helping break the ties with the dead, and thus lead societies to reintegrate more quickly. The rituals of secondary treatment are socially useful, as well as beneficial for the bereaved—particularly bereaved spouses, who in most societies are expected to remarry.

Another contrast between death rituals in our own society and in many others is the important role played by symbolic demonstrations of the themes of sexuality, fertility, and the continuation of life at funerals. These values are noticeable by their absence in America, where funerals are generally subdued, if not gloomy, affairs. In Madagascar, by contrast, among the Bara people, funerals involve "bawdy and drunken revelry enjoined upon the guests" (Huntington & Metcalf, 1979, p. 103). An important part of the funeral procession, during which the coffin is carried from the house to a cave in the hills, is a chase in which young girls run after the youths carrying the coffin, followed by adults and, finally, the family cattle. Only boys who have had sexual experience can participate in this, and it is viewed as essentially a sexual contest between boys and girls for possession of the corpse. About halfway up the mountain, the procession halts, the cattle are stampeded around the coffin, and the young men compete with each other in cattle wrestling. Then the procession begins again. Disorderly conduct of various kinds is essential at Bara funerals and secondary burial ceremonies. Toward this end, rum is served, and dancing, contests involving cattle, and sexual activities are part of the festivities.

This kind of behavior is not uncommon. Among the Cubeo of South America, simulated and actual ritual coitus is part of the mourning ritual. According to Goldman (1979) the dances, rituals, and dramatic performances, as well as the sexual license, have the purpose of transforming grief and anger at a death into joy. To understand sexual license as part of funeral and mourning ceremonies, we can view it as an introduction of the life principle into the fact of death. Given the trauma of death to the social fabric, it is not surprising that the aim of many death rituals is to restore a feeling of vitality and joy to the group. Rosenblatt et al. (1976) have also shown that attendance at funerals appears to be correlated with the distribution of food and drink, and with sexual license. Since they further demonstrate that attendance at funerals correlates with a relatively rapid working through of grief, it would appear that such festivities have important psychological and social functions related to resuming normal behavior.

Mourning

This section focuses on mourning rituals as they function to integrate persons, particularly the spouse of the deceased, into society. Undoubtedly, one of the important functions of a mourning period is to limit the grief of the bereaved so that they may eventually return to more or less normal patterns of behavior. Just as funerary rites provide a passage in status for the deceased, so mourning rites provide a passage in status for the survivors. In all societies bereavement is not expected to be permanent. To the extent that a culturally defined mourning ritual exists, it both supports the expression of grief in a culturally approved way and limits the period of grief by limiting the period of mourning.

Two widespread mourning practices are marking and isolating the close survivors of the deceased. Isolation involves a limited time period during which close and specified kin of the deceased are kept apart from the rest of society. Isolation occurs more frequently for widows than for widowers, and more for spouses than for parents of a dead child or for adult children of aged parents. This suggests that grief may be less when the deceased is economically marginal. Where concepts of pollution or certain taboos must be observed involving isolation or marking, it is most frequently the spouse who is most subject to them. Among the Tlingit, for example, all those who participated in touching the corpse in preparation for its cremation were under taboos of various sorts; but the deceased's widow, in particular, "was the prisoner of taboo" (Fried & Fried, 1980, p. 158). She was not allowed to speak for 12 days after the death of her husband, nor allowed to do work of any kind. She was not allowed to use a knife or cup. It was believed that if she broke a cup, it could cause the death of her next husband. Her clothing and bedding were taken from her and burned along with the clippings of her hair, which she had cut for the cremation. A rock was placed on her bed, which was supposed to assure her next husband of a long life. A rope was placed around her waist, and this was said to guarantee long life for her relatives. These customs clearly imply a responsibility in the widow for the life and well-being of her closest kin, as well as the expectation that she would remarry.

Among the Berawan, spouses were subjected to even severer restrictions. Widows and widowers had to stay for 10 days in a tiny cell made of mats, next to the corpse. They were not allowed to bathe and had to wear filthy clothes, eating only the poorest food, which was "shared" with the deceased. They could sit or sleep only with their legs tucked up in a cramped position. Huntington and Metcalf (1979) suggest that these restrictions are a way for the spouse to take on the burden for the whole community of appeasing the ghost of the deceased, by appearing to share the conditions of discomfort in which the deceased's soul resides. More general functions of isolation and restrictions may be to treat the bereaved with more consideration, or to help enlist aid for the bereaved, or to deflect aggression by putting distance between the most immediately affected by the death and the rest of the community.

In a cross-cultural survey of mourning behavior, Rosenblatt et al. (1976) found that the mourning of spouses for each other finds the most frequent ritual and emotional expression in most societies. The average time of mourning was found to be 305 days for widows, 215 days for widowers, and 198 days for adult children who had lost a parent. Clearly, the practice of sutee in India, where the widow was enjoined to throw herself on her husband's funeral pyre, was an extreme example of the asymmetry of mourning behavior. A widower was not expected to act in this way, and this was obviously related to his greater ability to remarry. Remarriage for widows was forbidden.

It is also true cross-culturally that women are permitted, and perhaps expected, to behave more emotionally than men when a death occurs. There are several possible explanations for this. Men may actually experience a loss less deeply, since women in their roles as wives and mothers may experience stronger attachments than men do in their roles. Another explanation may be that women are more strongly coerced than men by the normative requirements of mourning (and other) behavior. Still another explanation may be that women, being generally of lower status then men, are expected to take on the symbolic burden of distress and grief for the whole community. Finally, it should be pointed out that a lifetime of economic dependence on a man may lead women to experience the loss of a spouse more keenly than a man does. In the following lament from a widow among the Jivaro, the themes of dependency and loss are clearly mixed:

> O my dear husband, why have you left me alone, why have you abandoned me? . . . Who will hereafter fell the trees for me and clear the ground to make the manioc and banana plantations, or help me with

cleaning and tending the fields? Who will hereafter make a red-striped *tarachi* for me for the feasts, who will bring me game from the forest or the gaily colored birds which you used to shoot with you blowgun and your poisoned arrows? All this you did for me, but now you lie there mute and lifeless. . . . O, dear me, what will become of me? (Karsten; quoted in Rosenblatt et al., 1976, p. 2)

As has already been suggested, in many societies remarriage is expected and encouraged after a suitable mourning period. In these societies, there are various mourning ceremonies that have the effect of breaking ties with the dead spouse and thus encouraging remarriage. The most common of these are destroying or giving away the deceased's personal property, observing a taboo on the name of the deceased, changing the residence of the survivor, and changing feelings about the spouse through ghost fears. All these practices may be viewed as moving the spouse of the deceased to undertake new personal commitments more readily. Such rituals also make it easier for others to relate to the deceased's spouse in terms of new relationships. Tie-breaking rituals appear to be particularly frequent in societies that have the levirate or the sororate—that is, where the deceased's spouse is expected to marry the brother or sister of the deceased (Rosenblatt et al., 1976).

The LoDagaa, previously mentioned, are such a group. Among the LoDagaa, the funeral ritual is, above all, a time at which the social roles that the dead man, especially, played throughout his life are reallocated. Funeral ceremonies provide institutionalized procedures for other persons to take over these roles. This is done through the mechanism of funeral orations, accompanied by gifts. A person in a particular relationship to the deceased makes a speech about him, telling of his good qualities that were important in that relationship. The speaker then produces gifts of food and beer, which are offered to the dead man, but also to the person who is prepared to fill his place in the relationship. In these ceremonies the dead man's roles as husband and father, as friend and even lover, are handed over to others. The persons who accept the gifts also accept the responsibility of the roles, and of filling them not merely perfunctorily but satisfactorily (Goody, 1962).

It seems appropriate to end this chapter with the preceding account of the funeral customs of the LoDagaa, which contrast so strongly with our own. In the United States, the absence of funeral or mourning rituals that satisfactorily reintegrate the closest survivors of the deceased, especially widows, into new statuses and new social networks appears to underlie many of the emotional problems that death causes us. Almost without exception, studies have shown that widows, particularly, suffer increased isolation and feelings of depression at their husbands' death. The LoDagaa, and other cultures like them, appear wiser than we in preparing for death and in developing their rituals, which—though they may seem outlandish and extreme to us—appear to be more than reasonably successful in meeting the needs of individuals and societies in their moments of greatest crisis.

SUMMARY

Death is universally regarded as a significant event both for the individual and the social group. In every culture there are beliefs about death, rituals that are carried out at death, and emotions that are considered appropriate at death. Many cultures have beliefs and rituals that express the idea of the continuity of society and the ongoing relationship between the living and the dead. In our own society, such beliefs are noticeable by their absence. The social and psychological functions of such beliefs are many: at an individual level such beliefs may comfort a person who is dying; at the social level these beliefs help society reorganize itself around the vacuum caused by the death of one of its members.

The emotions that surround dying and death in different cultures vary, although grief is one of the most common. Grief may be expressed in different ways, however: in some cultures it is accompanied by wailing and aggressive behavior, whereas in other cultures its expression is inhibited. In most cultures the expression of grief is tempered by the age, sex, social status, and social relationships of the deceased, all of which are reflected in the mourning ritual. The aim of culturally normative grief reactions is to console the persons closest to the deceased: mourning ritual in general is a useful social mechanism because it puts limits on grieving, and thereby aids in the reintegration of the survivors into normal social life. This appears to be particularly important for widows, who—in the absence of such meaningful rituals in our own society—appear to suffer particularly intense feelings of isolation and depression.

By examining cultural variation in death reactions and rituals, we can begin to think about alternative kinds of responses that might be useful in our society in aiding individuals to deal with death and dying more adequately.

AUDIOVISUAL MATERIAL

Magical Death. 28 min/color/1973. Pennsylvania State University.
The film documents a ceremony during which a Yanomamo (Amazon) shaman launches a magical attack on the souls of children in a distant village. The monograph on which the film is based is *The Yanomamo* by Napoleon Chagnon, published by Holt, Rinehart, and Winston, 1968.

Dear Birds. 83 min/color/1963. Pennsylvania State University.
Shows various rituals including, prominently, a funeral among the Dugum Dani people of Western New Guinea; narration; teacher's guide available.

Death Is Afraid of Us. 26 min/color/1980. Granada Television International.
A beautifully produced documentary about the men and women who live in the mountains of Soviet Georgia, and who live to be over 100 years old, leading active, vigorous lives.

The Spirit Possession of Alejandro Mamani. 27 min/color. Pennsylvania State University.
A documentary of the portrayal of an old man's battle with aging and bereavement among the Aymara Indians of South America; at 81 years old, feeling rejected, lonely, and possessed by evil spirits, he is drawn toward suicide.

REFERENCES

Benedict, R. *Patterns of culture.* Boston: Houghton Mifflin, 1961.

Bohannan, P. (Ed.). *African homicide and suicide.* New York: Atheneum, 1967.

Branch, M. F., & Paxton, P. P. *Providing safe nursing care for ethnic people of color.* New York: Appleton-Century Crofts, 1976.

Cannon, W. B. "Voodoo" death. *American Anthropologist,* April–June, 1942, *44,* 169–181.

Devereux, G. *Mohave ethnopsychiatry and suicide: the psychiatric knowledge and the psychic disturbances of an Indian tribe* (Smithsonian Institution, U.S. Bureau of American Ethnology Bulletin #175). Washington, D.C.: United States Government Printing Office, 1961.

Elkin, A. P. *The Australian aborigines.* Garden City, N.Y.: Doubleday, 1964.

Firth, R. *Tikopia Ritual and Belief.* London: Allen and Unwin, 1967.

Fortune, R. *Sorcerers of Dobu: The social anthropology of the Dobu islanders of the Western Pacific.* New York: Dutton, 1932.

Freed, R., & Freed S. Shanti Nagar: The effects of urbanization in a village in North India. 3. Sickness and health. *Anthropological Papers of the American Museum of Natural History* (Vol. 55, Part 5). New York: American Museum of Natural History, 1979.

Freed, R., & Freed, S. Rites of passage in Shanti Nagar. *Anthropological Papers of the American Museum of Natural History* (Vol. 56, Part 3). New York: American Museum of Natural History, 1980.

Freuchen, P. *Book of the Eskimo.* Greenwich, Conn.: Fawcett, 1961.

Fried, M. N., & Fried, M. H. *Transitions: Four rituals in eight cultures.* New York: Norton, 1980.

Goldman, I. *The Cubeo: Indians of the Northwest Amazon.* Urbana, Ill.: University of Illinois Press, 1979.

Goody, J. Death, property and the ancestors: A study of the mortuary customs of the LoDagaa of West Africa. Stanford, Calif.: Stanford University Press, 1962.

Hendin, H. *Suicide and Scandinavia.* New York: Grune & Stratton, 1964.

Hertz, R. [*Death and the right hand*]. (R. & C. Needham, trans.). New York: Free Press, 1960.

Huntington, R., & Metcalf, P. *Celebrations of death: The anthropology of mortuary ritual.* Cambridge, England: Cambridge University Press, 1979.

Kakar, S. *The inner world: A psychoanalytic study of childhood and society in India.* Delhi: Oxford University Press, 1978.

Kenyatta, J. *Facing Mt. Kenya.* New York: Random House, 1965.

Lewis, O. *A death in the Sanchez family.* New York: Random House, 1970.

Lex, B. Voodoo death: New thoughts on an old explanation. In D. Landy (Ed.), *Culture, disease and healing: Studies in medical anthropology.* New York: Macmillan, 1977.

Mauss, M. [*Seasonal variation among the Eskimo: A study in social morphology*]. (James J. Fox, trans.). Boston: Routledge & Kegan Paul, 1979.

Myerhoff, B. *Number our days.* New York: Simon & Schuster, 1978.

Rosenblatt, P., Walsh, R., & Jackson, D. *Grief and mourning in cultural perspective.* New Haven: HRAF Press, 1976.

Sigerist, H. The special position of the sick. In D. Landy (Ed.), *Culture, disease and healing: Studies in medical anthropology*. New York: Macmillan, 1977.

Turnbull, C. *The Forest People: A study of the Pygmies of the Congo*. New York: Simon & Schuster, 1961.

van Gennep, A. [*Rites of passage*]. (M. B. Vizedom & G. L. Coffee, trans.). Chicago: University of Chicago Press, 1960.

Wolff, B. B., & Langley, S. Cultural factors and the response to pain. In D. Landy (Ed.), *Culture, disease and healing: Studies in medical anthropology*. New York: Macmillan, 1977.

11

Reformation or Reaction Formation: Society's Response to Death and Dying

In this final chapter we discuss some issues arising from the current emphasis on death and dying. Many professionals involved in the field of thanatology have expressed concern about the "commercialization of death," the fad/bandwagon phenomenon and what Simpson declares is "terminal chic." He (1979) observes that "death is a very badly kept secret; such an unmentionable taboo topic that there are over 750 books now in print that we are ignoring the subject" (p. 1). Death has always been around us. What forces in society are contributing to defining death as a "problem"? Has this upsurge of interest made an impact on and changed society's response to the terminally ill?

One result of media attention to problems related to the terminally ill is the controversy surrounding rational suicide. For better or worse, this form of suicide is increasingly linked with terminal illness. Does this represent an enlightened position or a covert message to the dying?

Increased interest in the subject has led to the development of courses on death and dying from the elementary school level through continuing adult education. What are students learning about death? Are there special criteria that death educators must meet? Are some

sort of credentials required for death educators and death counselors?
Is the thrust toward forming a subspecialty in thanatology advanta-
geous for the terminally ill?

WHY DEATH NOW?

Our present preoccupation with death flows from a variety of societal
forces. We live in the nuclear age, which gives rise to uncertainty and
meaninglessness. Lifton (1977) refers to a psychic numbing that occurs
in response to such events as the Nazi holocaust, Hiroshima, and our
involvement in Vietnam and Indochina, and that forces society to develop new ideas and hypotheses. We have the capacity for total annihilation. As society has become more secularized, emphasis has been
placed on immortality via descendants. This becomes threatened when
the individual recognizes the possibility of a "common epitaph" in the
event of a nuclear war (Feifel, 1977). The nuclear family and the fragmentation of family life isolate the individual from death, thus dimin-
ishing the number of social supports following the death of a significant other. As we noted in Chapters 3 and 4, death often occurs in
institutions where the primary goal is to prolong life. Increased medical technology frequently ignores or negates the feelings of the individual patient. The aged in our society are frequently segregated in nursing homes or retirement communities. Family members, particularly
children, are not exposed to a "personal death." At the same time,
everyone is exposed to megadeaths, fictional death, and violent death
in the media. Each individual is faced with the dilemma of integrating
personal death against the backdrop of nonpersonal death. Our society
emphasizes individualism, achievement, and futurity (Charmaz, 1980;
Feifel, 1977). It is un-American to die. "If death is un-American, our
response to it, however, is characteristically American—we form a committee" (Maddocks, 1978, p. 15). Perhaps "the death movement" in
America is that committee.

"THE DEATH MOVEMENT"

"The Death Movement" has both advocates and critics. It calls to mind
the old saw—there's good news and bad news. Vaisrub (1978) questions the premises and the outcome of the emphasis on death and
dying. He challenges the belief that secularization has increased the
fearfulness of death and that physicians and families have abandoned

patients. He contends that the fear of death is universal. "Perhaps because it is so easy to write about dying, so much is written about it without saying anything new. Words cannot bridge the infinite chasm of eternity" (Vaisrub, 1978, p. 35).

Dr. Michael Simpson (1980), a psychiatrist/internist, outlines some "unwholesome elements":

1. *Death Voyeurism.* This includes visits to oncology units, special centers for terminal care, and interviewing dying patients. Simpson (1980) queries, "Doesn't anyone die where you come from?" (p. 3). There is the danger of not paying attention to ethical issues surrounding patients' and families' privacy. Intrusive care is not synonymous with good care.

2. *Death Exhibitionism.* This applies to caregivers who try to impress people with their capacity to help terminally ill patients and who attempt to "display patients."

3. *Prescriptive Stages.* This is a criticism of the belief that Kübler-Ross's stages have shifted from a descriptive model to a prescriptive model, which implies that patients have to behave in a certain way. "There aren't five stages. There aren't 575 stages. There are only 2 stages—the stage when you naively believe that there are stages, and the stage when you realize that there are not" (Simpson, 1980, p. 3)

4. *Death Ghettos.* Simpson (1980) remains skeptical about the hospice movement, which he feels gained momentum when "it became clear that a lot of dollars might be available" (p. 4). Many hospice advocates would take exception to this criticism. The current bête noire in the movement is the lack of funding for adequate services. Simpson reiterates the dilemma, Should the dying be cared for by "death doctors," "death nurses," and "death volunteers," or should we be seeking redundancy when most physicians and nurses can provide appropriate care for the dying patient? Simpson does not stand alone in this regard. Drs. Krant (1974), Geltman (1981), and Magno (1981) have all voiced similar concerns. Krant believes that hospices will add to fragmentation, overspecialization, and discontinuity in health care. He fears that hospices will become another discontinuous phenomenon and will relieve hospitals and physicians of their true responsibilities to patients and the community. "If I had my way all hospices would go out of business in a few years" (Geltman, 1981, p. 29). "Hospice care should be self-destructing after 30 or 40 years, once their message and techniques have spread throughout the medical community" (Magno, 1981, p. 29).

5. *Smothering.* This includes the deliberate fostering of overdepen-

dency in patients. Simpson is concerned that the initiative of the patient will be restricted and lead to unnecessary early social death. This also encompasses the extremisms of incessant communication about dying with patients and family members.

6. *The Personality Cult.* Although there are vast numbers of pioneers in the death-and-dying field, a few have achieved celebrity status. "Hagiography is a powerful human instinct, making saints and heroes in a world that seems to have so few" (Simpson, 1980, p. 4). The personality cult fosters burnout, leads to decreased creativity, and diminishes discussion and criticism essential to continued growth. Another aspect of this category is the "dying superstar," the person who publicizes his or her dying, yet continues to live. Simpson names no specific individuals. A controversial program, "Joan Robinson: One Women's Story," was aired on PBS television on January 21, 1980. It depicted the last two years of Joan's life after she was diagnosed as having ovarian cancer. Many experts in the field were critical of the film's lack of clarity and its emphasis on Joan's unremitting pain. The film contributes to the general public's preexisting fears and distortions about dying from cancer.

In her analysis of death work—processing the death and dying—Charmaz (1980) describes a process she calls flaunting. It is similar to Simpson's exhibitionism and smothering. "Flaunting consists of a new mode of handling death—by ostentatious identification with death and forced confrontation of others" (Charmaz, 1980, p. 179). She hypothesizes that this stance may represent an overreaction to the previous avoidance and denial. Caretakers adopting this stance create an impression of superiority over their colleagues, and through zealousness attempt to coerce patients and coworkers into confronting their feelings about death. This behavior is not only intrusive; it also robs patients of choice about their own dying.

Herman Feifel's keynote address at the Second Annual Conference of the Forum for Death Education and Counseling, December 5–7, 1979, included both the strengths and the weaknesses of "the death movement." He believes the movement has three major accomplishments. First, information about the role of attitudes toward death, dying, and grief has been examined and the scope, broadened. Death is multifaceted and requires varying coping strategies. Advocates in this area have affirmed the idea that therapy must include the meaning of a patient's life as well as his or her symptoms. Second, it has validated the need for a multidisciplinary approach rather than a parochial one in dealing with dying patients and survivors. Third, it has pointed to the need for change in professional curricula, as well as institutional and communal structures.

The weaknesses are threefold. First, we don't possess a sophisticated research instrument that encompasses methodology and outcome measurement to assess adequately the multimeanings of death. Second, the movement has neglected the life-threatening behaviors of substance abuse and personal violence, as well as the social issues of abortion, capital punishment, mercy killing, and war. We would like to underscore a third area of neglect. In researching this book, we became aware of the lack of minority-group content in the literature related to terminally ill patients. Sudnow's (1967) study contrasting care at two institutions indicated that different social classes received different care. Patients received better care if caretaking staff assumed their "social value" was worth the effort. We lack information, however, on the needs of dying blacks, Hispanics, Mexican Americans, and American Indians based on their respective values and cultural backgrounds.

Davidson (1978) provides an excellent example of staff members inappropriately responding to a patient because they are unable to account for or accept the reality of that patient. In his discussion, he proposes that "it is the health care worker's taboos and methodological presuppositions that are honored" (Davidson, 1978, p. 150). We agree, but would add that behavior is also based on knowledge. If the caretaker is unfamiliar with the patient's cultural background, it will be excluded. Upon admission, the patient was labeled "Puerto Rican," "Roman Catholic," "violating his care plan," and "easily excited and nervous." Staff recommended no visitors. A psychiatric evaluation reported that the patient was using excessive denial, was obsessed with immortality, and was talking of taking a trip; and that visitors accentuated his condition. Family became increasingly agitated about restrictions placed upon them and finally announced that the patient was the "Son of the Gypsy King." The team members finally recognized and were able to "relabel" much of the patient's behavior. Since Gypsies are uncomfortable around *gadje* (non-Gypsies), the patient was moved, and visitors were allowed to circulate in and out of his room. Secondly, "what the psychiatrist had taken in the first interview as a sign of denial was the patient's symbolic reference to his destiny, for which appropriate preparation was vital" (Davidson, 1978, p. 153). For this patient to die surrounded by strangers would have been inappropriate and painful. He needed to perform the required rituals in the context of his own beliefs. We are not suggesting that every health care worker should become an expert in anthropology. Not many of us know that Gypsies conceive of death as a journey across the river that encircles the world. We do believe that caretakers must be sensitized to cultural differences and must consider appropriate behavior within this context.

An unpublished survey of 24 hospices indicated that only 10.8 percent of hospice patients served were Hispanic and that 5.2 percent were black (Buckingham, 1981). Their underrepresentation in this particular study is partially related to eligibility requirements. These were limited prognosis, physician participation, and presence of a caregiver in the home. Due to economic status, many minority-group people are unable to obtain private medical care, and family members must work outside the home.

The third weakness is that the public's increasing receptivity to death and dying has included the entrance "into our midst of dabblers, dilettantes and seekers of the fast buck" (Feifel, 1979). In this, Feifel is referring to the "instant experts" who, after reading a few books, feel they know all about the field. Another example is the entrepreneur who writes a grant proposal to begin a hospice project because funding is available, although he or she has no notion of the hospice concept. A third example is the media blitz, including television programming to secure high audience ratings, the development of poor-quality teaching aids, and the publication of articles in magazines and newspapers that emphasize sensationalism related to the terminally ill.

RATIONAL SUICIDE?

The media, notably television, have frequently been criticized for "dabbling" with death. Programming has been labeled "death porn," created to secure high Nielson ratings. "They present cancer as automatically meaning pain; that nothing can be done for this pain, that medical caregivers don't care. Carried to its extreme [as depicted] conclusion, suicide is shown to be least painful to all concerned" ("TV's Plot," 1980, p. 3). The CBS-TV Sunday evening program "60 Minutes" ran a segment titled "Rational Suicide?" hosted by Mike Wallace on October 15, 1980. The program was sparked by the controversy over the publication of *How to Die with Dignity*, a how-to handbook for successful suicides. The book was written by Dr. George Muir, the chairman of EXIT (previously known as the Voluntary Euthanasia Society). The handbook was available to members of three months' duration or more and, to prevent impulsive action, one month after an initial request. "After widespread publicity of the group's plans, its membership soared just in a few months from 2,000 to 9,000 including many Americans" (Borders, 1980, p. 7). Publication was halted because the organization feared prosecution under an English law against aiding and abetting suicide.

The program included a discussion with Derek Humphrey, a British journalist who helped his wife Jean commit suicide when dying from cancer. Humphrey expressed no regrets about his actions. In *Jean's Way* (1978), a book about her suicide, he explains that he helped her commit suicide so she could "die on her own terms, not those of the disease that ravaged her body" (quoted in Borders, 1980, p. 7). He presently is involved in an organization, Hemlock, that plans to publish a similar guide to suicide in the United States. The EXIT booklet is available in Scotland, which has a different criminal code than England. There is no problem about publishing this type of book in the United States. The book would not be considered aiding and abetting a suicide. The actual abettor might be accused of murder. "The question is, how do you draw the line between murder and what you're doing? A jury would have to be convinced that you were or were not actively murdering the person, that you were or were not helping him or her to do something they had a legal right to do: commit suicide. It's more a matter of proof than anything else" (Annas, 1980, p. 5).

The program included an interview with a cancer patient (identity withheld), his wife, and his daughter. The patient also expressed plans to kill himself if the pain became unbearable. His wife, a nurse, was ambivalent about the role she would play if he took such steps. The family ultimately did reach agreement that the suicide would be understood and the patient, assisted as much as possible.

Dr. Cicely Saunders appeared to state her opposition to the notion of rational suicide. Dr. Saunders, a pioneer in the hospice movement, believes in sound medical management of terminal cancer pain. She considers suicide unnecessary. With proper pain control, the terminal stage represents "the unique period in the patient's illness when the long defeat of living can be gradually converted into a positive achievement in dying" (Holden, 1980, p. 61).

A Public Broadcasting System program entitled "Choosing Suicide," shown in June 1980, evoked a strong reaction across the country. Many stations in Connecticut, Maine, and Mississippi canceled showings of the documentary. They did not want to broadcast a program that "seemed to advocate suicide." The documentary shows Jo Roman planning suicide and discussing it with family and friends. The videotape was done at her request to record her philosophy about "rational suicide." "Society needs to say to people, your life belongs to you . . . to provide a human way." Jo Roman had always planned to take her own life. Her original "target date" was at age 75. When she discovered she had breast cancer at age 62, she changed the date. In the documentary she talks about not wanting to accept "scraps on the banquet table of life"; "I do not want to have one day of pain. I don't want to have a minute of pain." During the program a representative sample of the population in Columbus, Ohio, was asked a series of questions related to the content of the program. Some of these responses are tabulated in Table 11.1.

Table 11.1. Instant Audience Response to PBS Special "Choosing Suicide," June 1980

1. Do you agree with Jo Roman's decision?
   Yes — 48%
   No — 32%
   Unsure — 20%
2. What statement most nearly reflects your opinion?
   Suicide is: a natural human right — 20%
   a right for some — 47%
   always wrong — 33%
3. If you believe suicide is sometimes justifiable, when?
   Deep depression — 7%
   Disgrace/humiliation — 1%
   Onset of senility — 4%
   Painful terminal illness — 71%
   Conviction — 16%
4. If you believe suicide is always wrong, why?
   My religious beliefs — 65%
   My personal conviction — 25%
   Other — 10%
5. Assuming that an individual is determined to commit suicide, which is a better way?
   A solitary secret — 45%
   After discussion with family and friends — 55%
6. In dealing with a dying patient, what should a doctor do?
   Dissuade — 26%
   Not give an opinion — 15%
   Advise about means — 7%
   Actively assist — 3%
   Case-by-case — 50%
7. Do you think doctors sometimes do, in fact, help patients to die?
   Yes — 66%
   No — 13%
   Unsure — 21%

The program included discussion by a panel made up of Ronald Maris, Ph.D., President of the Association of Suicidology; Dr. Robert Neale, Professor of Psychiatry and Religion, Union Theology Seminary; David Peretz, M.D.; Rev. Kevin O'Rourke, Professor of Ethics, St. Louis University; and David Richards, Professor of Law, New York University. The responses were a reflection of each panelist's orientation. Only Prof. Richards agreed that Jo Roman's suicide was "rational." Maris suggested that "too much was left out," that she wasn't "genuinely hopeless"; he wondered about her desire "to escape intolerable pain." Peretz believed that her suicide was "not really related to her cancer" but reflected "her need to control events" and her "difficulty facing limits." O'Rourke observed, "Affective powers were limited—she couldn't respond to love around her." Much of the videotape of Jo Roman's decision-making process related to her diagnosis of cancer. Autopsy results revealed that she did not have advanced cancer. (What is most noteworthy is that while half the audience did not agree or was unsure about Jo Roman's decision, 71 percent believed suicide was sometimes justifiable in "painful terminal illness.")

When can suicide be considered rational? Hoche proposed "balance-sheet suicide" to describe where mentally normal people decide to take their lives when they believe that life is intolerable and/or unacceptable, and when they anticipate no improvement. "In classical antiquity, as well as in the contemporary Western world, loneliness and isolation of the aged and painful terminal illness have been accepted as such mitigating circumstances" (Choron, 1972, p. 98). He (1972) provides an example that would pass muster as a rational suicide: "A few days ago he sent for me and some of his intimate friends and told us to ask the doctors what the outcome of his illness would be, so that if it was to be fatal he could deliberately put an end to his life" (p. 98).

Wertenbaker (1974) poignantly describes her husband's choice to take his life.

"All I should like to ask is to know if you decide to," I told him.

"You're sure?" asked Wert. He stood as far away from me as he could get when he asked this and spoke very coolly as if he would prefer a different answer.

"Yes," I said.

"Or if I do it any other way?"

"Yes." (P. 99)

"When he wants to die he can do that too," I said.

"You let him kill himself!" said Carter. "You cannot."

"Why not?"

"You would not kill him?"

"No! And I don't want him to die one day sooner, God knows, but do you understand me, it's up to him what he does!"

"You would help him do that!" he said in horrified comprehension. "I believe you would. This is serious. You must not." (P. 144)

In the book she describes the numerous attempts before her husband was successful. These accounts in literature could be objected to on the grounds that suicide is romanticized. Whether or not suicide related to terminal illness should be considered rational is still unresolved. Caretakers must be sensitive to "acceptance" of this possibility, for their behavior can be interpreted as a command or instruction. Neale (1970) observes: "We are prone to have powerful and rigid opinions on matters relating to death. We are prone to enforce these opinions on others" (p. 203).

DEATH EDUCATION

Death education for all has been proposed as the modus operandi to change our attitudes toward death. The basic assumption is that we will live more meaningful lives if we are able to accept death. "Death comes not to the dead but the living. To deny it is to distort life's pattern" (Feifel, 1971, p. 12). Attitudes toward death start early in childhood and continue through adulthood. On an informal basis, everyone "learns" about death from their environment. Brantner (1971) discusses the content of nursery rhymes: "Thirty-one of these deal directly with human death. Twenty-six deal with the subjects of animals being killed. Two of them deal with both human and animal deaths. One, 'Jack is Dead,' deals with the death of an inanimate object" (p. 16). He believes the purpose of death education is to dispel the misinformation, unhealthy attitudes, and fears people accumulate through their lifetimes.

Leviton (1971, 1977) and Knott (1979) examine the who, what, where, when, and how in suggesting death education for all. Leviton (1971) makes analogies between sex education and death education. As with sex education, formalized death education serves to complement that received in the home and church. He, too, believes the goal of death education is to disseminate scientific information and promote philosophical thought. He (1977) outlines 12 goals for death education:

1. Gently remove the taboo aspect of death language so students can read and discourse upon death rationally without becoming anxious.
2. Promote comfortable and intelligent interaction with the dying as human beings who are living until they are dead.
3. Educate children about death so they grow up with a minimun of death-related anxieties. Anxieties are too often based upon irrationality and myth rather than fact.
4. Assist the individual in developing a personal eschatology by specifying the relationship between life and death.
5. Perceive the health-care giver as a professional and human being, neither omnipotent nor omniscient, who has an obligation to give competent and humane service, attention, and information without mendacity to the dying and their families.
6. Understand the dynamics of grief and the reactions of differing age groups to the death of a "significant other."
7. Understand and be able to interact with the suicidal person.
8. Understand the role of those involved in what Kastenbaum and Aisenberg (1972) call the "death system" and the assets and liabilities of that system.
9. Educate consumers to the commercial death market.
10. Recognize that war and other holocausts are related to feelings of personal immortality and omnipotence. War might be avoided if we realize that it may be ourselves or our children who would be killed or mutilated as well as an amorphous "enemy."
11. Recognize the variations involved in aspects of death both within and between cultures. Death means different things to different people.
12. Know the false idols and mythology existing in the growing field of thanatology, the salient heuristic questions, and the great need for research. (Pp. 258–259)

Knott (1979) develops a triad of goals: (1) information sharing; (2) values clarification; and (3) coping behaviors. A study of college courses on death in 1973 offered a different way of studying the meaning of death and dying. Instruction emphasized (1) death as a personal phenomenon; (2) examination of the sociocultural aspects and effects of death; and (3) a limited study of singular aspects of death, such as self-destructive behavior, religion, and funeral practices (p. 391).

Formalized death education will vary in content depending on its audience. Young children can be helped to understand "what is dead" and can be encouraged to discuss their religious beliefs and rituals about dying.

When Sampson, the resident guinea pig in a San Francisco classroom died, Roni Howard had her fifth graders place the animal in a coffin fashioned from a cardboard box and write epitaphs to him. The children dug a grave in the schoolyard and buried Sampson in an ecumenical service in which they sang the folk song "Shenandoah" simply because it was the only tune to which they all knew the words. (Maeroff, 1978, p. 8)

Most elementary programs are designed to take advantage of the "teachable moment."

Adolescents can be exposed to a more structured curriculum, including assessment of attitudes and the use of fiction and community resources such as a funeral director, a psychologist, different clergy, physicians, and so on. Fontenot (1974) describes how death can be integrated into an eleventh- and twelfth-grade English course. Students were asked to analyze articles and books, keeping in mind, "How was death faced by the major character of the book?" Class discussion covered suicide, euthanasia, and accepting one's death and the death of loved ones.

Leviton has developed a course to serve as a model for large audiences of college students and caregivers. His approach is hierarchical. "Topics, initially, are of an impersonal, objective nature and then evolve into personal and affect-arousing aspects" (Leviton, 1977, p. 267). The course includes use of literature, films, and objective tests. He has another format for smaller groups. Classes meet biweekly, with one session devoted to didactic material and one session for small group discussion. He assumes that individual counseling by the instructor is an essential component of formal death education.

> Frequently the student has developed some confidence in his teacher and feels at ease discussing his personal problems with him. Of course, we refer students . . . when professional or psychiatric help is indicated, but the role of helping people better enjoy life, face death or prevent suicide is not the special providence of any one profession. (Leviton, 1971, p. 35)

This is a critical issue in death education. It has been our experience that some students enroll in a course to resolve personal issues related to suicidal feelings or to conflict about the death of a significant other. Leviton (1977) reports that in one of his course, 8 of 230 students admitted to a previous suicide attempt; 15 were contemplating suicide when beginning the course; 8 reported still contemplating suicide when the course was completed; and 1 student eventually did commit suicide (p. 261).

Since these issues do arise, how can one judge the appropriateness or competence of the death educator? The Forum for Death Education and Counseling has consistently articulated as one of its goals "to promote and upgrade the quality of death education and counseling." It offers courses during each of its annual meetings. Some of the objectives of the 1979 workshop were (a) to list and understand the goals of death education; (b) to describe historical conditions affecting death attitudes and behavior; (c) to understand the complexity of the interplay of the individual and the community; (d) to understand the effects of death language; (e) to know sociological and psychological variables affecting death-related behavior; (f) to recommend resources; (g) to understand the nature and needs of death, the dying, and the bereaved; and (h) to develop a death education curriculum (Forum *Newsletter*, Summer 1979, pp. 1–2). The 1980 Annual Conference again sponsored workshops with similar goals.

The Professional Standards and Ethics Committee of the forum, chaired by Jeanne Quint-Benoliel, has developed a set of standards for death educators and counselors. The committee has recommended professional certification and licensing; identification of thanatology professionals as educators or counselors with evidence that the professional has the appropriate educational background in the field; and identification of basic technical competencies (Forum *Newsletter*, February 1980, p. 5). "The Board charged the Professional Standards and Ethics Committee to move ahead to develop a final plan of (1) workable criteria for certification and (2) implementation for certification procedures before the next Board Meeting in June 1981" (Forum *Newsletter*, November–December, 1980, p. 1). This thrust for specialization can be a double-edged sword. It may provide some criteria for judging qualifications, but also underscores the specialization that has already contributed to fragmentation, issues of territoriality, and "kingdom building." The motivations of the Forum in offering courses are understandable, but can also contribute to creating "instant experts."

Leviton (1971) adapted Johnson's criteria for sex educators to apply to death educators. These are:

1. The teacher must have come to terms with his or her own [death] feelings and to have admitted not only to its existence but to its full status in the dynamics of his total personality functioning.
2. It should go without saying that the teacher needs to know the appropriate subject matter that he is to teach.
3. The teacher of [death] education needs to be able to use the language of [death] easily and naturally, especially in the presence of the young. This is impossible for many people; however, most can probably learn to do it.
4. He or she needs to be familiar with the sequence of [psychothanatolog-

ical] developmental events throughout life; and to have a sympathetic understanding of common problems associated with them.

5. The teacher needs an acute awareness of the enormous social changes that are in progress and of their implications for changes in our patterns of attitudes, practices, laws, and institutions [concerning death]. (P. 39)

Much more research is needed to measure the criteria for judging the competency of death educators and counselors effectively. Further, it is difficult to draw conclusions about the effectiveness of the students' exposure to death education. Schulz (1978) sums up the current state of the art: "The point is that death education, like most things, can be good or bad depending upon the specific teacher, student, and method of instruction" (p. 169).

SUMMARY

From the foregoing, one can conclude, like Dickens, that it is "the best of times and the worst of times." The current questioning, examining, and reorganizing are to be expected. Every social reform, no matter how enthusiastically it is received, encounters professional, philosophical, political, economic, and legal problems. "All reform movements have a missionary zeal; a zeal with blessings and problems" (Foster, Wald, & Wald, 1978, p. 22). It will take time to formulate the principles necessary for reform related to the basic meaning of life. Feifel (1979) cautions, "No quick fixes are usually available."

The death-and-dying movement has been a major force in helping to humanize medical care. One branch of the movement, the hospice concept, has represented a challenge to the status quo of care versus cure, personal care versus technological care, family inclusion versus exclusion, the team concept versus specialization and compartmentalization. In 1980 more than 80 hospice programs were providing care for the terminally ill and their families. The death-and-dying movement challenges one aspect of our socioeconomic system. Kastenbaum has called this our death system. Health care and care for the dying are two elements in this complex system. It is too early to tell if principles underlying humanized care for the dying will be adequately integrated to insure scope, quality, and longevity.

Rational suicide, when applied almost inclusively to the terminally ill, has ramifications that extend beyond the usual ethical-moral arguments about an individual's right to choose to die. There is the added dimension of the economic and emotional burden society assumes in relation to the terminally ill. Careful consideration is required to assess the overt and covert messages implied in this aspect of rational suicide.

Finally, death education continues to be a topic of interest for every segment of society. Only the elderly have limited access to formal death education courses. It is too soon to judge what death education can achieve. It cannot be viewed as a panacea. Our society constantly seeks answers. We assume adequate scientific research will always provide solutions. The meaning of life and death does not readily lend itself to the scientific model. Paradoxically, we may be searching for answers when questioning may be the only solution.

LEARNING EXERCISES

1. Review the chapter content on Jo Roman's death. If you were a member of her family, would you have tried to stop her suicide? Give reasons for your response.
2. Has the recent so-called media blitz influenced your attitudes or perception of death and dying? If so, in what manner?
3. What preventive measures should be taken to insure that hospices will not parallel the scandals associated with nursing homes, and that they will avoid becoming the death ghettos of the next decade?
4. Discuss the query, "Are we 'death-and-dying' our patients to death?"

AUDIOVISUAL MATERIAL

Death Education. 30 min/color video or film. Allied Memorial Council.
  A variety of death educational materials for school use is demonstrated by George Daugherty. The focus is primarily on courses implemented in grade and high schools.

Role of Schools in Death Education. 27 min/audiocassette. Bowie, Maryland: The Charles Press.
  The value of and need for death education in the schools is expressed by David Leviton.

The Mortal Body. 12 min/black and white/1976. Filmmakers Library.
  The wonders of life are stressed, without forgetting the inevitability of death, through photographic collage.

The Promise of Death. 3 h, 50 min/4 audiocassettes. The Thomas More Association.

The basic issues related to death and dying are conveyed through interviews with various members of the health care professions and with dying patients.

REFERENCES

Annas, G. Lawyer does not favor suicides or helpers, does favor discussions. *Thanatology Today*, October 1980, *2*(7), 5–6.

Borders, W. Suicide guide stirs debate in Britain. *New York Times*, September 28, 1980, p. 7.

Brantner, J. Death and the self. In B. R. Green & D. P. Irish (Eds.), *Death education: Preparation for living.* Cambridge, Mass.: Schenkman, 1971.

Buckingham, R., & Luper, D. *An empirical study of hospice social services in the United States.* Unpublished study, University of Arizona, College of Business and Public Administration, Tucson, Arizona, 1981.

Charmaz, K. *The social realities of death.* Reading, Mass.: Addison-Wesley, 1980.

Choron, J. *Suicide.* New York: Scribner's, 1972.

Davidson, G. In search of models of care. In G. Davidson (Ed.), *The hospice: Development and administration.* Washington, D.C.: Hemisphere, 1978.

Feifel, H. The meaning of death in American society. In B. R. Green & D. P. Irish (Eds.), *Death education: Preparation for living.* Cambridge, Mass.: Schenkman, 1971.

Feifel, H. Death in contemporary America. In H. Feifel (Ed.), *New meanings of death.* New York: McGraw-Hill, 1977.

Feifel, H. *The death movement.* Keynote Address, Second Annual Conference of the Forum for Death Education and Counseling, Orlando, Florida, December 5–7, 1979.

Fontenot, C. The subject no one teaches. *English Journal*, 1974, *63*(2), 62–63.

Forum for Death Education and Counseling. *Newsletter*, Summer 1979, *3*(5), 1–8.

Forum for Death Education and Counseling. *Newsletter,* February 1980, *4*(2), 1–8.

Forum for Death Education and Counseling. *Newsletter,* November–December 1980, *4*, 9–10.

Foster, Z., Wald, F., & Wald, H. The hospice movement. *New Physician,* May 1978, 21–24.

Geltman, R., M.D. Quoted in C. Calvert, Hospices: Leaving life gracefully, *New York Daily News,* January 5, 1981, p. 29.

Holden, C. Hospices for the dying, relief from pain and fear. In M. Hamilton & H. Reid (Eds.), *A hospice handbook: A new way to care for the dying.* Grand Rapids, Mich.: W. Eerdsmans, 1980.

Humphrey, D. *Jean's way.* New York: Quartet Books, 1978.

Kastenbaum, R., & Aisenberg, R. *The psychology of death.* New York: Springer, 1972.

Knott, J. E. Death education for all. In H. Wass (Ed.), *Dying: Facing the facts.* New York: Hemisphere, 1979.

Krant, M. J. *Dying and dignity: The meaning and control of a personal death.* Springfield, Ill.: Charles C Thomas, 1974.

Leviton, D. The role of the schools in providing death education. In B. R. Green & D. P. Irish (Eds.), *Death education: Preparation for living.* Cambridge, Mass.: Schenkman, 1971.

Leviton, D. Death education. In H. Feifel (Ed.), *New meanings of death.* New York: McGraw-Hill, 1977.

Lifton, R. The sense of immortality. In H. Feifel (Ed.), *New meanings of death.* New York: McGraw-Hill, 1977.

Maddocks, M. Life and death in the USA. In R. Fulton, E. Marhusen, G. Ower, & J. Scheiber (Eds.), *Death and dying: Challenge and change.* Reading, Mass.: Addison-Wesley, 1978.

Maeroff, G. Schools take up study of death. *New York Times,* March 6, 1978, pp. 1; 8.

Magno, Dr. J. Quoted in C. Calvert, Hospice: Leaving life gracefully. *New York Daily News,* January 5, 1981, p. 29.

Neale, R. E. Psychiatry and religion: Death. *Archives of the Foundation of Thanatology,* 1970, *2*(4), 200–210.

Schulz, R. *The psychology of death, dying and bereavement.* Reading, Mass.: Addison-Wesley, 1978.

Simpson, M. *Dying death and grief: A critically annotated bibliography and source book of thanatology and terminal care.* New York: Plenum Press, 1979.

Simpson, M. The future of death: Exploration or exploitation? (Part II). *Thanatology Today,* October 1980, *2*(7), 3–4.

Sudnow, D. *Passing on: The social organization of death.* Englewood Cliffs, N.J.: Prentice-Hall, 1967.

TV's plot: Cancer = pain = suicide? *Thanatology Today,* October 1980, *2*, 7.

Vaisrub, S. Dying is worked to death. In R. Fulton, E. Marhusen, G. Ower, & J. Scheiber (Eds.), *Death and dying: Challenge and change.* Reading, Mass.: Addison-Wesley, 1978.

Wertenbaker, L. *The death of a man.* Boston: Beacon Press, 1974.

Appendix: Addresses of Audiovisual Distributors

Abbott Laboratories
Professional Relations
Abbott Park
North Chicago, Illinois 60064

ABC News
7 West 66th Street
New York, New York 10023

Allied Memorial Council
P.O. Box 30112
Seattle, Washington 98103

American Journal of Nursing
% Association Films
600 Grand Avenue
Ridgefield, New Jersey 07657

Billy Budd Films
235 East 57th Street
New York, New York 10022

Bureau of Community Health Services
Program Services Branch
5600 Fishers Lane
Rockville, Maryland 20852

Center for Death Education
University of Minnesota
Minneapolis, Minnesota 55455

Centron Educational Films
P.O. Box 687
1621 West Ninth Street
Lawrence, Kansas 66044

Charles Press
Bowie, Maryland 20715

Concern for Dying
250 West 57th Street
New York, New York 10019

CRM/McGraw-Hill Films
1221 Avenue of the Americas
New York, New York 10020

Eccentric Circle Cinema Workshop
P.O. Box 4085
Greenwich, Connecticut 06830

Educational Perspectives Associates
P.O. Box 213
Dekalb, Illinois 60115

Encyclopedia Britannica
Educational Concern
425 North Michigan Ave.
Chicago, Illinois 60611

Filmmakers Library
290 West End Avenue
New York, New York 10023

Films, Inc.
1144 Wilmette Ave.
Wilmette, Illinois 60091

Dr. Charles Garfield
Cancer Research Institute
University of California Medical Center
San Francisco, California 94143

Grenada Television Int. Ltd.
36 Golden Square
London WIR-4AH
England

Learning Corporation of America
1350 Avenue of the Americas
New York, New York 10019

Mass Media Associates
1720 Chouteau Avenue
St. Louis, Missouri 63103

McMillan Films
34 MacQuesten Parkway South
Mount Vernon, New York 10550

National Audio-Visual Center
General Services Administration
Washington, D.C. 20409

National Film Board of Canada
1251 Avenue of the Americas
16th Floor
New York, New York 10020

National Medical Audiovisual Center
Station K
Atlanta, Georgia 30324

Pacifica Tape Library
Pacifica Foundation
5316 Venice Blvd.
Los Angeles, California 90019

The Pennsylvania State University
Audio Visual Services
17 Willard Building
University Park, Pennsylvania 16802

Perspective Films
65 East South Water St.
Chicago, Illinois 60601

Phoenix Films
470 Park Avenue South
New York, New York 10016

Professional Research Inc.
American Video Network
660 South Bonnie Brae St.
Los Angeles, California 90057

The Public Television Library Video
Program Service
475 L'Enfant Plaza, S.W.
Washington, D.C. 20024

Spectrum Motion Picture Laboratory
399 Gundersen Drive
Carol Stream, Illinois 60187

The Thomas More Association
180 North Wabash Avenue
Chicago, Illinois 60601

Time/Life Multi-Media
Time/Life Building
1271 Avenue of the Americas
New York, New York 10020

University of Arizona Bureau of
AV Services
Tucson, Arizona 85724

University of California Extension
Media Center
2223 Fulton Street
Berkeley, California 94720

University of Iowa
Audiovisual Center
Iowa City, Iowa 52242

University of Minnesota
AV Library Service
3300 University Ave., S.E.
Minneapolis, Minnesota 55414

University of Oregon
Division of Continuing Education
P.O. Box 1491
1633 S.W. Park Avenue
Portland, Oregon 97201

Viewfinders
Box 1665
Evanston, Illinois 60204

WGBH-TV
125 Western Avenue
Boston, Massachusetts 02134

Wombat Productions, Inc.
Little Lake, Glendale Road
P.O. Box 70
Ossining, New York 10562

Photo Credits

Chapter 1.   Prehistoric burial from site of Chalula, Puebla, Mexico. Photo by Serena Nanda.

Chapter 2.   Picasso, Pablo. *Guernica* (1937, May–early June). Oil on canvas, 11′5½″ × 25′5¾″. On extended loan to The Museum of Modern Art, New York, from the estate of the artist.

Chapter 3.   Photo by Nina Leake.

Chapter 4.   Detail of a hieroglyphic tomb in Egypt. Photo by Gary C. Croland.

Chapter 5.   From McFarlane: Contemporary Pediatric Nursing: A Conceptual Approach. New York: John Wiley & Sons, Inc., 1980.

Chapter 6.   EEG demonstrating a flat EEG.

Chapter 7.   From McFarlane: Contemporary Pediatric Nursing: A Conceptual Approach. New York: John Wiley & Sons, Inc., 1980.

Chapter 8.   A gravesite in Sweden. Photo by Suzanne Kaufman.

Chapter 9.   Photo by Susan Kuklin.

Chapter 10.   Bolivian funeral. Photo courtesy of the United Nations.

Chapter 11.   Mural by Art Guerra, American Nursing Home, East 5th Street and Avenue B, New York, New York. Photo by Art Guerra.

Index